WASTE GENERATION AND UTILIZATION

ENV BOOKS SERIES

WASTE GENERATION AND UTILIZATION

Editors

Dr. Priya Bajaj
Assistant Professor
Govt., Raza PG College
Rampur (U.P.)
(INDIA)

Dr. B. Tabassum
Assistant Professor
Govt., Raza PG College
Rampur (U.P.)
(INDIA)

Dr. Pawan Kumar 'Bharti'
Vice President (Executive)
Society for Environment, Health, Awareness of Nutrition & Toxicology (SEHAT)
1775, Sohan Ganj, Near Clock Tower
Delhi - 110 007 (INDIA)
E-mail - gurupawanbharti@rediffmail.com

Associate Editor

Mr. Jaswant Ray
Society for Environment, Health, Awareness of Nutrition and Toxicology (SEHAT)
H.O.- F/119, Pandav Nagar
Meerut (U.P.) - 250 003 (INDIA)

DPH

DISCOVERY PUBLISHING HOUSE PVT. LTD.
NEW DELHI-110 002

Published by:

Namit Wasan

DISCOVERY PUBLISHING HOUSE PVT. LTD.
4383/4B, Ansari Road, Darya Ganj
New Delhi-110 002 (India)
Phone : +91-11-23279245, 43596064-65
Fax : +91-11-23253475
E-mail : discoverypublishinghouse@gmail.com
namitwasan9@gmail.com
sales@discoverypublishinggroup.com

website: www.discoverypublishinggroup.com

***First Edition:* 2016**

ISBN: 978-93-5056-792-0

Waste Generation and Utilization

Printed at:
Infinity Imaging Systems
Delhi

ENV Books Series, India

Calls descriptive and error free chapters for upcoming volumes of books on various environmental issues. Send your manuscripts to envbooks@gmail.com

Founding Editor (Editor-in-Chief)

Dr. Pawan Kumar 'Bharti'

Society for Environment, Health, Awareness of Nutrition & Toxicology (SEHAT-India)

1775, Sohanganj, Near Clock Tower, Delhi - 7, India

E-mail: *gurupawanbharti@rediffmail.com*

Other Titles by Editor-in-Chief:

1. **Advances in Biotechnology and Ecological Sciences (2013)**
   Bharti, P.K., Chauhan, A. and Ray, J. (eds.)
   (ISBN: 978-93-5056-358-8).
2. **Advances in Agriculture and Ecology (2013)**
   Bharti, P.K., Chauhan, A. and Ezeaku Peter Ikemefuna (eds.)
   (ISBN: 978-93-5056-362-5).
3. **Agriculture Development and Sustainable Environment (2015)**
   Ray, J. and Bharti, P.K. (eds.)
   (ISBN: 978-93-5056-759-3).
4. **Agriculture, Environment and Nano-science (2015)**
   Bharti, Pawan K. (ed.)
   (ISBN: 978-93-5056-760-5).
5. **Agriculture Ecology and Environment (2014)**
   Bharti, P.K. and Olubukola O. Babalola (eds.)
   (ISBN: 978-93-5056-480-6).
6. **Agriculture and Environmental Biotechnology (2014)**
   Bharti, P.K. and Chauhan, A. (eds.)
   (ISBN: 978-93-5056-479-0).
7. **Agro-biodiversity: *Conservation and Sustainable Development* (2016)**
   Sharma Pankaj; Singh Narayan and Bharti, P.K. (eds.)
   (ISBN: 978-93-5056-782-1).
8. **Agro-forestry and Climate Change (2014)**
   Bharti, Pawan K. and Singh, Narayan (eds.)
   (ISBN: 978-93-5056-514-8).
9. **Agro-forestry and Sustainable Agriculture (2016)**
   Sharma Pankaj, Bharti Pawan K. (eds).
   (ISBN: 978-93-5056-786-9).

10. **Aquatic Biodiversity and Pollution (2013)**
Bharti, P.K., Chauhan, A. and Kaoud, H.A.H. (eds.)
(ISBN: 978-93-5056-359-5).
11. **Aquatic Ecology and Biotechnology (2014)**
Bharti, P.K. and Zaki, M.S.A. (eds.)
(ISBN: 978-93-5056-451-6).
12. **Aquatic Environment and Toxicology (2013)**
Bharti, Pawan K. (ed.)
(ISBN: 978-93-5056-236-9).
13. **Aquaculture and Fisheries Environment (2014)**
Gupta, S.K. and Pawan K. Bharti (eds.)
(ISBN: 978-93-5056-408-0).
14. **Biodiversity, Biotechnology and Environmental Conservation (2015)**
Bharti, P.K. and Bhandari, G. (eds.)
(ISBN: 978-93-5056-750-4).
15. **Biotechnological Approaches and Water Ecosystem (2016)**
Zaki S.A. Mona and Pawan K. 'Bharti' (eds.)
(ISBN: 978-93-5056-779-1).
16. **Biotechnology, Agro-ecology and Environment (2015)**
Avnish Chauhan and Bharti, P.K. (eds.)
(ISBN: 978-93-5056-757-9).
17. **Bioremediation and Microbial Biotechnology (2016)**
Gupta Sandeep; Bharti, P.K. (eds.)
(ISBN: 978-93-5056-783-8).
18. **Biodiversity of Aquatic Ecosystem: *Significance, Threat and Conservation* (2013)**
Bharti, P.K. and Kaoud, H.A.H. (eds.)
(ISBN: 978-93-5056-297-0).
19. **Biological Diversity and Ecology (2016)**
Arya Manoj Kumar; Bharti, P.K., and Joshi Ritesh (eds.)
(ISBN: 978-93-5056-785-2).
20. **Clean Technology for Environmental Protection (2015)**
Chauhan, A., Sharma, S. and Bharti, P.K. (eds.)
(ISBN: 978-93-5056-731-9).
21. **Climate Change and Agriculture (2012)**
Bharti, P.K. and Chauhan, Avnish (eds.)
(ISBN: 978-93-5056-148-5).
22. **Climate Change and Biodiversity (2013)**
Bharti, P.K., and Chauhan, Avnish (eds.)
(ISBN: 978-93-5056-360-1).

23. **Climate Change, Disaster Management and Environment (2016)**
Chauhan Alka; Bharti, P.K. (eds.)
(ISBN: 978-93-5056-784-5).

24. **Conservation and Cultivation of Medicinal Plants (2015)**
Narayan Singh and Bharti, P.K. (eds.)
(ISBN: 978-93-5056-740-1).

25. **Crop Productivity and Plant Disease Management (2016)**
Chauhan Alka; Bharti, P.K. (eds.)
(ISBN: 978-93-5056-791-3).

26. **Eco-toxicology and Eco-technology (2013)**
Bharti, P.K. and Zaki, M. (eds.)
(ISBN: 978-93-5056-313-7).

27. **Environmental Biotechnology and Application (2013)**
Bharti, P.K. and Chauhan, Avnish (eds.)
(ISBN: 978-93-5056-262-8).

28. **Environmental Conservation and Biotechnology (2014)**
Chauhan, A. and P.K. Bharti (eds.)
(ISBN: 978-93-5056-512-4).

29. **Environmental Health and Problems (2013)**
Bharti, P.K. and Gajananda, Kh. (eds.)
(ISBN: 978-93-5056-263-5).

30. **Environmental Pollution and Biodiversity (2012)**
Bharti, P.K., Chauhan, Avnish and Kumar, P. (eds.)
(ISBN: 978-93-5056-149-2).

31. **Fish Habitat and Aquaculture (2015)**
Gupta, S.K. and Bharti, P.K. (eds.)
(ISBN: 978-93-5056-744-9).

32. **Fisheries and Toxicology (2014)**
Zaki, M.S.A., Bharti, P.K. and Chauhan, A. (eds.)
(ISBN: 978-93-5056-452-3).

33. **Fisheries and Sustainable Aquaculture (2016)**
Kumar, G.S. and 'Bharti' P.K. (eds.)
(ISBN: 978-93-5056-797-5).

34. **Freshwater Ecosystem and Xenobiotics (2013)**
Bharti, P.K., Zaki, M. and Chauhan, A. (eds.)
(ISBN: 978-93-5056-299-4).

35. **Food Processing, Mangement and Nanotechnolgy (2016)**
Chauhan Avnish and 'Bharti' P.K. (eds.)
(ISBN: 978-93-5056-796-8)

36. **Limnology and Aquatic Science (2015)**
Sharma, S. and Bharti, P.K. (eds.)
(ISBN: 978-93-5056-735-7).

37. **Medicinal Plants: *Status, Distribution and Significance* (2015)**
Sharma, P., Bharti, P.K. and Narayan Singh (eds.)
(ISBN: 978-93-5056-734-0).
38. **Microbial Applications and Environment (2014)**
Bharti, Pawan K. (ed.)
(ISBN: 978-93-5056-515-5).
39. **Microbial Ecology and Habitat (2014)**
Bharti, Pawan K. (ed.)
(ISBN: 978-93-5056-514-8).
40. **Natural Ecosystem and Climate Change (2015)**
Bharti, P.K. and Gajananda, Kh. (eds.)
(ISBN: 978-93-5056-749-0).
41. **Pest Management and Agro-techniques (2016)**
Biswas Asim, Bharti, Pawan K., Chauhan Avnish (eds.)
(ISBN: 978-93-5056-794-4).
42. **Prakriti me Aushadhi (*in Hindi*) (2012)**
Singh, J.R., Bharti, P.K. and Bharti, B. (eds.)
(ISBN: 978-93-5056-200-0).
43. **Seed Technology, Plant Growth and Cropping System (2015)**
Tyagi, P.K. and Bharti, P.K. (eds.)
(ISBN: 978-93-5056-738-8).
44. **Soil Contamination and Conservation (2015)**
Ezeaku, P.I. and Bharti, P.K. (eds.)
(ISBN: 978-93-5056-737-1).
45. **Soil Characteristics and Agro-ecology (2015)**
Avnish Chauhan and Bharti, P.K. (eds.)
(ISBN: 978-93-5056-758-6).
46. **Soil Quality and Contamination (2013)**
Bharti, P.K. and Chauhan, Avnish (eds.)
(ISBN: 978-93-5056-361-8).
47. **Waste Disposal and Management (2015)**
Bharti, P.K., Tabassum, B. and Bajaj, P. (eds.)
(ISBN: 978-93-5056-729-6).
48. **Waste Management and Environmental Health (2016)**
Tabassum B; Bajaj Priya and Bharti, P.K. (eds.)
(ISBN: 978-93-5056-777-7).
49. **Water Resources and Agriculture (2014)**
Bharti, P.K. and Ezeaku Peter Ikemefuna (eds.)
(ISBN: 978-93-5056-481-3).
50. **Water Resources Management: *Monitoring and Assessment* (2016)**
Bharti, P.K. and Gupta Sandeep Gupta (eds.)
(ISBN: 978-93-5056-799-9).

Preface

Development of any country is largely based on its magnitude of industrial growth. India after independence laid stress on industrial revolution. Presently in India, about 960 million tonnes of solid waste is being generated annually as by-products during industrial, mining, municipal, agricultural and other processes. Of this 350 million tonnes are organic wastes from agricultural sources, which is degradable thus manageable; 290 million tonnes are inorganic waste of industrial and mining sectors and 4.5 million tonnes are hazardous in nature. Growth of population, increasing urbanization, rising standards of living due to technological innovations have contributed to an increase in both the quantity and variety of solid wastes generated by industrial, mining, domestic and agricultural activities. Globally the estimated quantity of wastes generation was 12 billion tonnes in the year 2002 of which 11 billion tonnes were industrial wastes and 1.6 billion tonnes were municipal solid wastes (MSW). About 19 billion tonnes of solid wastes are expected to be generated annually in India by the year 2025; and MSW generation is expected to reach 300 MT by the year 2047, and land requirement for disposal of this waste would be 169.6 km^2 as against which only 20.2 km^2 were occupied for management of 48 MT.

Waste management involves management of such materials which have apparently no value and is based on the concept of reduce, reuse and recycle. The generation of hazardous waste is to be reduced or eliminated as expeditiously as possible. Waste that is nevertheless generated should be treated, stored, or disposed of so as to minimize the present and future threat to human health and the environment. Waste Utilization is using an agricultural or other waste on land in an environmentally acceptable manner while maintaining or improving soil and plant resources.

Prior to its management, proper characterization of wastes through physical, mineralogical and chemical analysis is very important because, if the composition is not exactly known, the 'Eco saving' to be gained by the utilization of rejects can be lost. With the scenario changing, on passage of time and with the technologies getting regularly upgraded, there is need for use of such waste materials continuously being produced in large quantum through conversion of work materials to either by-products or in-process material for recycling.

Waste generation and utilization is a thrust area. Advances in solid waste management resulted in alternative materials as a substitute to traditional materials like: bricks, blocks, tiles, aggregates, ceramics, cement, lime, soil, timber and paint. To safeguard the environment, efforts are being made for recycling different wastes and utilize them in value added applications.

Use of waste plastic in bituminous mixes for road construction is a good example of waste utilization. Of the various waste materials, plastic waste and municipal solid waste are of great concern. Disposal of waste materials including waste plastic bags has become a serious problem and waste plastics are burnt for apparent disposal which cause environmental pollution. On the other side, the road traffic is increasing. The traffic intensity is increasing. The load bearing capacities of the road are to be increased. Utilization of waste plastic bags in bituminous mixes has proved that these enhance the properties of mix in addition to solving disposal problems. Plastic waste, consisting of carry bags, cups and Thermocoles (Polystyrene) can be used as a coating over aggregate and this coated stone can be used for road construction. By this process a road of 1 km., length and 3.375M width of single lane can consumes 10, 00000 carry bags and the road strength is increased by 100 per cent and there found no any pot hole. The mix polymer coated aggregate have shown higher strength. Use of this mix for road construction helps to use plastics waste. Once the plastic waste is separated from municipal solid waste, the organic matter can be converted into manure and used. The use of the innovative technology will not only strengthen the road construction but also increase the road life as well as will help to improve the environment. Plastic roads would be a boon for India's hot and extremely humid climate, where temperatures frequently cross 50°C and torrential rains create havoc, leaving most of the roads with big potholes.

Because of obsolete production equipment and old technology, the generation of industrial solid wastes is very high. The rates of treatment, disposal and comprehensive utilization of industrial solid wastes are relatively low, so that a large volume goes to landfill. On the other hand, since the urbanization process has speeded up; the numbers of cities and the urban population has increased rapidly, leading to substantial increase in municipal solid wastes. The funds used for solid waste pollution control are woefully inadequate, so sound control of solid wastes is at a low level, leading to serious environmental problems. In this book, present status on generation and utilization of both non-hazardous and hazardous solid wastes in India, their recycling potentials and environmental implication are reported and discussed in details. The main object of this book is to analyze how all type of waste materials could be successfully utilized.

The present book updates the subject matter and issues related to waste generation, disposal problems, waste treatment technology, environmental health issues, utilization of waste, waste to energy, wealth from waste, biotechnology for waste minimization and integrated waste management. Thanks are due to contributors from various institutions and publisher for their interest in this book. The book will definitely provide a multidisciplinary forum to explore emerging areas in the field of waste generation, disposal problems, waste treatment technology, environmental health issues, utilization of waste, waste to energy, wealth from waste, biotechnology for waste minimization and integrated waste management.

Editors
(envbooks@gmail.com)

Acknowledgements

"Appreciation is the highest form of Prayers for it acknowledges the presence of Good wherever you shine the light of your Thankful Thoughts".

Behind every success there is certainly an unseen power of Almighty *'God'*. Firstly we are very much thankful to Almighty *'God'*, whose gracious blessings enabled us to complete this work. Above all, we want to thank our beloved parents and whole family, who supported and encouraged us in spite of all the time it took us away from them. It was a long and difficult journey for them.

We are whole heartedly thankful to Mr. Pavan Kumar, Department and Science and Technology, New Delhi and Dr. M K J Siddiqui, Director, CST UP, Lucknow for their inspiration and beholden support. Thanks are also due to all contributors and Publisher for playing their part in all view.

Though this book is a short episode in the long journey of mission, many hands were there to help us and to make it a memorable experience. We would like to express our deepest sense of gratitude to all those people who saw us through this book; to all those who provided support, talked things over, read, wrote, offered comments, allowed us to quote their remarks and assisted in the editing, proof reading and design.

Last but not least, we beg forgiveness of all those who have been with us over the course of the years and whose names we have failed to mention.

– Editors

Contents

Pages: 1-23

WASTE GENERATION AND UTILIZATION

Edited by: **Dr. Priya Bajaj; Dr. B. Tabassum** and **Dr. Pawan Kumar 'Bharti'**

ISBN: 978-93-5056-792-0

Edition: **2016**

Published by: **Discovery Publishing House Pvt. Ltd., New Delhi (India)**

CHAPTER – 1

Wastewater

An Alternate Source of Irrigation Water for Agricultural Production

N. Jagathjothi and M. Mohamed Amanullah

ABSTRACT

Pot culture and field experiment were conducted at the Common Effluent Treatment Plant (CETP), Dindigul, Tamil Nadu, India to study the effect of using wastewater as alternate source of irrigation water for agricultural production especially to investigate the of irrigating treated tannery effluent and domestic wastewater with amendments on marigold growth, yield attributes and yield. The pot culture was laid out in a factorial completely randomized design and field experiment was laid out in factorial randomized block design with four replications. The results of study revealed that the mixing proportion of 1:3 ratio (25% treated tannery effluent + 75% domestic wastewater irrigation) recorded higher growth parameters *viz;* plant height, number of primary branches plant^{-1}, internode length and number of leaves plant^{-1} compared to other mixing proportions. Similarly the physiological parameters *viz;* leaf area index (LAI), leaf area ratio (LAR), leaf area duration (LAD) and SPAD reading were also higher under 25 per cent treated tannery effluent with 75 per cent domestic wastewater irrigation application when compared to other mixing proportions.

Department of Agronomy, Tamil Nadu Agricultural University, Coimbatore - 641 003, Tamil Nadu, India.

Significantly the yield attributes *viz;* number of days to flower bud appearance, days to flower bud opening, days to first harvest were earlier and flower diameter was higher under normal water and 100 per cent domestic wastewater irrigation application which were comparable each other. This was followed by 1:3 ratio which was recorded higher yield attributes among the mixing proportions. Irrigation of 25 per cent treated tannery effluent (TTE) + 75 per cent domestic wastewater (DWW) registered higher yield of marigold with the yield reduction of around 15 per cent compared to normal water irrigation both in pot culture and field experiment. But it was lowest in application of 100 per cent treated tannery effluent alone. With regard to amendments, gypsum application was positively influenced the performance of different irrigation sources on mariold growth, yield attributes and yield compared to control (without amendments) and VAM (Vesicular Arbuscular Mycorrhiza) addition. Among the mixing proportion of irrigation source and amendments, irrigation of 25 per cent TTE + 75 per cent DWW with gypsum recorded higher marigold yield and keeping quality of flower compared to other mixing proportions and 100 per cent TTE with gypsum application.

Keywords: Effluent, taning industry, marigold, pollution, environment.

INTRODUCTION

The leather industry is a major industry on global level and is of noteworthy economic importance. Tannery operations involve conversion of raw hides or skins into leather which can be used for manufacturing of large number of products. The tannery industry is a water and chemical demanding industry, wherein a large number of multipart chemical and mechanical processes are involved. The tannery industry operation is as follows: Process in tanning industry can be broadly classified as pre-tanning, tanning and post tanning process.

Pre tanning is employed mainly for the removal of impurities from the raw materials. The impurities consist of mainly blood, hairs, *etc.,* which has composition of protein. This process involves salt, lime and sulphides as process chemicals. Tanning process is used for altering the characteristics of skin. The effluents of tannery process contains chromium and vegetable or synthetic tanning. Post tanning processes include colouration and produce effluents containing residues of dyestuffs and auxiliary chemicals. Hence, these industries are one of the most polluting industries causing environmental pollution.

The European Union is the world's largest supplier of leather in international market. Italy is the major contributor to the supply of leather in Europe in terms of production, employment, establishments and turnover. Worldwide around 80-90 per cent of the tanneries use Cr (III) salts in their tanning processes. While in India there are about 2500 tanneries and most of them (nearly 80%) are engaged in chrome tanning process (Shukla *et al.* 2009). In India, Tamil Nadu, Uttar Pradesh, West Bengal and Punjab are the dominant states for tanning business. Thus, the natural resources are experiencing an increasing threat of pollution coming from urbanization and industrial development activities.

To deal with the pollution coming out from industries, adoption of cleaner production technologies and waste minimization strategies are being encouraged. Common Effluent Treatment Plants (CETPs) are considered as one of the feasible solution for small to medium enterprises for efficient wastewater treatment. Till 2005, around 88 CETPs had been established across the India. The number of CETPs rose to more than 150 by the year 2011. Even though Tamil Nadu has the highest number of CETPs, Gujarat treats the highest amount of wastewater. Delhi, Maharashtra, Rajasthan and Uttar Pradesh also have a large number of CETPs and also treat a high volume of wastewater. Tamil Nadu has the distinction of being the state that has the maximum number of CETPs. This is due to large concentration of small processing units.

Dindigul district in Tamil Nadu, India, where the study was taken up is known for its leather industries, some of them have been established as early as 1939. Since then tanneries are spreading and at present there are more than 60 well established tanneries. Most of these are located in the central part of town along Madurai, Batlagundu and Ponmandurai roads. During the past few decades, the groundwater is being contaminated giving potential risk to soil ecosystem and human health. To minimize these pollution hazards, the effluent generated in these tanneries are treated by pumping through five pump stations into the Common Effluent Treatment Plant (CETP). Nearly 80 per cent of tanneries in our country are engaged in the chrome-tanning process. But, particularly this CETP is collecting vegetable tanning effluent from 61 leather industries receiving about 1500 m^3 of effluent per day. Domestic wastewater generation in this city is more than 5 time of tannery effluent generation per day.

Generally Dindigul region is drought affected area with minimal water sources due to overexploitation of water table for irrigation and tanning through dug wells, dug-cum-bore wells and bore wells (Mondal *et al.* 2005). In this condition, reuse of treated tannery effluent and domestic wastewater for agriculture will help to reduce pressure on the environment by reducing the use of good quality fresh water.

One of the major pollutants in vegetable tanning effluent is high TDS. So, mixing of treated tannery effluent with abundantly available domestic wastewater may help to reduce the TDS based on the dilution concept and it may also act as efficient and low cost technology to dispose the effluent in a safer way. Apart from the dilution of treated tannery effluent, addition of some soil amendments will favourably be helpful to minimize its redundant effect on crop growth and soil properties. With this back drop, the present study was carried out to study the effect of combined use of treated tannery effluent and domestic waste water an alternate source of irrigation water for agricultural production that is on growth and yield of flower crop of marigold.

Materials and Methods

The pot culture and field experiments were carried out at CETP, Dindigul, Tamil Nadu during 2011-12 to study the effect of using wastewaters from tannery industry and urban area as an alternate source of irrigation water for agricultural production specially in flower crop (Marigold) production. The soil of the pot culture and field was red sandy loam and red sandy clay loam in texture, respectively. The experimental soils were low in available nitrogen, medium in available phosphorus and high in available potash. The pot culture was laid out in a factorial completely randomized design and field experiment laid out in factorial randomized block design with four replications. Treatment comprised six levels of irrigation sources *viz;* I_1 - 25 per cent treated tannery effluent (TTE) + 75 per cent domestic wastewater (DWW), I_2 - 50 per cent TTE + 50 per cent DWW, I_3 - 75 per cent TTE + 25 per cent DWW, I_4 - 100 per cent TTE, I_5 - 100 per cent DWW and I_6 - control (normal water) treatments under factor A and three amendments *viz;* A_0 - control (without amendment), A_1 - gypsum and A_2 - VAM as treatments under factor B. Well decomposed FYM @ 12.5 tonnes per hectare was applied at the time of land preparation. The recommended dose of 90:90:75 kg of NPK ha^{-1} was applied in the form of urea, single super phosphate and muriate of potash, respectively. Half the dose (50%) of N and full dose of P and K were applied as basal. The remaining 50 per cent of the N was top dressed on 45th day after planting (DAP).

In pot culture, all the manures and fertilizers were applied to the crop based on the quantity of (10 kg) soil contained in mud pot (1 ha = $2x10^6$ kg soil). VAM inoculum (*Glomus intraradices*) at the rate of 5g $plant^{-1}$ was at the time of planting. Gypsum was finely powdered and uniformly applied to all the treatments as basal at the rate of 20g pot^{-1}. As per the treatment, equal quantity of irrigation water for each pot was added throughout the experiment period. The half litre of water $irrigation^{-1}$ was given at weekly twice and totally 20 irrigations were given to the crop.

In field experiment, thirty days old healthy and uniform marigold seedlings were transplanted at one seedling $hill^{-1}$ with a spacing of 45 x 30 cm. The variety MDU-1 was used as test crop for cultivation. VAM was applied at the rate of 100 kg ha^{-1} and gypsum applied as basal at the rate of 4 t ha^{-1} as general recommendation. As per the treatment, equal quantity of irrigation water was given for each plot throughout the experiment period with the help of scale marked water tanks.

Five plants were selected at random in each treatment and tagged for taking growth observations. The mean of observations of five plants was arrived and expressed.

Growth Parameters of Marigold

Plant Height

The height was measured from the ground level to growing point of the plant at 40, 80 and 120 DAP and expressed in cm.

Number of Primary Branches Plant^{-1}

The primary branches arising from the main stem alone were counted at 40, 80 and 120 DAP and expressed as number of primary branches plant^{-1}.

Internode Length

The internodal length was recorded at 40, 80 and 120 DAP by measuring the 3rd, 4th and 5th internodes from the tip of the selected plants. The mean value of these three was taken as the internode length for a particular treatment.

Number of Leaves Plant^{-1}

The number of leaves was counted at 40, 80 and 120 DAP and expressed as number plant^{-1}.

Physiological Parameters of Marigold

Leaf area Index

The leaf area index of flower crops was computed by adopting the following formula suggested by Williams (1946). The observations were made at 40, 80 and 120 DAP.

$$\text{LAI} = \frac{\text{Leaf area of plant}}{\text{Land area occupied by plant (cm}^2\text{)}}$$

Leaf area Ratio (LAR)

LAR was calculated by using the formula given by Radford (1967) and expressed in cm^2 g^{-1}.

$$\text{LAR} = \frac{\text{Leaf area per plant}}{\text{Total plant dry weight}}$$

Leaf area Duration (LAD)

Leaf area and its functional duration determine the productivity of crop plants. The duration of the leaf was determined by using the formula suggested by Power *et al.* (1967) and expressed in days.

$$\text{LAD} = \frac{\text{Li} + \text{L(i+1)}}{2} \times (t_2 - t_1)$$

Where,

Li	=	Leaf area index at ith stage.
L(i+1)	=	Leaf area index at (i+1)th stage.
$t_2 - t_1$	=	Time interval between two stages (days).

Chlorophyll Content (SPAD value)

The chlorophyll content was measured through chlorophyll meter (SPAD 502 model) at 40, 80 and 120 DAP.

Yield Components and Yield

Days to flower bud appearance

The number of days taken for visible appearance of the flower bud from the date of planting was recorded and expressed in days.

Days to flower bud opening

The number of days taken from the date of planting to the 50 per cent of the flower bud opening was counted and expressed in days.

Days to first harvest

The number of days taken from the date of planting to the first harvest was counted and expressed in days.

Flower Size

The diameter of the flower was measured across the middle portion of fully opened flower and expressed in cm.

Flower yield plant^{-1}

Marigold flowers were harvested in the morning hours at weekly intervals when the central whorls of petals were fully opened. Total weight of flowers harvested from plant was recorded and expressed in g plant^{-1}.

Keeping Quality of Flowers

Ten flowers from each treatment of selected plants were harvested and kept in plastic plates under room temperature. Every 24 hrs., recorded percentage of flower petal necrosis and flower petal drop over is used as index of keeping quality and the mean value expressed in number of days.

Results and Discussion

Effect on Plant Height

Plant height was significantly influenced by irrigation water and amendments. The plant heights increased progressively with advancement in the age of the crop from 40 to 120 DAP in both the experiment (Table 1.1).

Regarding pot culture, at 40 and 80 DAP, taller plants (46.83 and 96.50 cm) were recorded under normal water irrigation. With regard to mixing ratios, 1:3 ratio of TTE and DWW recorded taller plants compared to other mixing ratios. The least plant height was observed under 100 per cent TTE. However, at 120 DAP irrigation with domestic wastewater recorded taller plants of 118.15 cm. This was comparable with normal water irrigation. The least plant height was recorded under 100 per cent TTE. Among the amendments, gypsum application recorded taller plants of 40.33, 82.89 and 100.58 cm at 40, 80 and 120 DAP compared to VAM and control.

Table 1.1: Effect of wastewaters and amendments on plant height (cm) of marigold

Treatment	Pot Culture			Field Experiment		
	40 DAP	80 DAP	120 DAP	40 DAP	80 DAP	120 DAP
Irrigation water						
I_1: 25% TTE + 75% DWW	38.76	85.88	100.71	39.50	82.70	101.83
I_2: 50% TTE + 50% DWW	35.23	68.64	82.63	36.55	74.20	89.80
I_3: 75% TTE + 25% DWW	33.33	62.13	76.21	35.35	66.95	83.95
I_4: 100% TTE	31.89	56.43	68.72	34.18	58.28	75.60
I_5: 100% DWW	42.74	96.08	118.15	56.55	99.23	124.50
I_6: Control (Normal Water)	46.83	96.50	115.83	50.28	104.55	127.10
SEd	0.61	0.72	0.95	1.97	4.15	6.04
CD *(P=0.05)*	1.22	1.45	1.90	4.19	8.85	12.88
Amendments						
A_0: Control	35.43	72.45	84.64	39.09	75.60	90.75
A_1: Gypsum	40.33	82.89	100.58	44.49	86.49	107.83
A_2: VAM	38.63	77.50	95.90	42.62	80.86	102.82
SEd	0.43	0.51	0.67	1.39	4.35	4.27
CD *(P=0.05)*	0.86	1.03	1.34	2.96	9.26	9.11

TTE – Treated tannery effluent, DWW – Domestic wastewater.

In the field experiment also, at 40 DAP, taller plants (56.55 cm) were recorded under 100 per cent DWW. The least plant height was observed under 100 per cent TTE (34.18 cm). At 80 and 120 DAP, application of normal water recorded taller plants of 104.55 and 127.10 cm, respectively. This was comparable with 100 per cent DWW. The least plant height was recorded under 100 per cent. The plants were taller under irrigation with normal water and 100 per cent DWW which were comparable each other. Better soil conditions for growth, sufficient nutrient availability and the resultant uptake of nutrients resulted in taller plants. With regard to different mixing proportions, application of 25 per cent TTE + 75 per cent DWW (1:3) registered taller plants. Increase in the concentration of tannery effluent reduced the plant height and 100 per cent TTE recorded the least plant height. Higher level of salts in the effluent had inhibiting effect on plant growth (Mishra and Bera, 1995).

Regarding amendments, the gypsum application recorded taller plants of 44.49, 86.49 and 107.83 cm at 40, 80 and 120 DAP compared to VAM and control. Gypsum application improved the plant height compared to other treatments. Gypsum addition ameliorated the injurious effect of salts in the soil which ultimately showed positive effect on the crop growth by better nutrient uptake (Rashid *et al.* 2009).

Effect on Number of Primary Branches Plant^{-1}

The different irrigation sources and amendments significantly influenced the number of primary branches plant^{-1} at all the stages of observation in both pot culture and field experiments (Table 1.2).

Table 1.2: Effect of wastewaters and amendments on number of primary branches plant^{-1} of marigold

Treatment	Pot Culture			Field Experiment		
	40 DAP	80 DAP	120 DAP	40 DAP	80 DAP	120 DAP
Irrigation water						
I_1: 25% TTE + 75% DWW	8.18	10.16	10.97	8.55	12.60	13.45
I_2: 50% TTE + 50% DWW	7.26	8.85	9.43	8.20	11.50	12.50
I_3: 75% TTE + 25% DWW	6.54	8.23	8.92	7.95	10.85	11.95
I_4: 100% TTE	6.02	7.71	8.42	7.80	10.10	11.10
I_5: 100% DWW	11.25	13.30	14.00	9.45	14.10	15.55
I_6: Control (Normal Water)	9.57	11.88	13.58	9.70	14.85	16.35
SEd	*0.14*	*0.15*	*0.17*	*0.32*	*0.44*	*0.60*
CD *(P=0.05)*	0.27	0.31	0.35	0.69	0.93	1.27
Amendments						
A_0: Control	6.93	8.60	9.50	7.33	10.58	11.76
A_1: Gypsum	9.14	11.04	11.96	9.67	13.59	14.81
A_2: VAM	8.34	10.42	11.20	8.82	12.83	13.88
SEd	0.10	0.11	0.12	0.23	0.31	0.42
CD *(P=0.05)*	0.19	0.22	0.25	0.49	0.66	0.90

TTE – Treated tannery effluent, DWW – Domestic wastewater.

In pot culture, higher number of primary branches plant^{-1}was observed under 100 per cent DWW (11.25, 13.30 and 14.00 at 40, 80 and 120 DAP, respectively). Among the combinations, irrigation of 25 per cent TTE with 75 per cent DWW showed higher number of primary branches plant^{-1} of 8.18, 10.16 and 10.97 at 40, 80 and 120 DAP, respectively. The least number of primary branches plant^{-1} was observed under 100 per cent TTE.

With respect to amendments, gypsum addition recorded higher number of primary branches plant^{-1} (9.14, 11.04 and 11.96 at 40, 80 and 120 DAP, respectively). The least number of primary branches plant^{-1} was observed under control (without amendments).

Pertaining to field experiment, higher number of primary branches plant^{-1} was observed under normal water (9.70, 14.85 and 16.35 at 40, 80 and 120 DAP, respectively). Kumar and Reddy (2007) recorded increased number of branches and leaves in tomato with municipal wastewater.

Among the combination, application of 25 per cent TTE with 75 per cent DWW showed higher number of primary branches plant^{-1} of 8.55, 12.60 and 13.45 at 40, 80 and 120 DAP, respectively. The least number of primary branches plant^{-1} was observed under 100 per cent TTE. Regarding amendments, gypsum application recorded higher number of primary branches plant^{-1} compared to VAM and control.

Effect on Internode Length

The irrigation treatments had significant influence on the internode length at all the stages of observation (Table 1.3). Higher internode length of 3.95, 6.39, and 7.28 cm at 40, 80 and 120 DAP, respectively was observed under 100 per cent DWW which was comparable with normal water. Among the combinations, irrigation of 25 per cent TTE with 75 per cent DWW recorded higher internode length of 3.78, 5.92 and 6.79 cm at 40, 80 and 120 DAP, respectively. The least internode length was observed under 100 per cent TTE.

Table 1.3: Effect of wastewaters and amendments on internode length (cm) of marigold

Treatment	Pot Culture			Field Experiment		
	40 DAP	80 DAP	120 DAP	40 DAP	80 DAP	120 DAP
Irrigation water						
I_1: 25% TTE + 75% DWW	3.78	5.92	6.79	3.90	6.63	7.55
I_2: 50% TTE + 50% DWW	3.66	5.65	6.39	3.68	6.43	7.20
I_3: 75% TTE + 25% DWW	3.41	5.27	5.93	3.60	6.15	7.00
I_4: 100% TTE	3.26	4.96	5.52	3.53	5.80	6.68
I_5: 100% DWW	3.95	6.39	7.28	4.50	6.73	7.63
I_6: Control (Normal Water)	3.92	6.20	7.09	5.00	7.10	7.80
SEd	0.04	0.11	0.13	0.18	0.25	0.26
CD *(P=0.05)*	0.08	0.22	0.25	0.39	0.54	0.55
Amendments						
A_0: Control	3.57	5.53	6.29	3.93	6.25	7.07
A_1: Gypsum	3.83	5.99	6.73	4.22	6.76	7.56
A_2: VAM	3.59	5.67	6.49	3.95	6.40	7.29
SEd	0.03	0.08	0.09	0.13	0.18	0.18
CD *(P=0.05)*	0.06	0.16	0.18	0.27	0.38	0.39

TTE – Treated tannery effluent, DWW – Domestic wastewater.

Application of amendments also had significant effect on the internode length. Gypsum application recorded higher internode length of 3.83, 5.99 and 6.73 cm at 40, 80 and 120 DAP, respectively than VAM and control.

Similarly, in the field experiment also, higher internode length was observed under normal water (5.00, 7.10, and 7.80 cm at 40, 80 and 120 DAP, respectively) which was comparable with 100 per cent DWW. This was followed by 25 per cent TTE with 75 per cent DWW. The least internode length was observed under 100 per cent TTE. Gypsum application recorded higher internode length of 4.22, 6.76 and 7.56 cm at 40, 80 and 120 DAP, respectively than VAM application and control. Gypsum application reduced the salinity stress thereby enhanced the growth morphology. This is in conformity with the earlier findings of Jimenez *et al.* (1997) in rose.

Effect on Number of Leaves Plant^{-1}

There existed significant difference on number of leaves plant^{-1} due to irrigation treatments at all the stages of observation (Table 1.4). Irrigation with 100 per cent DWW registered higher number of leaves plant^{-1} (62.53, 85.49 and 100.02 at 40, 80 and 120 DAP, respectively) compared other treatments. This was followed by normal water. Among the mixing ratios, 25 per cent TTE + 75 per cent DWW (1:3) recorded higher number of leaves plant^{-1}. The least number of leaves plant^{-1} was recorded under 100 per cent TTE. Application of amendments exhibited significant effect on number of leaves plant^{-1}. Gypsum recorded higher number of leaves plant^{-1} compared to VAM and control.

Table 1.4: Effect of wastewaters and amendments on number of leaves plant^{-1} of marigold

Treatment	Pot Culture			Field Experiment		
	40 DAP	80 DAP	120 DAP	40 DAP	80 DAP	120 DAP
Irrigation water						
I_1: 25% TTE + 75% DWW	48.59	64.72	80.07	50.61	80.26	98.13
I_2: 50% TTE + 50% DWW	40.95	55.86	66.80	46.19	72.64	88.42
I_3: 75% TTE + 25% DWW	35.81	53.04	63.30	43.54	69.87	83.77
I_4: 100% TTE	31.16	49.19	58.88	40.31	64.38	77.46
I_5: 100% DWW	62.53	85.49	100.02	52.37	95.37	110.92
I_6: Control (Normal Water)	54.46	85.16	94.56	55.11	98.62	115.89
SEd	0.71	0.89	1.05	1.99	2.90	4.40
CD *(P=0.05)*	1.42	1.79	2.11	4.24	6.18	9.39
Amendments						
A_0: Control	38.83	56.85	68.16	40.91	69.52	84.48
A_1: Gypsum	51.21	71.93	84.67	53.95	87.97	104.93
A_2: VAM	46.71	67.95	78.98	49.21	83.09	97.88
SEd	0.50	0.63	0.74	1.41	2.05	3.11
CD *(P=0.05)*	1.01	1.27	1.49	3.00	4.37	6.64

TTE – Treated tannery effluent, DWW – Domestic wastewater.

In field experiment, irrigation of normal water registered higher number of leaves plant^{-1} (55.11, 98.62 and 115.89 at 40, 80 and 120 DAP, respectively) which was comparable with 100 per cent DWW. Among the mixing proportions, 1:3 (25% TTE + 75% DWW) recorded higher number of leaves plant^{-1}. The least number of leaves plant^{-1} was recorded under 100 per cent TTE. This may be due to higher concentration of salts. These results endorse the findings of Abhijeet (2010). With regard to amendments, gypsum recorded higher number of leaves plant^{-1} compared to other treatments.

Effect on Leaf area Index

Leaf area index (LAI) was recorded at three stages *viz;* 40, 80 and 120 DAP. Significant difference in LAI was observed due to irrigation sources and amendments in both the experiments (Table 1.5). In the pot culture experiment, at 40 DAP, 100 per cent DWW registered higher LAI but at 80 and 120 DAP, irrigation with normal water recorded higher LAI of 3.89 and 3.09, respectively. This was followed by 100 per cent DWW irrigation. This might be due to the lesser concentration of salts in soil compared to other treatments (Britto, 1993). Among the mixing proportions, 25 per cent TTE + 75 per cent DWW recorded higher LAI. The least LAI was recorded under 100 per cent TTE at all the stages.

Table 1.5: Effect of wastewaters and amendments on leaf area index (LAI) of marigold

Treatment	Pot Culture			Field Experiment		
	40 DAP	80 DAP	120 DAP	40 DAP	80 DAP	120 DAP
Irrigation water						
I_1: 25% TTE + 75% DWW	1.13	3.11	2.29	1.18	3.86	2.81
I_2: 50% TTE + 50% DWW	0.96	2.42	1.69	1.09	3.14	2.23
I_3: 75% TTE + 25% DWW	0.87	2.23	1.55	1.06	2.93	2.07
I_4: 100% TTE	0.78	2.05	1.34	1.01	2.68	1.76
I_5: 100% DWW	1.46	3.69	2.92	1.23	4.25	3.35
I_6: Control (Normal Water)	1.40	3.89	3.09	1.39	4.46	3.80
SEd	0.02	0.04	0.03	0.04	0.14	0.11
CD *(P=0.05)*	0.04	0.08	0.06	0.09	0.30	0.24
Amendments						
A_0: Control	0.95	2.49	1.86	1.00	3.05	2.31
A_1: Gypsum	1.23	3.19	2.37	1.29	3.91	2.95
A_2: VAM	1.12	3.02	2.21	1.18	3.70	2.75
SEd	0.01	0.03	0.02	0.03	0.10	0.08
CD *(P=0.05)*	0.03	0.06	0.04	0.06	0.21	0.17

TTE – Treated tannery effluent, DWW – Domestic wastewater.

With regard to amendments, addition of gypsum recorded higher LAI of 1.23, 3.19 and 2.37 at 40, 80 and 120 DAP, respectively followed by VAM.

Likewise, in field experiment also, normal water registered higher LAI of 1.39, 4.46 and 3.80 at 40, 80 and 120 DAP. Among the mixing ratios, 25 per cent TTE + 75 per cent DWW recorded higher LAI than the other ratios. The least LAI was recorded under 100 per cent TTE at all the stages. Application of gypsum recorded higher LAI of 1.29, 3.91 and 2.95 at 40, 80 and 120 DAP, respectively followed by VAM and control.

Effect on Leaf area Ratio

Significant variation in leaf area ratio (LAR) was observed between different irrigation sources and amendments (Table 1.6). LAR increased from 40 to 80 DAP and then declined in both the experiments.

Table 1.6: Effect of wastewaters and amendments on leaf area ratio ($cm^2\ g^{-1}$) of marigold

Treatment	Pot Culture			Field Experiment		
	40 DAP	80 DAP	120 DAP	40 DAP	80 DAP	120 DAP
Irrigation water						
I_1: 25% TTE + 75% DWW	51.21	65.40	43.96	55.90	69.95	38.00
I_2: 50% TTE + 50% DWW	47.88	51.51	33.48	55.17	64.35	34.15
I_3: 75% TTE + 25% DWW	40.64	45.69	30.44	54.53	61.69	33.44
I_4: 100% TTE	36.14	39.88	26.35	53.67	61.08	32.40
I_5: 100% DWW	60.20	79.17	59.26	56.70	68.13	40.85
I_6: Control (Normal Water)	59.22	84.31	61.19	62.64	71.95	45.48
SEd	0.72	1.07	0.68	1.88	2.57	1.63
CD *(P=0.05)*	1.44	2.14	1.36	4.01	5.47	3.46
Amendments						
A_0: Control	42.71	49.29	35.82	48.97	53.49	31.55
A_1: Gypsum	57.38	69.12	47.81	65.80	75.00	42.10
A_2: VAM	47.56	64.58	43.71	54.54	70.08	38.50
SEd	0.51	0.75	0.48	1.33	1.82	1.15
CD *(P=0.05)*	1.02	1.51	0.96	2.84	3.87	2.45

TTE – Treated tannery effluent, DWW – Domestic wastewater

In the pot culture experiment, application of 100 per cent DWW recorded higher LAR at 40 DAP and the least was noticed under 100 per cent TTE. But, at 80 and 120 DAP, irrigation of normal water recorded higher LAR of 84.31 and 61.19 $cm^2\ g^{-1}$, respectively. This was followed by 100 per cent DWW. The least LAR was registered under 100 per cent TTE. Among the amendments, gypsum recorded higher LAR compared to VAM and control.

Regarding field experiment, normal water application recorded higher LAR of 62.64, 71.95 and 45.48 cm^2 g^{-1}, respectively. This was followed by 100 per cent DWW. Regarding mixing ratios, 25 per cent TTE + 75 per cent DWW recorded higher LAR due to dilution of salts. This is in conformity with the earlier findings of Karunyal *et al.* (1994) in *Lycopersicon esculentum*. The least LAR was registered under 100 per cent TTE.

With respect to amendments, gypsum applied treatment recorded higher LAR compared to other treatments.

Effect on Leaf area Duration

The leaf area duration (LAD) was significantly influenced by irrigation water and amendments at all the stages in both the experiments (Table 1.7).

Table 1.7: Effect of wastewaters and amendments on leaf area duration (days) of marigold

Treatment	Pot Culture		Field Experiment	
	40-80 DAP	80-120 DAP	40-80 DAP	80-120 DAP
Irrigation water				
I_1: 25% TTE + 75% DWW	84.78	108.01	100.65	133.25
I_2: 50% TTE + 50% DWW	67.67	82.16	84.50	107.25
I_3: 75% TTE + 25% DWW	61.97	75.54	79.80	99.95
I_4: 100% TTE	56.69	67.78	73.90	88.90
I_5: 100% DWW	103.08	132.29	109.50	152.00
I_6: Control (Normal Water)	105.76	139.56	116.95	165.30
SEd	1.28	1.26	3.83	6.14
CD *(P=0.05)*	2.57	2.74	8.15	13.09
Amendments				
A_0: Control	68.68	86.83	80.89	107.10
A_1: Gypsum	88.49	111.31	104.23	137.29
A_2: VAM	82.80	104.53	97.53	128.93
SEd	0.91	0.97	2.71	4.34
CD *(P=0.05)*	1.82	1.94	5.77	9.26

TTE – Treated tannery effluent, DWW – Domestic wastewater.

In pot culture, irrigation of normal water recorded higher LAD of 105.76 and 139.56 days between 40-80 and 80-120 DAP, respectively. This was followed by 100 per cent DWW. The least LAD (56.69 and 67.78 days at 40-80 and 80-120 DAP) was registered under 100 per cent TTE.

There existed significant difference in LAD due to amendments. Higher LAD was recorded under gypsum application than VAM and control.

Regarding the field experiment, irrigation of normal water recorded higher LAD of 116.95 and 165.30 days between 40-80 and 80-120 DAP, respectively. This was followed by 100 per cent DWW. The least LAD was registered under 100 per cent TTE. Higher LAD was recorded under gypsum application than VAM and control.

Effect on SPAD Reading

SPAD reading was significantly influenced by different irrigation sources and amendments in both pot culture and field experiment. In general, SPAD readings increased upto 80 DAP and then declined (Table 1.8).

Table 1.8: Effect of wastewaters and amendments on SPAD reading of marigold

Treatment	Pot Culture			Field Experiment		
	40 DAP	80 DAP	120 DAP	40 DAP	80 DAP	120 DAP
Irrigation water						
I_1: 25% TTE + 75% DWW	41.10	43.03	39.96	40.30	40.35	36.95
I_2: 50% TTE + 50% DWW	38.43	39.67	37.47	38.10	39.60	36.10
I_3: 75% TTE + 25% DWW	36.87	38.42	36.02	36.68	38.60	35.35
I_4: 100% TTE	35.85	37.38	35.20	35.33	37.95	34.73
I_5: 100% DWW	45.14	46.48	42.81	42.98	44.05	39.20
I_6: Control (Normal Water)	44.21	45.34	41.30	44.18	44.75	40.40
SEd	*0.53*	*0.57*	*0.48*	*1.10*	*1.21*	*0.99*
CD *(P=0.05)*	1.07	1.14	0.97	2.33	2.59	2.11
Amendments						
A_0: Control	39.18	40.07	37.32	38.52	39.27	35.71
A_1: Gypsum	41.23	43.05	40.01	40.54	42.19	38.29
A_2: VAM	40.40	42.04	39.05	39.72	41.20	37.36
SEd	0.38	0.40	0.34	0.77	0.86	0.70
CD *(P=0.05)*	0.76	0.81	0.69	1.65	1.83	1.49

TTE – Treated tannery effluent, DWW – Domestic wastewater.

Irrigation of 100 per cent DWW showed higher SPAD readings of 45.14, 46.48 and 42.81 at 40, 80 and 120 DAP, respectively. This was comparable with normal water irrigation. Among the mixing ratios, 25 per cent TTE + 75 per cent DWW recorded higher SPAD readings. The least SPAD readings were recorded under 100 per cent TTE.

Among the amendments, gypsum recorded higher SPAD readings of 41.23, 43.05 and 40.01 at 40, 80 and 120 DAP, respectively.

Regarding field experiment, irrigation of normal water showed higher SPAD readings of 44.18, 44.75 and 40.40 at 40, 80 and 120 DAP, respectively.

Among the mixing ratios, (1:3) 25 per cent TTE + 75 per cent DWW recorded higher SPAD readings compared to other mixing ratios. This was comparable with 100 per cent DWW. Increasing concentration of TTE reduced the photosynthetic pigments with increasing level of salts as indicated by Amini and Ehsanpour (2006) in tomato might be the reason for reduced LAD and SPAD reading. The least SPAD readings were recorded under 100 per cent TTE.

With respect to amendments, gypsum recorded higher SPAD readings of 40.54, 42.19 and 38.29 at 40, 80 and 120 DAP, respectively compared to VAM and control.

Effect on days to Flower bud Appearance

Days to flower bud appearance was significantly influenced by different irrigation treatments and amendments in both the experiments (Table 1.9).

In pot culture, early flower bud appearance (49.75 days) was observed under normal water irrigation which was comparable with 100 per cent DWW (50.42 days). This was followed by the mixing ratio of 25 per cent TTE + 75 per cent DWW (54.11 days) among the mixing ratios. There was delay in flower bud appearance under 100 per cent TTE (58.89 days). Regarding amendments, application of gypsum recorded early flower bud appearance (52.15 days) compared to other treatments.

In the field experiment, early flower bud appearance (54.26 days) was early under normal water irrigation which was comparable with 100 per cent DWW (55.14 days) and 25 per cent TTE + 75 per cent DWW (57.92 days). Flower bud appearance was late under 100 per cent TTE (64.05 days). With respect to amendments, application of gypsum recorded early flower bud appearance (56.90 days) compared to VAM and control.

Effect on days to Flower bud Opening

Days to flower bud opening was significantly influenced by different irrigation sources and amendments in both the experiments (Table 1.9).

In pot culture, among the irrigation treatments, the days to flower bud opening was lesser in 100 per cent DWW (56.01 days). This was comparable with normal water irrigation (56.79 days) while, 100 per cent TTE (68.35 days) took more number of days for flower bud opening. With respect to amendments, earlier flower bud opening (60.71 days) was observed under gypsum application.

Regarding field experiment, flower bud opening was earlier under normal water (59.26 days). This was comparable with 100 per cent DWW irrigation (60.34 days) and 100 per cent TTE (70.60 days) took more number of days to flower bud opening. Regarding amendments, flower bud opening (62.82 days) was early under gypsum application.

Effect on days to First Harvest

The days to first harvest differed significantly due to different irrigation treatments and amendments in both the experiments (Table 1.9).

Table 1.9: Effect of wastewaters and amendments on yield attributes of marigold

Treatment	Pot Culture			Field Experiment		
	No. of Days for Flower bud Appearance	No. of Days for Flower bud Opening	No. of Days for First Harvest	No. of Days for Flower bud Appearance	No. of Days for Flower bud Opening	No. of Days for First Harvest
Irrigation water						
I_1: 25% TTE + 75% DWW	54.11	60.08	72.20	57.92	63.75	76.00
I_2: 50% TTE + 50% DWW	56.02	63.35	74.49	60.37	66.51	78.84
I_3: 75% TTE + 25% DWW	55.50	65.92	74.59	62.53	69.02	81.37
I_4: 100% TTE	58.89	68.35	79.01	64.05	70.60	83.08
I_5: 100% DWW	50.42	56.01	67.29	55.14	60.34	73.39
I_6: Control (Normal Water)	49.75	56.79	67.62	54.26	59.26	71.34
SEd	0.63	0.97	0.99	2.21	2.38	2.77
CD *(P=0.05)*	1.27	1.95	1.98	4.70	5.06	5.89
Amendments						
A_0: Control	56.59	62.80	74.72	61.75	67.01	80.17
A_1: Gypsum	52.15	60.71	70.94	56.90	62.82	75.14
A_2: VAM	53.61	61.75	71.94	58.49	64.91	76.70
SEd	0.45	0.69	0.70	1.56	1.68	1.96
CD *(P=0.05)*	0.90	1.38	1.40	3.33	3.58	4.17

TTE – Treated tannery effluent, DWW – Domestic wastewater.

In pot culture, irrigation of 100 per cent DWW (67.29 days) took lesser number of days for first harvest compared to other treatments. This was comparable with normal water irrigation (67.62 days) and followed by the mixing ratios of (1:3) 25 per cent TTE + 75 per cent DWW (72.20 days). It took more number of days to first harvest under 100 per cent TTE (79.01 days). Regarding amendments, application of gypsum took less number of days (70.94 days) to first harvest compared to VAM and control.

Similarly, in the field experiment also, irrigation of normal water (71.34 days) took less number of days to first harvest compared to other treatments. This was comparable with 100 per cent DWW (73.39 days) and 25 per cent TTE + 75 per cent DWW (76.00 days). It took more number of days to first harvest under 100 per cent TTE (83.08 days). Application of gypsum recorded the least number of days (75.14 days) to first harvest compared to VAM and control.

Effect on Flower Diameter

The flower diameter varied with different irrigation treatments and amendments in both the experiments (Table 1.10). Irrigation of normal water recorded higher flower diameter (5.73 cm) which was comparable with 100 per cent DWW and was followed by 25 per cent TTE + 75 per cent DWW.

Table 1.10: Effect of wastewaters and amendments on flower diameter (cm) of marigold

Treatment	Pot Culture				Field Experiment			
	Amendments				Amendments			
	A_0	A_1	A_2	Mean	A_0	A_1	A_2	Mean
I_1: 25% TTE + 75% DWW	4.70	5.43	5.28	5.13	5.15	5.95	5.78	5.63
I_2: 50% TTE + 50% DWW	3.97	4.55	4.40	4.31	4.38	5.02	4.85	4.75
I_3: 75% TTE + 25% DWW	3.52	3.93	3.78	3.74	3.93	4.38	4.21	4.18
I_4: 100% TTE	2.70	3.08	2.93	2.90	3.09	3.53	3.36	3.33
I_5: 100% DWW	5.22	6.05	5.90	5.72	5.65	6.55	6.39	6.20
I_6: Control (Normal Water)	5.09	6.13	5.98	5.73	5.57	6.71	6.54	6.28
Mean	4.20	4.86	4.71		4.63	5.36	5.19	
	SEd		CD (*P*=0.05)		SEd		CD (*P*=0.05)	
I	0.07		0.13		0.23		0.49	
A	0.05		0.09		0.16		0.35	
I x A	0.11		0.23		0.40		0.85	

TTE – Treated tannery effluent, DWW – Domestic wastewater.
A_0 – Without amendment (control), A_1 – Gypsum, A_2 – VAM.

The least flower diameter was observed under 100 per cent TTE. Regarding amendments, higher flower diameter was observed under gypsum application (4.86 cm) and the least diameter of flower was recorded under control (without amendments).

The interaction between irrigation water and amendments on flower diameter was significant. Higher flower diameter (6.13 cm) was recorded under treatment combination of normal water along with gypsum application. However, the flower diameter under this combination was comparable with the flower diameter obtained under normal water along with VAM. With regard to mixing ratios and amendments, irrigation of 25 per cent TTE + 75 per cent DWW (1:3) along with gypsum recorded higher flower diameter (5.43 cm). The least diameter of flower was recorded under 100 per cent TTE without amendments.

With respect to the field experiment, irrigation with normal water recorded higher flower diameter (6.28 cm) which was comparable with 100 per cent DWW and was followed by 25 per cent TTE + 75 per cent DWW. The least flower diameter was observed under 100 per cent TTE.

Regarding amendments, higher flower diameter was observed under gypsum application (5.36 cm). The interaction between irrigation water and amendments on flower diameter was significant. Higher flower diameter

(6.71 cm) was recorded under treatment combination of normal water along with gypsum application. However, the flower diameter under this combination was comparable with the flower diameter obtained under normal water along with VAM. The least flower diameter was recorded under 100 per cent TTE without amendments.

With regard to yield components *viz;* number of days to flower bud appearance, days to flower bud opening, days to first harvest were earlier and flower diameter was higher under normal water and 100 per cent DWW application which were comparable each other. This may be due to availability and uptake of sufficient amount of nutrients for their growth and development as reported by Safi *et al.* (2007) in *Lilium aziatische.*

Among the mixing ratios of TTE and DWW, irrigation with 25 per cent TTE + 75 per cent DWW showed higher yield parameters but the yield parameters reduced with increasing concentration of effluent *viz;* 2:2 and 3:1 ratios. Similarly, 100 per cent TTE recorded the least yield parameters. Reduced metabolic activity due to lesser growth and uptake of nutrients under high effluent concentration as reported by Babyshakila and Usha (2009) might be the reason for the reduction in yield parameters.

Application of gypsum enhanced the yield parameters compared to the other treatments which might be due to reduced salt concentration of soil due to addition of gypsum and the resultant higher uptake of nutrients as reported by Saeed and Ahmad (2009) in tomato.

Effect on Flower yield Plant^{-1}

Significant differences among the irrigation sources and amendments were observed with regard to flower yield plant^{-1} in both the experiments (Table 1.11).

In the pot culture, regarding irrigation treatments, irrigation with normal water recorded higher flower yield plant^{-1} (309.2 g) which was comparable with irrigation of 100 per cent DWW (295.7 g). This was followed by the mixing ratio of 25 per cent TTE + 75 per cent DWW (264.0 g). The least flower yield plant^{-1} was recorded under 100 per cent TTE. Among the amendments, gypsum application recorded higher flower yield plant^{-1} (263.9 g) compared to VAM and control. The interaction between irrigation water and amendments on flower yield plant^{-1} was significant. Higher flower yield plant^{-1} (340.4 g) was registered under normal water along with gypsum application. Among the mixing ratios and amendments, 25 per cent TTE + 75 per cent DWW along with gypsum recorded higher flower yield plant^{-1} (295.5 g). The least flower yield plant^{-1} was obtained under 100 per cent TTE without amendments.

Table 1.11: Effect of wastewaters and amendments on flower yield plant^{-1} (g) of marigold

Treatment	Pot Culture				Field Experiment			
	Amendments				Amendments			
	A_0	A_1	A_2	Mean	A_0	A_1	A_2	Mean
I_1: 25% TTE + 75% DWW	225.7	295.5	271.0	264.0	224.9	294.4	270.0	263.1
I_2: 50% TTE + 50% DWW	173.4	231.2	211.9	205.5	190.6	254.2	233.0	225.9
I_3: 75% TTE + 25% DWW	158.0	214.2	196.9	189.7	165.7	224.7	206.6	199.0
I_4: 100% TTE	128.2	178.5	161.2	156.0	129.0	179.7	162.3	157.0
I_5: 100% DWW	267.2	323.7	296.3	295.7	278.8	337.7	309.1	308.5
I_6: Control (Normal Water)	274.1	340.4	312.9	309.2	277.1	344.1	316.3	312.5
Mean	204.4	263.9	241.7		211.0	272.5	249.5	
	SEd		CD *(P=0.05)*		SEd		CD *(P=0.05)*	
I	1.9		3.9		16.2		34.6	
A	1.4		2.7		11.5		24.5	
I x A	3.3		6.7		27.7		59.1	

TTE – Treated tannery effluent, DWW – Domestic wastewater.
A_0 – Without amendment (control), A_1 – Gypsum, A_2 – VAM.

In the field experiment, irrigation of normal water recorded higher flower yield plant^{-1} (312.5 g) was comparable with 100 per cent DWW application (308.5 g). Better vegetative growth of the crop and yield attributes under stress free environment has resulted in good flower yield. Among the mixing ratio of TTE and DWW, 1:3 ratio (25% TTE + 75% DWW) recorded higher yield plant^{-1} (263.1 g). The yield reduction under 25 per cent TTE + 75 per cent DWW was 15.85 per cent and 49.72 per cent under 100 per cent TTE (field experiment) compared to normal water. Similarly, pot culture also showed less than 14.62 per cent and 47.24 per cent yield reduction in the respective treatments compared to normal water application. The lesser reduction in yield under 25 per cent TTE + 75 per cent DWW compared to 100 per cent treated tannery effluent was due to reduced concentration of toxic ions in the root zone which enhanced the crop growth and yield (Castilhos *et al.* 2002).

Among the amendments, gypsum application recorded higher flower yield plant^{-1} (272.17 g) compared to VAM and control. This might be due to reduction in sodicity as evidenced by reduction in ESP in this study and addition of sulphur present in gypsum as reported by Chen *et al.* (2010) in *Broccoli*.

The interaction between irrigation water and amendments on flower yield plant^{-1} was significant. Higher (344.1 g) flower yield plant^{-1} was registered under normal water along with gypsum application. Among the combination of mixing ratios and amendments, irrigation with 25 per cent TTE + 75 per cent DWW with gypsum recorded higher flower yield plant^{-1} (294.4 g). The least flower yield plant^{-1} was obtained under 100 per cent TTE without amendments.

Effect on keeping Quality of Flower

Different irrigation treatments and amendments showed significant effect on keeping quality of flowers in both the experiments (Table 1.12).

Table 1.12: Effect of wastewaters and amendments on keeping quality (days) of marigold

Treatment	Pot Culture				Field Experiment			
	Amendments				Amendments			
	A_0	A_1	A_2	Mean	A_0	A_1	A_2	Mean
I_1: 25% TTE + 75% DWW	3.30	4.04	3.42	3.58	3.61	4.42	3.74	3.92
I_2: 50% TTE + 50% DWW	2.79	3.39	2.88	3.02	3.12	3.80	3.23	3.38
I_3: 75% TTE + 25% DWW	2.57	2.85	2.75	2.73	2.86	3.17	3.06	3.03
I_4: 100% TTE	1.96	2.30	2.05	2.10	2.28	2.68	2.39	2.45
I_5: 100% DWW	4.00	4.81	4.31	4.37	4.31	5.17	4.65	4.71
I_6: Control (Normal Water)	3.91	4.68	4.29	4.30	4.32	5.18	4.72	4.74
Mean	3.09	3.68	3.28		3.42	4.07	3.63	
	SEd		CD (P=0.05)		SEd		CD (P=0.05)	
I	0.05		0.10		0.21		0.44	
A	0.04		0.07		0.15		0.31	
I x A	0.09		0.18		0.36		0.75	

TTE – Treated tannery effluent, DWW – Domestic wastewater.

A_0 – Without amendment (control), A_1 – Gypsum, A_2 – VAM.

In the pot culture, the keeping quality of flower was significantly higher under 100 per cent DWW (4.37 days) and normal water (4.30 days) which were comparable with each other. This was followed by the mixing proportion of 25 per cent TTE + 75 per cent DWW (3.58 days). The least keeping quality of flowers was observed under 100 per cent TTE. Regarding amendments, higher keeping quality of flowers (3.68 days) was observed under gypsum application compared to other treatments. The interaction between irrigation water and amendments was significant on keeping quality of flower. Irrigation of normal water along with gypsum recorded better keeping quality of flower (4.68 days) and the least keeping quality of flower (1.96 days) was observed under 100 per cent TTE without amendments.

Pot culture experiment

Field Experiment

In the field experiment, the keeping quality of flower was higher under normal water (4.74 days) and 100 per cent DWW (4.71 days) which were significantly comparable with each other. In normal water irrigation, better keeping quality of flowers might be due to optimum nutrient content of crop as reported by Shubha (2006) in marigold. This was followed by the mixing ratios of 25 per cent TTE + 75 per cent DWW (3.92 days). The least keeping quality of flower was observed under 100 per cent TTE. This might be due to higher accumulation of excess salt in flowers and lesser nutrients. Regarding the amendments, higher keeping quality of flower (4.07 days) was observed under gypsum application compared to other treatments. Gypsum addition subsequently released Ca which enhanced the availability and uptake of Ca that moves very slowly from root to end of the transport system. This might be the reason for improved keeping quality of flower as reported by Heckman (2008) in tomato.

The interaction between irrigation water and amendments on keeping quality of flower was significant. Irrigation of normal water along with gypsum recorded higher keeping quality of flower (5.18 days) and the least keeping quality of flower (2.28 days) was observed under 100 per cent TTE without amendments.

Conclusion

Irrigation of 25 per cent treated tannery effluent with 75 per cent domestic wastewater (1:3 ratio) is best option for effective utilization of wastewater as alternate source of irrigation water for marigold production. Therefore, use of diluted treated tannery effluent with domestic wastewater helpful for irrigating crop without significant loss in the marigold yield compared to irrigation of raw treated tannery effluent.

REFERENCES

Abhijeet, K.S. (2010): Impact of Mixed Treated Tannery Effluent along with Domestic Wastewater Irrigation and Soil Amendments on Crops. *M.Sc., (Ag.) Thesis,* Department of Environmental Science, Tamil Nadu Agric. Univ., Coimbatore.

Amini, F. and Ehsanpour, A.A. (2006): Response of Tomato Cultivars to MS, Water Agar and Salt Stress *In vitro* Culture. *Pak. J. Biol. Sci.,* 9: 170-175.

Babyshakila, P. and Usha, K. (2009): Effect of Diluted Effluent on Soil Properties and Plant Growth. *Adv. Studies in Biol.,* 1(8): 391-398.

Britto, A.J.D. (1993): Morphological and Physiological Response of *Sorghum vulgare* to Sewage Treatment. *J. Ecotoxicol. Environ. Monit.,* 3(4): 233-236.

Castilhos, D.D., Tedesco, M.J. and Vidor, C. (2002): Crop Yields and Chemical Alterations in Soil Treated with Tannery Waste and Hexavalent chromium. *R. Bras. Ci. Solo.,* 26: 1083-1092.

Chen, L., Tubail, K., Kost, D. and Dick, W.A. (2010): Effects of gypsum enhanced composts on Yields and Mineral Compositions of Broccoli and Tall fescue. *J. Plant Nutrition,* 33: 1040-1055.

Heckman, J.R. (2008): Can Soil Fertility Influence Tomato Flavour. *New Jersey Annual Vegetable Meeting Proceedings*, pp. 11-13.

Jimenez, M.S., Gonzales, A.M., Rodring, Morales, D., Cid, M.C., Soccoro, R.A. and Cabrello. (1997): Evaluation of chlorophyll fluorescence as a tool for salt Stress Detection in Roses. *Photosynthetica*, 33(2): 291-301.

Karunyal, S., Renuga, G. and Paliwal, K. (1994): Effects of Tannery Effluent on Seed Germination Leaf area, Biomass and Mineral Content of some Plants, *Biores. Technol.*, 47(3): 215-218.

Kumar, A.Y. and Reddy, M.V. (2007): Effect of Municipal Sewage Irrigation on the Growth of Tomato Plants on Sandy Soils at Kalpakkam, Tamil Nadu, India. *Nature Environ. Poll. Technol.*, 6(4): 549-556.

Mishra, P. and Bera, A.K. (1995): Effect of Tannery Effluent on Seed Germination and Early Seedling Growth in wheat. *Seed Res.*, 23: 129-131.

Mondal, N.C, Saxena V.K. and Singh, V.S. (2005): Impact of Pollution due to Tanneries on Groundwater regime. *Curr. Sci.*, 88 (12): 1988-1994.

Power, J.E., Wills, W.O., Granes D.L. and Reichman, G.A. (1967): Effect of Soil Temperature, phosphorus and Plant age on Growth Analysis of Barley. *Agron. J.*, 59: 231-234.

Radford, D.J. (1967): Growth Analysis Formula, their use and abuse. *Crop Sci.*, 7: 171-175.

Rashid, A., Khan, R.U. and Marwat, S.K. (2009): Response of Wheat to Soil amendments with Poor Quality Irrigation Water in Salt Affected Soil. *World J. Agric. Sci.*, 5(4): 422-424.

Saeed, R. and Ahmad, R. (2009): Vegetative Growth and Yield of Tomato as Affected by the Application of Organic mulch and gypsum under saline rhizosphere. *Pak. J. Bot.*, 41(6): 3093-3105.

Safi, M.I., Bulad, A. and Blawenah, A. (2007): Flower Yield and Quality of *'Lilium aziatische'* Irrigated with different Types of Water. *Bulgarian J. Agric. Sci.*, 13: 51-54.

Shubha, B.M. (2006): Integrated Nutrient Management for Growth, Flowering and xanthophyll yield of marigold (*Tagetes erecta L.*). *M.Sc., (Ag.) Thesis*, Department of horticulture, UAS, Dharwad.

Shukla, O.P., Rai, U.N. and Dubey, S. (2009): Involvement and Interaction of Microbial Communities in the Transformation and Stabilization of Chromium during the Composting of Tannery Effluent Treated biomass of *Vallisneria spiralis L. Bioresource Technology*, 100: 2198-2203.

Williams, R.F. (1946): The Physiology of Plant Growth with Special Referance to the Concept of net assimilation rate. *Ann. Bot.*, 10: 41-72.

Pages: 24-43

WASTE GENERATION AND UTILIZATION

Edited by: **Dr. Priya Bajaj; Dr. B. Tabassum** and **Dr. Pawan Kumar 'Bharti'**

ISBN: 978-93-5056-792-0

Edition: **2016**

Published by: **Discovery Publishing House Pvt. Ltd., New Delhi (India)**

CHAPTER - 2

Vermicomposting Biotechnology

An Eco-friendly Technology for Bioconversion of Organic Wastes in to Biofertilizers

Nitin Prakash Pandit;[1] **Jaswant Ray;**[2] **Indu Bhati;**[1]
Dipti Chaudhary;[1] **Mukul Chaudhary**[1] and **Priti Gupta**[3]

ABSTRACT

Day-by-day vigorous changes in the human population, indiscriminate growth of urban cities, industrialization, and agricultural practices have led to an increased accumulation of solid organic waste materials in the environment. The recovery of nutrients by modification of wastes like: municipal solid waste, industrial solid waste, agricultural residues, and animal wastes, etc., is important for their management and for reducing environmental degradation. Recycling of organic wastes through vermicomposting biotechnology is an emerging trend as an 'environmentally sustainable', 'economically viable' and 'socially acceptable' technology all over the world. The review assesses the following topics in detail: Vermicomposting biotechnology, earthworm species for waste management, raw materials for vermicomposting, environmental factors effecting vermicomposting, applications of vermicompost and future prospects.

Keywords: Solid organic wastes, earthworm species, environmental factors, vermicomposting.

1. Department of Biotechnology, Vinayak Vidyapeeth (A Unit of Rudra Group of Institution), Modipuram, Meerut - 250 110, Uttar Pradesh, India.
2. Society for Environmental, Health, Awareness of Nutrition and Toxicology (SEHAT) India.
3. Directorate of Agricultural Marketing, Government of NCT of Delhi, 49 Shamnath Marg, Delhi - 110 054, India.

INTRODUCTION

In past 20 years population pressure, urbanization, industrialization, and mechanized agricultural activities have increased, due to which organic waste materials have been accumulated in the environment as Solid Organic Waste (SOW). On one hand tropical soils are deficient in all necessary plant nutrients and on the other hand large quantities of such nutrients available in SOW. Treatment of Solid Organic Wastes has therefore become an essential part of life almost all over the world, the alarming increase in their quantity and the mixing of biodegradable and non-biodegradable wastes at the generation points make it complicated to handle them with limited resources. The overall objective of SOW management is to minimize the adverse environmental effects caused by the indiscriminate disposal of SOWs (Pevey *et al.* 1985). Further, the disposal of wastes through the use of earthworms also upgrade the value of original waste materials in situ and allows a final product to be obtained free of chemical or biological pollutants (Bouche, 1979; Divya, 2001). Vermicomposting is a decomposition process involving the joint action of earthworms and microorganisms. Although microorganisms are responsible for the biochemical degradation of organic matter, earthworms are crucial drivers of the process, by fragmenting and conditioning the substrate and dramatically altering its biological activity. Earthworms act as mechanical blenders and by comminuting the organic matter they modify its physical and chemical status, gradually reducing its C:N ratio, increasing the surface area exposed to microorganisms and making it much more favorable for microbial activity and further decomposition. Greatly during passage through the earthworm gut, they move fragments and bacteria-rich excrements, thus homogenizing the organic material. Earthworms involved directly or indirectly in organic matter decomposition, stabilization, and nutrient turn-over (Edwards and Lofty, 1977; Edwards *et al.* 1988; Edwards and Bohlen, 1996; Singh, 1997a; Lavelle and Spain, 2001).

The cast produced after bioconversion of organic wastes through earthworm is a special type of Bio-fertilizer (Vermicompost). The term 'Biofertilizer' or more appropriately a 'Microbial inoculants' can generally be defined as preparation containing live or latent cells of efficient strains of Nitrogen fixing, Phosphate solublising or cellulolytic microorganisms used for application to seeds, soil with the objective of increasing the number of such microorganisms and accelerate those microbial process which augment the availability of nutrients that can be easily assimilated by plants. It is generally accepted that microbial biomass and respiration are greater in earthworm casts/vermicompost than in the parent soil (Tiunov and Scheu, 2000; Aira *et al.* 2003). However earthworms can feed on these selective raw materials (Moody *et al.* 1995; Edwards, 2004), resulting in an increase in culturable aerobic microorganisms and micro and macro nutrients in the cast of earthworms, as seen with studies on *Lumbricus terrestris* and *Lumbricus rubellus* (Kristufek *et al.* 1992; Fisher *et al.* 1995; Schonholzer *et al.* 1999). Earthworms are therefore considered as potential for use in SOW management through the use of Vermicomposting Technology.

Vermicomposting Biotechnology

Millions of tonnes of solid waste (SW) generated from the modern society are ending up in the landfills every day, creating extraordinary economic and environmental problems for the local government to manage and monitor them (may be up to 30 years) for environmental safety (emission of GHG, toxic gases and leach ate discharge into ground water and soil). Another serious cause of concern today is the emission of greenhouse gases (GHG) methane (CH4) and nitrous oxides (N2O) resulting from the disposal of SW either in the landfills or from their management by conventional composting systems. We are facing the escalating socio-economic and environmental cost of dealing with current and future generation of mounting solid wastes (SW). A considerable portion of SW consist of 'Organic Wastes' that are 'biodegradable' and can be vermicomposted into a highly 'nutritive bio-fertilizer' 4-5 fold more powerful than conventional composts and even superior to chemical fertilizers for better crop growth and safe food production.

Waste degradation and composting by earthworms is proving to be economically and environmentally preferred technology over the conventional microbial degradation and composting technology as it is rapid and nearly odorless process, reducing composting time by more than half and the end product is both 'disinfected' and 'detoxified' (Loehr *et al.* 1984; Edwards, 1998). One million worms doubling every two months can become 64 million worms at the end of the year. Considering that each adult worm (particularly *Eisenia fetida*) consume organics waste equivalent to its own body weight everyday, 64 million worms (weighing 64 tons) would consume 64 tons of waste everyday and produce 30-32 tonnes of vermicompost per day at 40-50 per cent conversion rate.

Types of Solid Organic Wastes (SOW) and Earthworm Species used in Vermicomposting Biotechnology

Solid Organic Substrates have been classified by Thomas and Trivedy (2002) on the basis of physical and chemical characteristics is presented in Table 2.1. The use of different organic substrates and species of earthworms employed and their suitability in vermicomposting is presented in Table 2.2. Substrates, especially agricultural residues, have been tested extensively in combination with an easily biodegradable substrate such as: Cow Dung (CD). Kale *et al.* (1986) reported the suitability of neem cake as an additive in earthworm feed and its significance in the establishment of micro flora. *E. eugeniae* was tolerant to neem cake in the culture medium up to a concentration of 1.6-6.4 per cent and had a positive effect on earthworm biomass production.

Table 2.1: Rating of substrates for vermicomposting

Sl. No.	Types of Substrates	C:N Ratio	Suitability
1.	Fish, scrap poultry manure, night soil, activated sludge, pig manure, sheep dropping, meat scraps, cotton seed meal and other oil seed residues	1-19	Most suitable due to high Nitrogen content
2.	Garbage, sea weed, butter cup, amaranthus, lettuce, cabbage and vegetable waste which are fresh, green and succulent including wastes from food processing industries	19-27	Moderately suitable
3.	Saw dust flax, waste straw, coir waste, etc., including all crop residues with high lignocelluloses content, high carbon and low moisture	27-208	Less suitable

Source: Thomas and Trivedy, 2002.

Table 2.2: Earthworm species employed for vermicomposting of Solid Organic Wastes (SOW)

Sl. No.	Solid Organic Waste (SOW)	Species Employed	Reference
1.	Potato peels	*Pheretima elongate*	Munnoli *et al.* 2000
2.	Press mud	*Pheretima elongate Eudrilus eugeniae, Eisenia fetida, Megascolex megascolex*	Singh, 1997b Munnoli, 2007 Munnoli and Bhosle, 2008
3.	Canteen waste	*Eisenia fetida*	Kale, 1994; Narayan, 2000
4	Tomato skin seed	*Pheretima elongate*	Singh, 1997a
5.	Onion residue	*Eisenia fetida/Eudrilus eugeniae*	White, 1996
6.	Sericulture waste	*Perionyx excavates*	Gunthilingaraj and Ravignanam, 1996
7.	Sericulture waste	*Phanerochaete chrysosporium*	Kallimani, 1998
8.	Board mill sludge	*Lumbricus terrestris*	Butt *et al.* 2005
9.	Sugar cane residues	*Pheretima elongate*	Bhawalkar, 1995
10.	Gaur gum	*Eudrilus eugeniae*	Suthar, 2006, 2007
11.	Agricultural residues	*Eudrilus eugeniae*	Kale, 1994
16.	Sago waste	*Lampito mauritii*	Rajesh *et al.* 2008
17.	Sago waste	*Eisenia fetida*	Subramaniana *et al.* 2010
18.	Onion waste	*Eudrilus eugeniae*	Mishra *et al.* 2009
19.	Garlic waste	*Eisenia fetida*	Mishra *et al.* 2009
20.	Source separated from human feces	*Eisenia fetida*	Yadav *et al.* 2010
21.	Paper mill sludge	*Eisenia fetida*	Kaur *et al.* 2010
22.	Press mud, bagassi, sugar cane trash	*Drawida willsi*	Kumar *et al.* 2010
23.	Press mud	*Perionyx ceylanensis*	Mani and Karmegam, 2010

E. eugeniae was mass cultured on 6 different feed formulate prepared by mixing CD, sheep and horse dung with other OWs such as: rice polish, wheat barn and green gram bran vegetable waste and eggshell powder in various combinations (Bano *et al.* 1987). A laboratory-scale study was conducted to access the suitability of powdered rubber leaf litter as vermiculture substrate for *P. excavatus*, *E. eugeniae*, and *E. fetida.*

Some Important Studies on Vermicomposting Biotechnology

- Visvanathan *et al.* (2005) studied vermicomposting in great details and found that most earthworms consume, at the best, half their body weight of organics in the waste in a day. *Eisenia fetida* can consume organic matter at the rate equal to their body weight every day. Earthworm participation enhances natural biodegradation and decomposition of organic waste from 60 to 80 per cent over the conventional aerobic and anaerobic composting. Given the optimum conditions of temperature (20-30°C) and moisture (60-70%), about 5 kg of worms (numbering approx. 10,000) can vermiprocess 1 tonne of waste into vermicompost in just 30 days. Upon vermicomposting the volume of solid waste is significantly reduced from approximately 1 cum to 0.5 cum of vermicompost indicating 50 per cent conversion rate, the rest is converted into worm biomass.
- Kale (1998); Kale *et al.* (1992); Seenappa *et al.* (1995); Gunathilagraj (1996) and Lakshmi *et al.* (2000) studied the degradation and composting of 'wastewater sludge' from paper pulp and cardboard industry, brewery and distillery, sericulture industry, vegetable oil factory, potato and corn chips manufacturing industry, sugarcane industry, aromatic oil extraction industry, and logging and carpentry industry by earthworms. These organic wastes offer excellent feed materials for vermicomposting by earthworms. Kale *et al.* (1995) also studied the vermicomposting of waste from the mining industry which contains sulfur residues and creates disposal problems. They can also be fed to the worms mixed with organic matter. Optimum mixing ratio of the sulfur waste residues to the organic matter was 4 per cent.
- Saxena *et al.* (1998) studied the vermicomposting of 'fly-ash' from the coal power plants which is considered as a hazardous waste and poses serious disposal problem due to heavy metal contents. As it is also rich in nitrogen and microbial biomass it can be vermicomposted by earthworms. They found that 25 per cent of fly-ash mixed with sisal green pulp, parthenium and green grass cuttings formed excellent feed for *Eisenia fetida* and the vermicompost was higher in NKP contents than other commercial manures. The earthworms ingest the heavy metals from the fly-ash while converting them into vermicompost.

- Bajsa *et al.* (2004) successfully studied vermicomposting of 'human excreta' (feces). It was completed in six months, with good physical texture, odourless and safe pathogen quality. Sawdust appeared to be the best covering material that can be used in vermicomposting toilets to produce compost with a good earthy smell, a crumbly texture and dark brown colour.

Mechanism of Earthworm action during Vermicomposting of Solid Organic Wastes

Grinding Action

The waste feed materials ingested is finely ground (with the aid of stones in their muscular gizzard) into small particles to a size of 2-4 microns and passed on to the intestine for enzymatic actions. The gizzard and the intestine work as a 'bioreactor'.

Enzymatic Action

The gizzard and the intestine work as a 'bioreactor'. Worms secrete enzymes proteases, lipases, amylases, cellulases and chitinases in their gizzard and intestine which bring about rapid biochemical conversion of the cellulosic and the proteinaceous materials in the waste organics. They ingest the food materials, cull the harmful microorganisms, and deposit them mixed with minerals and beneficial microbes as 'vermicasts' in the soil (Dash 1978).

Worms Reinforce Decomposer Microbes and act Synergistically

Worms promotes the growth of 'beneficial decomposer microbes' (bacteria, actinomycetes and fungi) in waste biomass (Dash, 1978; Binet *et al.* 1998). They hosts millions of decomposer microbes in their gut which is described as 'little bacterial factory'. They devour on microbes and excrete them out (many times more in number than they ingest) in soil along with nutrients nitrogen (N) and phosphorus (P) in their excreta. The nutrients N and P are further used by the microbes for multiplication and vigorous action (Singleton *et al.* 2003). Edwards *et al.* 1988 showed that the number of bacteria and 'Actinomycetes' contained in the ingested material increased up to 1000 fold while passing through the gut. A population of worms numbering about 15,000 wills in turn faster a microbial population of billions of millions. Earthworms and microbes act 'symbiotically and synergistically' to accelerate and enhance the decomposition of the organic matter in the waste. It is the microorganisms that break down the cellulose in the food waste, grass clippings and the leaves from garden wastes (Morgan *et al.* 1982).

Humification

Dominguez and Edwards (2004) reported that organic wastes, to be compatible with their agricultural uses and to avoid adverse effects on plant growth, must be transformed into a humus-like material and become stabilized, decreases in the carbon from fulvic acids (FA) and increases in the percentages of the carbon from humic acids (HA) were observed throughout the vermicomposting process, and this was also much more marked at the end of the process, so clearly earthworm activity accelerates humification of organic matter. Moreover, during Vermicomposting, the humic materials increased from 40 to 60 per cent, which was more than the values obtained in a composting process using the same materials. Humification processes are enhanced not only by the fragmentation and size reduction of the organic matter, but also by the greatly increased microbial activity within the intestines of the earthworms and by aeration of the soil through earthworm movement and feeding.

Parameters change during Vermicomposting of Solid Organic Waste

pH

Earthworms are very sensitive to pH, thus pH of soil or waste is sometimes a factor that limits the distribution, numbers and species of earthworms. In a vermicomposting experiment with different soil proportions (1:3, 1:4, 1:5, 1:6) of CD the earthworms reduced the pH: *E. fetida*, 6.7 to 6.1; *E. eugeniae*, 6.7 to 6.0 and *M. megascolex*, 6.7 to 6.4 (Munnoli and Bhosle, 2009). Several researchers have stated that most species of earthworms prefer a pH of about 7.0 (Singh, 1997a; Narayan, 2000; Pagaria and Totwat, 2007; Suthar, 2008a). Edwards (1995) reported a wide pH range (5.0-9.0) for maximizing the productivity of earthworms in SOW management. Bhawalkar (1989) suggested a neutral substrate pH for vermicomposting using deep burrower species *Pheritima elongata*. Satchell (1955) reported that *Bimastos eiseni*, *Dendrobaena octaedra* and *Dendrobaena rubida* were acid-tolerant species, while *Allolobophora caliginosa*, *Allolobophora nocturna*, *Allolobophora longa* were acid-tolerant. Singh *et al.* (2005) reported that *P. excavatus* performs well in a wide range of substrate pHs. The decrease in pH values when press mud was treated with *M. megascolex*, *E. eugeniae* and *E. fetida* showed a decreasing trend in pH from 8.6 to 6.7 during vermicomposting over a period of 60 days (Munnoli, 2007). A decrease in pH was recorded in CD vermicomposting using *E. fetida* and *L. mauritti* (Suthar, 2008a) and *Pheritima elongate* using tomato skin seed waste as substrate (Singh, 1997b), or kitchen waste (Narayan, 2000).

Moisture

In the natural soil-earthworms interaction, when there is a loss of soil moisture, earthworms tend to move to a safer area with more moisture. When the whole area is dry the earthworms adjust themselves and survive through large water loss from the body: *L. terrestris* can lose up to 70 per cent and *A. caliginosa* 75 per cent (Edwards and Lofty, 1977). Experiments conducted using *P. elongata* showed optimum moisture of 70 per cent for the treatments of potato peel waste (Munnoli, 1998) whereas press mud required 60-70 per cent. Trials for vermicomposting CD showed optimum moisture of 60-70 per cent with a higher number of *E. eugeniae*, *E. fetida* and *M. megascolex* earthworms (Munnoli, 2007; Munnoli and Bhosle, 2009).

Strains associated with endospore-forming Bacillus survive extreme weather conditions and become active when favorable soil moisture conditions are regained (Munnoli, 2007). Evans and Guild (1948) reported that *A. chlorotica* produced more cocoons at moisture contents of 28 to 48 per cent. Juveniles, who show high tolerance to low moisture, when transferred to a new environment with favorable moisture, adjust faster than adult worms (Edwards and Lofty, 1977; Singh, 1997b). Such experiments were also carried out with the cocoons of *E. fetida* and *E. eugeniae,* which were transferred to culture boxes containing CD while adult earthworms were separately transferred. More juveniles were found in culture boxes with cocoons than in culture boxes with adults (Singh, 1997b; Munnoli, 1998, 2007). Therefore, moisture level is a significant factor in the set-up of a vermicomposting unit (Scheu, 1987; Parthasarathi and Rangnathan, 2001; Parthasarathi, 2006); in village environments units need to be carefully designed to hold water without causing water logging.

Temperature

Evans and Guild (1948) reported that the activity, metabolism, growth, respiration, reproduction, fecundity and growth period from hatching to sexual maturity of earthworms are greatly influenced by temperature. Cocoons hatch sooner at higher temperatures (Edwards and Lofty, 1977). A temperature range of 20-30°C for vermibeds was suggested using *E.fetida, E. eugeniae* and *P. excavatus* (Bhiday, 1994; Ruikar, 1997). The optimum temperature range for earthworm activity and for setting vermicomposting units are presented in Table 2.3 and Table 2.4 respectively.

Organic Matter

Earthworms use a wide variety of organic materials for food and even in adverse conditions; extract sufficient nourishment from the waste or soil to survive. The kind and amount of food available influences not only the size of an earthworm population but also the species present and their rate of growth and fecundity. Zezonc and Sedor (1990) reported that greatest weight increase in *E. fetida* was obtained when 50 g of soil was mixed with 150 g cellulose waste. Nayak and Rath (1996) claimed that organic residues comprising city, industrial, agricultural farms, household and kitchen wastes with dead or decaying materials can be used as bedding materials for vermicomposting. Joshi (1997) suggested that animal manure, dairy and poultry waste, food industry waste; slaughterhouse waste or biogas sludge could be used for recycling through vermicomposting. The best results of vermicomposting were obtained from paper and food manufacturing industries when treated with *E. fetida, E. andrei and P. excavatus* (Piccone *et al.* 1986).

Table 2.3: Optimum Temperature range for activity of earthworm species

Sl. No.	Temp. Range (°C)	Species	Reference
1.	26-35	*Pheretima californica*	El-Duweini and Ghabbour, 1965
2.	22-29	*Eudrilus eugeniae*	Viljoen and Reinecke, 1992
3.	25	*Eisenia fetida; Eudrilus eugeniae*	Reinecke *et al.* 1992
4.	20-35	*Perionyx excavates*	Bhoyar and Bhinde, 1996
5.	25-35	*Perionyx excavates*	Edwards, 1988
6.	15-35	*Eudrilus eugeniae; Eisenia fetida; Pheretima elongate*	Munnoli, 1998
7.	28-32	*Perionyx excavatus; Lampito mauritii; Drawida nepalensis*	Gautam and Chaudhuri, 2002
8.	25-34	*Eisenia fetida*	Paoletti *et al.* 2003
9.	25	*Eisenia fetida*	Tripathy and Bharadwaj, 2004
10.	20	*Eisenia fetida; Eisenia Andrei*	Dominguez *et al.* 2005
11.	20	*Eudrilus eugeniae*	Aira *et al.* 2006
12.	15-35	*Eudrilus eugeniae; Eisenia fetida; Megascolex megascolex*	Munnoli, 2007
13.	28.9	*Eisenia fetida; Lampito mauritii*	Suthar, 2008a
14.	26-35	*Eisenia fetida; Eudrilus eugeniae*	Mishra *et al.* 2009
15.	5-25	*Eisenia fetida*	Yadav *et al.* 2010
16.	28-32	*Lampito mauritii*	Kale *et al.* 2010
17.	27-28	*Octochatona serrata*	Kale *et al.* 2010

Table 2.4: Optimum temperature range for setting vermicomposting units

Sl. No.	Temp. Range (°C)	Species	Reference
1.	25-35	*Eudrilus eugeniae*	Munnoli, 2007
2.	20-35	*Eisenia fetida*	Munnoli, 2007
3.	20-35	*Megascolex megascolex*	Munnoli, 2007
4.	20-30	*Eisenia fetida, Eudrilus eugeniae*	Bhiday, 1994; Ruikar, 1997
5.	20-34	*Pheretima elongate*	Munnoli, 1998

Micro and Macro Nutrients Status and Microbial Population in Earthworm's Cast

There are varying reports on the nutrient contents of vermicasts (Narayan, 2000; Manna *et al.* 2003) whereas Ranganath *et al.* (2002) ascertained nutrient values for a good VC based on their study on urban wastes also suggested the rate of application of VC in Table 2.5. Ghilarov (1963) claimed that the number of microorganisms in earthworm casts was 1.64-, 1.35- and 1.97- fold higher than in regular soil in three different fields, namely: oak forest, rye and grass, respectively. A 5- and 40- fold higher level of bacterial counts was reported in vermicast more than the surrounding soil in the case of potato peel waste (Munnoli, 1998) and paper industry sludge (Kevian *et al.* 1996), respectively. An increase in hydrolytic microflora in vermicomposting of organic solid wastes was reported by Singh (1997b) and Munnoli (2007). Monson *et al.* (2007) reported an increase in nutrients of kitchen waste vermicomposted by *E. eugeniae*: in N, from 1.31 to 2.12 per cent; in P, from 0.121 to 0.7 per cent; in K, from 0.45 to 0.48 per cent and the C:N ratio decreased from 32.45 to 13.66 per cent. A higher microbial load was also observed in paddy fields to which VC was applied (Kale *et al.* 1992).

Table 2.5: Composition of good quality vermicompost and rate of application for various crops

Sl. No.	Parameter	Vermicompost	Crop	Rate/Th^{-1}
1.	pH	7-8.5	Cereals	5
2.	Organic Carbon (%)	20-30	Pulses	5
3.	Nitrogen (%)	1.5-2.0	Oil seeds	12.5
4.	Phosphorus (%)	1-2	Spices	10
5.	Potassium (%)	1-2	Vegetables	12.5
6.	Calcium (%)	1-3	Fruits	7.5
7.	Manganese (pap)	1-2	Cash crop	15-17.5
8.	Sculpture (%)	<1	Plantations	7.5
9.	Moisture (%)	15-20	*Horticulture Crops	100-200 g/tree
10.	C/N ratio	15-20:1	*Kitchen garden and pots	50 g/pot
11.	Micronutrients (pap)	200		

Sources: *Purakayastha and Bhatnagar, 1997; Ranganath *et al.* 2002.

An increase in the microbial population was recorded with potato waste using *Pheretima elongata* (Munnoli, 1998) and with press mud waste using *E. fetida*, *E. eugeniae* and *Megascolex megascolex* when compared with the surrounding soil (Munnoli, 2007). Meena and Renu (2009) reported an increase in nutrients when press mud was blended with saw dust and treated using three different earthworm species *E. fetida*, *E. eugeniae* and *P. excavatus* individually (Monocultures) and in combination (Polycultures). Kale *et al.* (1992) reported that earthworm's burrows lined with earthworm casts are an excellent medium for harbouring N-fixing bacteria; Loquet *et al.* (1977) and Bhattacharya *et al.* (2000) also recorded an increase in the microbial count of VCs compared to traditional compost in Table 2.6. Kumar *et al.* (2010) reported the contents of VCs in Table 2.7.

Table 2.6: Comparison of microbial count of traditional and vermicomposts

Sl.No.	Type of Microbes	Traditional Compost	Vermicompost
1.	Bacteria	$143 \times 10^3 \times 2$ /g	$167.29 \times 10^3 \times 2$ /g
2.	Fungi	$39.61 \times 10^2 \times 2$ /g	$96.25 \times 10^2 \times 2$ /g
3.	Actinomycetes	$365.27 \times 10^3 \times 2$ /g	$419.62 \times 10^3 \times 2$ /g
4.	PP solution	$195.61 \times 10^2 \times 2$ /g	$168.20 \times 10^2 \times 2$ /g
5.	N2 Fixing bacteria	$92.58 \times 10^2 \times 2$ /g	$96.62 \times 10^2 \times 2$ /g
6.	Thio-sulphate oxidizer	$315.38 \times 10^2 \times 2$ /g	$569.29 \times 10^2 \times 2$ /g

Source: Bhattacharya *et al.* 2000.

Table 2.7: Vermicompost Contents

Sl.No.	Contents	Percentage (%)
1.	Humus	30-50
2.	N	0.72
3.	K	0.74
4.	Carbon	40-57
5.	Hydrogen	4-8
6.	Oxygen	35-54
7.	pH	4 to 9
8.	C/N	20

Source: Senthil Kumar *et al.* 2000.

E. fetida vermicasts from sheep manure alone or mixed with cotton wastes were analyzed for their properties and chemical composition every 2 weeks for 3 months and compared with the same manure without earthworms. Earthworms accelerated the mineralization rate and resulted in castings with a higher nutritional value and degree of humification, suggesting that this kind of industrial wastes can be used in vermicomposting (Albanell *et al.* 1988). Madhukeshwar *et al.* (1996) claimed that any kind of organic waste generated in an agro-based industry or biotechnology unit when treated with earthworms would be resourceful VC. When *E. fetida* was used for vermicomposting it resulted in an increase in P, Ca, Mg and a decreased of K (Orozco *et al.* 1996). Giraddi and Tippanavar (2000) studied the biodegradation of waste from the fruit-pulp, biscuit and sugar industries were bio-degradable in field designs using *E. eugeniae, E. fetida* and *Perionyx excavatus,* for waste management. The wastes were bio-converted to compost in 40-90 days.

The quality of compost obtained had increased micro and macro nutrients. Butt (1993) explored the possibility of treating paper mill sludge with spent yeast from the brewery industry using *L. terrestris* whereas the same industrial waste was treated with *E. andrei* by Elvira *et al.* (1998). They also investigated the vermicomposting of sludge from paper mill and dairy industries mixed with cattle manure using *E. Andrei* in 6-months pilot scale experiments where the number of earthworms and biomass increased significantly. The VCs were rich in N, P, and K and had good structure, a low level of heavy metals, lower conductivity, high humic acid contents and good stability and maturity. They also reported the growth of *E. andrei* by using paper mill and dairy mill sludges in pure wastes by mixing with different proportions of cattle manure (Elvira *et al.* 1998). Studies of the possible use of paper and dairy mill sludge during vermicomposting confirmed that such material might be a valuable component of breeding medium for *E. fetida* earthworms. But the content of mineral N and total K were low (Zablocki *et al.* 1999).

Applications of Vermicomposting Biotechnology

Vermicomposting and Pathogen Destruction

Dominguez and Edwards (2004) showed that vermicomposting involves a great reduction in populations of human pathogenic microorganisms, as in composting. It is generally accepted that the thermophilic stage of the composting process eliminates pathogenic organisms, but we have shown that human pathogens do not survive vermicomposting. After 60 days of vermicomposting, amounts of faecal coliform bacteria in biosolids dropped from 39,000 MPN/g to 0 *MPN/g*. In that same time period, *Salmonella* sp. dropped from <3 MPN/g to <1 MPN/g. Similar results have been reported by Eastman (1999) and also for faecal coliforms, *Salmonella* sp., for enteric viruses, and for helminth ova.

Water Holding Capacity

The major losses of soil water are through the process of transpiration by plants and evaporation from the soil surface and the combined process is known as evapo-transpiration (Biswas and Mukharjee, 1994). If the organic content in a given soil/waste is more than about 10 per cent the max dry density of compaction decreases considerably. The optimum moisture content increases with an increase in organic content (Braja Das, 1987). A similar experiment on compaction conducted by adding 200 g of VC of press mud prepared by *E. fetida, E. eugeniae* and *M. megascolex* to 3 kg of soil showed lower densities compared to the density of soil indicating an increase in voids and water holding capacity (Munnoli, 2007). Therefore adding VCs with aggregation properties and higher water holding capacities will not only increase the yield of crops but also provide nutrients required for growth. When applied to the surface it takes part in maintaining the soil evaporation to a minimum by absorbing atmospheric moisture as a good adsorbent and influences the energy balance (Rodale, 1967; Nobel *et al.* 1970; Edwards and Lofty, 1977; Munnoli and Bhosle, 2008).

Carbon Mineralization during Vermicomposting

As other members of the organic matter decomposer community, earthworms can assimilate carbon from the most recently deposited organic matter fractions, consisting mainly of easily-degradable substances. In all cases the degradation process resulted in carbon losses by mineralization which produced a decrease in the amounts of total organic carbon and in the carbon contributions to the organic matter, which was much higher in the final stages of decomposition when the earthworm populations were bigger and more active (Dominguez *et al.* 2004). Although earthworms consume and process large amounts of organic matter, their contributions to the total heterotrophic respiration is very low due to their poor assimilation efficiency and only when there are large active earthworm populations, as in vermicomposting systems, can they contribute to an appreciable extent to the heterotrophic respiration.

Role in Nitrogen Cycle

Earthworms had a great impact on nitrogen transformations in the pig manure by enhancing nitrogen mineralization, so that most mineral nitrogen was retained as nitrate. The net total nitrogen, in all treatments and times, decreased; losses being more marked during the final stages when earthworm activity was higher. The different nitrogen fractions followed trends similar to the total nitrogen. In all treatments, during the final stages of the process, when the earthworm population was bigger and more active, important reductions in organic nitrogen content and a high nitrification rate were noted (Dominguez and Edwards 2004). This implies that earthworm (*Eisenia andrei* in this case), modified conditions in the manure that favoured nitrification, resulting in the rapid conversion of ammonium into nitrates. Similar results have been reported by Hand *et al.* (1988) who found that *Eisenia fetida* in cow slurry increased the nitrate concentration of the substrate.

Vermicomposting and Heavy Metal Availability

It is important to know the changes in total and available contents of heavy metals in the organic matter during the vermicomposting process, because they may cause problems in some animal manures, sewage sludges, and industrial organic wastes. Dominguez *et al.* (2004) studied that consequence of carbon losses by mineralization during vermicomposting, the total amounts of heavy metals increased (between 25 and 30%), the amounts of bioavailable heavy metals tended to decrease with a decrease of between 35 and 55 per cent in the bioavailable metals in two months. Similar results were reported in other studies for both composting and vermicomposting and this implies a lower availability of these elements for plants from vermicomposts. During vermicomposting, heavy metals tend to form complex aggregates with the humic acids and the most polymerized organic fractions.

Conclusion

Vermicomposting Biotechnology used for waste and land management and for improving soil fertility to promote crop productivity and production of valuable bioactive compounds of great medicinal values has grown considerably in recent years all over the world and has been scientifically improved (UNSW 2002). It is like getting 'gold from garbage' (solid organic waste to highly nutritive biofertilizer). The three versatile species *E. fetida, E. euginae* and *P. excavatus* performing wide social, economic and environmental functions occur almost everywhere.

The vermicomposting maintain the 'global human sustainability cycle' and 'circular economy' – using food wastes (negative economic and environmental value) of the society to produce food (positive socio-economic value) for the society again while also protecting farm soil and improving its fertility (positive economic and environmental value) and if vermicompost can 'replace' the 'chemical fertilizers' for production of 'safe organic foods' which has now been proved worldwide, it will be a giant step towards achieving global social, economic and environmental sustainability. With the growing global popularity of 'organic foods' which became a US $ 6.5 billion business every year by 2000, there will be great demand for vermicompost in future. US Department of Agriculture estimates 25 per cent of Americans purchase organically grown foods at least once a week (Li KM *et al.* 2010). In any vermiculture practice, 'worm biomass' comes as a valuable by-product. It is finding that uses and applications of earthworms in modern medicine and in several industries for sustainable production of essential goods for societal use and consumption (Dynes RA 2003). On commercial scale tons of worm biomass can result every year as under favorable conditions worms 'double' their number at least every 60-70 days.

All infrastructure based on vermicomposting biotechnology using earthworms are easy to construct, install and operate with minimum engineering considerations. They are highly economical and cost effective with highly valued by-products and end-products. It is basically a 'one-time investment' technology as the earthworms multiply at a fast rate under favorable conditions of temperature and moisture and increase the pace and rapidity of the technological process. Besides the advantages of this technique there are some disadvantages also; It can be quicker, but to make it so generally requires more labour; It requires more space because worms are surface feeders and won't operate in material more than a meter in depth; It is more vulnerable to environmental pressures, such as: temperature, freezing conditions and drought; Perhaps most importantly, it requires more start-up resources, either in cash (to buy the worms) or in time and labour.

It is also justifying the beliefs of Great Russian scientist Dr. Anatoly Igonin who said "*Nobody and nothing can be compared with earthworms and their positive influence on the whole living Nature. They create soil and improve soil's fertility and provide critical biosphere's functions: disinfecting, neutralizing, protective and productive"*. Future of mankind on earth beholds with the earthworms and our relationship must be maintained.

REFERENCES

Aira M., Monory F., Dominguez J. (2003): Effect of two Species of Earthworms (Allolobophora sp.) on Soil Systems: A Micro Faunal and Biochemical Analysis. *Pedobiologia* 47, 877-881.

Aira M., Monroy F., Dominguez J. (2006): Changes in Microbial Biomass and Microbial Activity of Pig Slurry after the Transit through the gut of the Earthworm *Eudrilus eugeniae* (Kinberg, 1867). *Soil Biology and Biochemistry* 42, 371-376.

Alabanell E., Plaixats J., Caberero T. (1988): Chemical Changes during Vermicomposting *Eisenia fetida* of sheep manure Mixed with Cotton Industrial Wastes. *Biology and Fertility of Soils* 63, 266-269.

Bajsa O., Nair J., Mathew K., H.O., G.E. (2004). Pathogen Die-Off in Vermicomposting Process. Paper Presented at the International Conference on *Small Water and Wastewater Treatment Systems*, Perth.

Bano K., Kale R.D., Vijayalakshmi D. (1987): Production and Reproduction trend in a Tropical Earthworm *Eudrilus eugeniae*. In: Palanichamy S (Ed) *Proceeding of 5th Indian Symposium of Invertibrate Reproduction*, Palani Paramount Publications, Palani, India, pp. 210-218.

Bhawalkar V.S. (1995): Vermiculture Bioconversion of Organic Residues. PhD. thesis, IIT Mumbai, India, pp. 15-45.

Bhawalkar S.V. (1989): A Promising Source of Biofertilizers. In: *Proceedings of National Seminar on Agricultural Biotechnology*, 7-8 March, 1989, Gujarat Agricultural University, Navasari, India, pp. 13-17.

Bhattacharya K.K., Mukhopadhyay N., Mukharjee D., Das S.K. (2000): Comparative Efficiency of Improved Compost Techniques. In: Jana BB, Banerjee RD, Guterstam B, Heeb J (Eds) *Proceedings of International Conference. Waste Recycling and Resource Management in Developing World*, Sapana Printing Works, Kolkata, India, pp. 219-224.

Bhiday M.R. (1994): Earthworms in Agriculture. *Indian Farming* March, 32.

Bhoyar R.V., Bhide A.D. (1996): Vermicomposting of Organic (vegetable) Solid Wastes. In: *International Conference on Environmental Planning and Management*, V.R.C.E. Nagpur, India, pp. 368-372.

Binet F., Fayolle L., Pussard M. (1998): Significance of Earthworms in Stimulating Soil Microbial Activity. *Biology and Fertility of Soils* 27 (1), 79-84.

Biswas T.D., Mukherjee S.K. (1994): *Soil Science*, Tata-McGraw Hill Publishers, Delhi, India, pp. 153-222.

Bouche M.B. (1979): Valorisation des dechetsorganiques parles lombricienns. *Collection Recherche of Environment* 11, 384.

Braja M.D. (1987): *Advanced Soil Mechanics*, McGraw Hill, New Delhi, India, pp. 36-47.

Butt K.R. (1993): Utilization of Solid Paper Mill Sludge and Spent Brewery Yeast Feed for Soil Dwelling Earthworms. *Bioresource Technology* 44, 105-107.

Butt K.R., Nieminen M.V., Siren T. (2005): Population and Behaviour Level Responces of arable Soil Earthworms to Broad Mill Sludge Application. *Biology and Fertility of Soils* 42, pp. 163-167.

Dash M.C. (1978): Role of Earthworms in the Decomposer System. In: J. S. Singh and B. Gopal, Eds., *Glimpses of Ecology*, India International Scientific Publication, New Delhi, pp. 399-406.

Divya UK (2001): Relevence of Vermiculture in Sustainable Agriculture. *Agriculture General* – World July, 9-11.

Dominguez J., Alberto V., Alfredo F. (2005): Are *Eisenia fetida* (Savingly 1826) and *Eisenia andrei* (Bouch 1972) (Oligocheata Lumbricidae) different Biological Species? *Pedobiologia* 49, 81-87.

Dominguez J., Edwards CA (2004). Vermicomposting Organic Wastes: A Review. *Soil Zoology for Sustainable Development in the 21st Century*, S.H. Shakir Hanna and W.Z.A. MikhaTl, eds, Cairo, 369-395.

Dynes R.A. (2003): "Earthworms: Technology Information to Enable the Development of Earthworm Production," Rural Industries Research and Development Corporation, Government of Australia, Canberra.

Edwards C.A. (1988): Breakdown of Animal, Vegetable and Industrial Organic Wastes by Earthworms. In: Edwards CA, Neuhauser EF (Eds) *Earthworms in Waste and Environmental Management*, SPB, The Hague, pp. 21-31.

Edwards C.A. (1995): *Earthworm*, McGraw Hill Encyclopedia, pp. 81-83.

Edwards C.A. (1998): The Use of Earthworms in the Breakdown and Management of Organic Wastes. In: C. A. Edwards, Ed., *Earthworm Ecology*, CRC Press, Boca Raton, pp. 327-354.

Edwards C.A. (2004): *Earthworm Ecology* (2nd Edn.), CRC Press LLC, Boca Raton, FL, USA, pp. 12-23.

Edwards C.A., Bohlen P.J. (1996): *Biology and Ecology of Earthworms* (3rd Edn), Chapman and Hall, London, pp. 35-55.

Edwards C.A., Fletcher K.E. (1988): Interaction between Earthworms and Micro-Organisms in Organic Matter Breakdown. *Agriculture Ecosystems and Environment* 24 (1-3), 235-247.

Edwards C.A., Lofty J.R. (1977): *Biology of Earthworms*, Chapman and Hall, Londan, pp. 129-147.

Edwards C.A., Stinne B.R., Stinner D., Rabatin S (Eds) (1988). Biological Interaction in Soil. *Agriculture, Ecosystem and Environment* 24 (1-3), 1-377.

EI-Duweini A.K., Ghabbour SI (1965): Population Density and Biomass of Earthworms in different Types of Egyptian Soil. *Journal of Applied Ecology* 2, 271-287.

Elvira C., Sampedro L., Benitez E., Nogales R. (1998). Vermicomposting of Sludge's from Paper Mill and Dairy Industries with *Eisenia andrei* a Pilot Scale Study. *Bioresource Technology* 63, 205-211.

Evans AC, Guild WJMcL (1948): Studies on the Relationships between Earthworms and Soil Fertility. 4th. On the life-cycles of some British Lumbricidae. *Annals of Applied Biology* 35, 471-484.

Fischer K., Hahn D., Amann R.I., Daniel O., Zeyer J. (1995). In situ Analysis of the Bacterial Community in the gut of the Earthworm *Lumbricus terrestris* L. by whole-cell hybridization. *Canadian Journal of Microbiology* 41, 666-671.

Gautam B., Chaudhuri P.S. (2002): Cocoon Production, Morphology, Hatching Pattern and Fecundity in Seven Tropical Earthworm Species – A Laboratory-based Investigation. *Journal of Bioscience* 27 (3), 283-294.

Ghilarov MS (1963): On the Interrelations between Soil Dwelling Invertibrates and Soil Microorganisms. In: Doekson J., Van der Drift J (Eds) *Soil Organisms*, North Holland Publishing Co., Amsterdam, pp. 255-259.

Giraddi R.S., Tippanavr P.S. (2000). Techniques of Biodegradation of Organic Wastes using Earthworms. In: *Proceedings of a National Seminar on Environmental Pollution*. November 2000, University of Agricultural Science, Dharwad, India, pp. 24-25.

Gunthilingaraj K., Ravignanam T. (1996): Vermicomposting of Sericulture Wastes. *Madras Agricultural Journal* 83 (7), 455-457.

Hand P., Hayes W.A., Frankland *lC,* Satchell J.E. (1988): Vermicomposting of Cow Slurry. *Pedobiologia* 31, 199-209.

Joshi S.N. (1997): Worm Composting. *Inora News Letter* 1, 2.

Kale R.D. (1994): *Vermicomposting of Waste Materials. Earthworm Cinderella of Organic Farrming,* Prism Book Pvt Ltd., New Delhi, India, pp. 47.

Kale R.D. (1998). "Earthworms: Nature's Gift for Utilization of Organic Wastes," In: C. A. Edward, Ed., *Earthworm Ecology*, St. Lucie Press, NY.

Kale R.D., Bano K., Vinayak, Bhagyaraj D.J. (1986): Suitability of Neem Cake as an Additive in Earthworm Feed and its Influence in the Establishment of Micro Flora. *Journal of Soil Biology and Ecology* 6, 98-103.

Kale R.D., Mallesh B.C., Kubra B., Bhagyaraj D.J. (1992): Influence of Vermicompost Application on Available Micronutrients and Selected Microbial Populations in Paddy Field. *Soil Biology and Biochemistry* 24, 1317-1320.

Kale R.D., Natchimuthu K. (2010): Role of Earthworms in Tropics with Emphasis on Indian Ecosystems. *Applied and Environmental Soil Science* 2010, Article ID 414356, pp. 16.

Kale R.D., Sunitha N.S. (1995): Efficiency of Earthworms (*E. Eugeniae*) in Converting the Solid Waste from Aromatic Oil Extraction Industry into Vermicompost. *Journal of IAEM* 22 (1) 267-269.

Kallimani C.S. (1998): Bioconversion of Sericulture Waste using *Eudrilus eugeniae* and *Phanerochaete crysosporium*. MSc thesis, University of Agricultural Science, Dharwad, pp. 1-10.

Kaur A., Singh J., Vig A.P., Dhaliwal S.S., Rup P.J. (2010). Co-composting with and without *Eisenia fetida* for Conversion of Toxic paper mill Sludge to a Soil Conditioner. *Bioresource Technology* 101 (21), 8192-8198.

Kavian M.F., Ghatnekar S.D. (1996). Biomanagement of Dairy Effluent using Cultures of Red Earthworms (*L. rubellus*). *Industrial Journal of Environmental Protection* 11, 680-682.

Kristufek V., Ravasz K., Pizi V. (1992). Changes in Densities of Bacteria and Micro Fungi during gut transit in *Lumbricus rubellus* and *Aporrectodea caliginosa* (Oligochaeta: Lumbricidae). *Soil Biology and Biochemistry* 12, 1499-1500.

Kumar R., Verma D., Singh B.L., Umesh U., Shweta (2010): Composting of Sugar-cane Waste By-products through Treatment with Microorganisms and Subsequent Vermicomposting. *Bioresource Technology* 101 (17), 6707-6711.

Lakshmi B.L., Vizaylakshmi G.S. (2000): Vermicomposting of Sugar Factory Filter Pressmud Using African Earthworms Species (*Eudrillus eugeniae*). *Pollution Research* 9 (3), 481-483.

Levelle P., Spain A.V. (2001). *Soil Ecology*, Kluwer Academic Publishers, Dordrecht, pp. 654.

Li KM., Li PZ (2010): "Earthworms Helping Economy, Improving Ecology and Protecting Health," In: R. K. Sinha, *et al.*, Eds., *International Journal of Environmental Engineering* (Special Issue on 'Vermiculture Technology').

Loehr R.C., Martin J.H., Neuhauser E.F. and Malecki M.R. (1984): Waste Management Using Earthworms – Engineering and Scientific Relationships, Project Report ISP-8016764, National Science Foundation, Washington, D.C.

Loquet M., Bhatnagar J., Bouche M.B., Ruvelle J. (1977): Estimation of Ecological Influence by Earthworms on Microorganisms. *Pedobiologia* 17, 400-417.

Madhukeshwar S.S., Anil K.N., Anandi Gowda, Laxminarayan M.T., Shreeramshetty T.A. (1996): Organic Farming and Sustainable Agriculture. In: *Proceedings of National Seminar*, University of Agricultural Science, Dharwad, India, pp. 9-11.

Mani P., Karmegam N. (2010): Vermistabilisation of Press-mud using *Perionyx celanensis*. *Bioresource Technology* 101 (21), 8464-8468.

Manna M.C., Jha S., Ghosh P.K., Acharya C.L. (2003): Comparative Efficacy of Three Epigeic Earthworms under Deciduous Forest Litters Decomposition. *Bioresource Technology* 88, 197-206.

Meena K., Renu B. (2009). Bioconversion of Filter mud using Vermicomposting Employing two Exotic and one Local Earthworm Species. *Bioresource Technology* 100, 5846-5852.

Mishra R.K., Singh B.K., Upadhyay R.K., Singh S. (2009): Technology for Vermicompost Production. *Indian Farming* July, 14-15.

Monson C.C., Damodharan G., Senthil Kumar, Kanakasbhai V. (2007): Composting of Kitchen Waste Using in Vessel and Vermibeds. In: *Proceedings of International Conference on Clear Tech and Environmental Management*, 4-6th January 2007, Pondichery Engineering College, Pondichery, India, pp. 678-682.

Moody S.A., Briones MJI, Pierce T.G., Dighton J. (1995): Selective Consumption of Decomposing Wheat Straw by Earthworms. *Soil Biology and Biochemistry* 28, 533-537.

Morgan M., Burrows I. (1982): Earthworms/Microorganisms Interactions. Rothamsted Experimental Station, USA.

Munnoli P.M. (1998): A Study on Management of Organic Solid Waste of Agro-based Industries Through Vermiculture Biotechnology. ME Thesis, TIET Patiala, India, pp. 11-30.

Munnoli P.M. (2007): Management of Industrial Organic Solid Wastes Through Vermiculture Biotechnology with Special Reference to Microorganisms. PhD thesis, Goa University, India, pp. 1-334.

Munnoli P.M., Arora J.K., Sharma S.K. (2000): Organic Waste Management through Vermiculture: A Case Study of Pepsi Food Channoo Punjab. In: Jana BB, Banarjee RD, Guterstam B, Heeb J. (Eds) *Waste Resource Recycling in the Developing World*, Sapana Printing Works Kolkatta, pp. 203-208.

Munnoli P.M., Bhosle S. (2008): Soil Aggregation by Vermicompost of Press Mud. *Current Science* 95 (11), 1533-1535.

Munnoli P.M., Bhosle S. (2009). Effect of Soil Cow Dung Proportion of Vermicomposting. *Journal of Scientific and Industrial Research* 68, 57-60.

Narayan J. (2000). Vermicomposting of Biodegradable Wastes Collected from Kuvempu University Campus using Local and Exotic Species of Earthworm. In: *Proceedings of a National Conference on Industry and Environment*, 28th to 20th December 1999, Karad, India, pp. 417-419.

Nayak A.K., Rath L.K. (1996): Vermiculture and Its Application. *Kisan World* December 1996, 61-62.

Nobel J.C., Garden W.T., Kieing C.R. (1970): The Influence on Earthworm on Development of Mats of Organic Matter under Irrigated Pasture in Southern Australia in Plant Nutrients and Soil Fertility. In: *Proceedings of 11th International Grassland Congress*, 13-23 April 1970, Queensland, Australia, pp. 465-468.

Orozco F.H., Cegara J., Trujillo L.M., Roing A. (1996): Vermicomposting of Coffee Pulp using the Earthworm, Eisenia fetida Effects on C and N Contents and the Availability of Nutrients. *Biology and Fertility of Soils* 22, 162-166.

Pagaria P., Totwat K.L. (2007): Effects of Press Mud and Spent Wash in Integration with Phosphogypsum on Metallic Cation Build up in the Calcareous Sodic Soils. *Journal of the Indian Society of Soil Science* 55 (1), 52-57.

Paoletti M.G., Buscardo E., Vanderjagt, Pastuszyn A., Pizzoferrato L., Haung Y.S., Chuang L.T., Millson M., Cerda H., Torres F., Glew R.H. (2003): Nutrrient Content of Earthworms Consumed by Ye'Kuana Amerindians of the Alto Orinoco of Venezuela. *Proceedings of Royal Society of London B* 270, 249-257.

Parthasarathi K. (2006): Aging of Press Mud Vermicast of *Lampito mauritti* (Kinberg) and *Eudrilus eugeniae* (Kinberg) – Reduction in Microbial Population and Activity. *Journal of Environmental Biology* 27 (2), 221-223.

Parthasarathi K., Ranganathan L. (2001): Aging Effect of Microbial Population, Enzyme Activities and NPK Contents in the Soil Worm Casts of *Lampito mauritti* (Kinberg) and *Eudrilus eugeniae* (Kinberg). *Pollution Research* 20 (1), 53-57.

Pevey H.S., Rowe D.R., Tchabonoglous G (1985). *Environmental Engineering*, McGraw Hill International, New Delhi, pp. 573-593.

Piccone G., Biosoil B., Deluca G., Minelli L. (1986): Vermicomposting of different Organic Wastes. In: *Compost Production and Use Symposium*, 17-19 April 1986, Udine, Italy, pp. 818-821.

Purakayastha T.J., Bhatnagar R.K. (1997): Vermicompost a Promising Source of Plant Nutrients. *Indian Farming* Feb, 35-37.

Rajesh B.J., Yeom I.T., Esakkiraj, Kumar N., Lee Y.W., Vallinayagam S. (2008): Bio Management of Sago-Sludge using an Earthworm, *Lampito mauritii*. *Journal of Environmental Biology* 29 (5), 753-757.

Ranganath Reddy R.L., Ramakrishnan Parama V.R., Bhargana M.M.V., Kale R.D. (2002): Vermicomposting a Method of Urban Solid Waste Management. In: *Proceedings of National Seminar on Solid Waste Management*, 12-14th December 2002, Bangalore, India, pp. 98-99.

Rodale J.I. and Staff of Organic Gardening and Farming Magazine (1967). *The Complete Book of Composting*, Rodale Books, Inc., Emmaus, PENNA, pp. 874-923.

Reinecke A.J., Viljoen S.A., Saayaman R.J. (1992): The Suitability of *Eudrilus eugeniae, Perionyx excavatus* and *Eisenia* (Oligochatea) for Vermicomposting in Southern Africa in Terms of their Temperature Requirements. *Soil Biology and Biochemistry* 24 (12), 1295-1307.

Ruikar S.K. (1997): Some useful Information about Vermicompost. *Inora* October (4), 2.

Satchell J.E. (1955): Some Aspects of Earthworm Ecology. In: Keven DKMcE (Ed) *Soil Zoology*, Butterworth's, London, pp. 180-201.

Saxena M., Chauhan A., Asokan P. (1998): Flyash Vemicompost from Non-Friendly Organic Wastes. *Pollution Research* 17 (1), 5-11.

Scheu S. (1987). Microbial Activity and Nutrient Dynamics in Earthworm Casts (Lumbricidae). *Biology and Fertility of Soils* 5, 230-234.

Schonholzer F., Hahn D., Zeyer J. (1999): Origins and Fate of Fungi and Bacteria in the Gut of *Lumbricus terrestris* L. Studied by Image Analysis. *FEMS Microbial Ecology* 28, 235-248.

Seenappa S.N., Rao J., Kale R. (1995): Conversion of Distillery Wastes into Organic Manure by Earthworm *Eudrillus euginae*. *Journal of IAEM* 22 (1), 244-246.

Senthil Kumar M., Sivalingam P.N., Sungathi A. (2000): Vermitech. *Kisan world* March, 57-88.

Singh J. (1997a): Habitat Preferences of Selected Indian Earthworm Species and their Efficiency in Reduction of Organic Material. *Soil Biology and Biochemistry* 29, 585-588.

Singh NB (1997b): Development of Process Package for Organic Solid Waste Management through Vermiculture Biotechnology, in Organic Waste Generating Industries in Punjab. ME thesis, TIET Patiala, Punjab, India, pp. 41-93.

Singh N.B., Khare A.K., Bhargava D.S., Bhattacharya S. (2005): Effect of Initial Substrate pH on Vermicomposting using *Perionyx excavatus* (Perrier 1872). *Applied Ecology and Environmental Research* 4 (1), 85-97.

Singleton D.R., Hendrix B.F., Coleman D.C., Whitemann W.B. (2003): Identification of Uncultured Bacteria Tightly Associated with the Intestine of the Earthworms *Lumricus rubellus*. *Soil Biology and Biochemistry* 35, 1547-1555.

Subramanian S., Sivarajan M., Saravanapriya S. (2010): Chemical Changes during Vermicomposting of Sago Industry Solid Wastes. *Journal of Hazardous Materials* 179 (1-3), 318-322.

Suthar S. (2006): Potential Utilization of Guar Gum Industrial Waste in Vermicomposting Production. *Bioresource Technology* 7, pp. 2474-2477.

Suthar S. (2007): Production of Vermifertilizer from Guar Gum Industrial Wastes by using Composting Earthworm *Perionyx sansibaricus* (Perrier). *Environmentalist* 27, pp. 329-335.

Suthar S. (2008a): Microbial and Decomposition Efficiencies of Monoculture and Polyculture Vermireactors based on epigeic and anecic Earthworms. *World Journal of Microbial Technology* 24, 1471-1479.

Thomas S., Trivedy R.K. (2002): Earthworm Biotechnology for Waste Management and Crop Improvement a Review of Research. In: *Proceeding of National Seminar on Solid Waste Management*, 12-14th December 2002, Allied Publication Pvt. Ltd., Bangalore, India, pp. 120-123.

Tiunov A.V., Scheu S. (2000): Microfungal Communities in Soil Litter and Casts of *Lumbricus terrestris* L. (Lumbricidae): A Laboratory Experiment. *Applied Soil Ecology* 14, 17-26.

Tripathi G., Bharadwaj P. (2004): Earthworm Diversity and Habitat Preference in Arid Regions of Rajasthan, India, *Zoos Print Journal* 19 (7), 1515-1519.

UNSW, ROU (2002): "Best Practice Guidelines to Managing On-Site Vermiculture Technologies," *University of New South Wales Recycling Organics Unit*, Sydney, [http:www.resource.nsw.gov.au/data/Vermiculture per cent 20BP G.pdf].

Viljoen S.A., Reinecke A.J. (1992): The Temperature Requirements of Epigeic worm *Eudrilus eugeniae* (Oligochaeta) Laboratory Study. *Soil Biology and Biochemistry* 24 (12), 1345-1350.

Visvanathan C., Trankler J., Jospeh K., Nagendran R. (2005). (Eds.) "Vermicomposting as an Eco-Tool in Sustainable Solid Waste Management," Asian Institute of Technology, Annamalai University, Chidambaram.

White S. (1996): Vermiculture Bioconversion in India. Worm Digest, June, 65.

Yadav K.D., Vinod T., Mansoor A.M. (2010): Vermicomposting of Source Separated Human Faeces for Nutrient Recycling. *Waste Management* 30, 50-56.

Zablocki Z., Keipas K.A., Tyburczy J. (1999): Conversion of Paper Mill Effluent with Municipal Sewage Sludges during Associated Vermicomposting Process. *Folia Universitatis Agriculturae Stetinensis* 77, 415-419.

Zajonc I., Sidar V. (1990): Use of some Wastes for Vermin Compost Preparation and their Influence on Growth and Reproduction of the Earthworm *Eisenia fetida*. *Polnophospodarstvo* 36, 742-752.

Pages: 44-63

WASTE GENERATION AND UTILIZATION
Edited by: **Dr. Priya Bajaj; Dr. B. Tabassum** and **Dr. Pawan Kumar 'Bharti'**
ISBN: 978-93-5056-792-0
Edition: **2016**
Published by: **Discovery Publishing House Pvt. Ltd., New Delhi (India)**

CHAPTER – 3

Waste Paper Generation, Collection, Disposal and Scope of Recycling

Ambo University, Oromia Regional State, Ethiopia

Yohanis Birhanu; Akhila S. Nair and **Natarajan P.**

ABSTRACT

Solid waste generation, collection and sustainable management are widely discussed topics world over. 'Reduce', 'Reuse' and 'Recycle' concept about solid waste has a large contribution towards the sustainable management of solid wastes especially in developing countries, where the generation and collection of solid wastes is a big hurdle. Among the material composition of solid wastes, used paper occupies a major share in the urban areas of developing countries. Many of the educational institutions and offices have been using white paper for academic and office purposes and are following a 'throw away culture' towards the used paper. In Ethiopia, some of the institutions have arrangements for collection and segregation of the waste paper. Most of the times these segregated waste papers are not sending for reuse or recycling but are simply ending up in open burning. Recycling refers to the removal of items from the waste stream to be used as raw materials in the manufacture of new products. Ambo University is a foremost educational institution in central Ethiopia. The objective of this

Environmental Science Programme, Department of Biology, College of Natural and Computational Science, Ambo University, Ambo, Oromia State, Ethiopia.

study was to determine the amount of waste paper generation of Ambo University and to demonstrate environmental benefits as well as economic importance of recycling of waste paper. Both qualitative and quantitative data were used in the study. To gather information about waste paper generation of Ambo University, five sites were selected purposively during the period from November 2011 to January 2012. The findings of the study revealed that the total waste paper generation per semester of Ambo University was 5960.65 kg. Field observations and survey results indicated that in Ambo University waste paper was segregated for burning, but not for recycling. Laboratory results of the pulp quality parameters including: consistency, beating degree and dewatering capacity, ash and cobb value of the waste paper collected from University were within the standard for recycling purpose. Hence the waste paper generated had a resource value for recycling industry that the University could have taken advantage of. The study could estimate that besides the environmental merits, an economic benefit of earning 71,527.8 Birr annually was possible through prompt supplying of the generated waste paper to a recycling company. In order to ameliorate the prevalent situation, the study has also recommended the departments of the University to practice using both sides of the paper, especially while preparing notes and exam papers in order to attain source reduction of waste paper. The paper recycling companies in turn should further their social responsibility of sensitizing the public community as well as relevant authorities to ensure that any waste paper generated from the Universities were promptly channelized for recycling.

Keywords: Economic importance, environmental benefit, recycling, waste paper.

INTRODUCTION

Solid waste generation and its management are big hurdles for most of the developing countries. Population growth and urbanization in developing countries contribute to the generation of solid wastes. Improper management of solid wastes creates health, environment and social issues. The way of solid waste generation and management in an area give an important insight into how the people in that particular are lives. Now-a-days solid waste management is one of the challenges for the administrations of the cities in many developing countries. The attitude of the people and their environmental awareness are also other factors which are contributing to the specific issue. Figure 3.1 shows the Hierarchy of waste management as advised by the European Union. According to the diagram, recovery, recycling and reuse can make the waste management process much sustainable. Recycling is considered as one of the most sustainable methods of solid waste management.

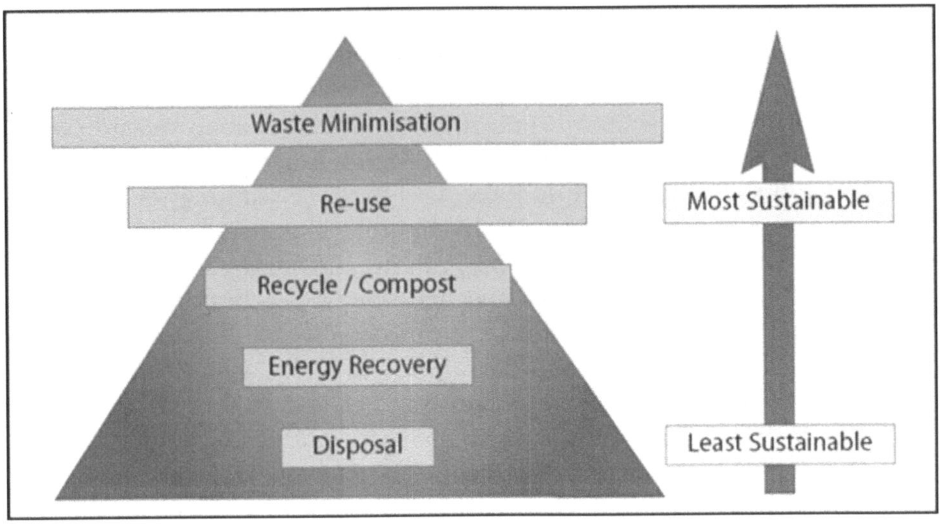

Fig. 3.1: **Hierarchy of waste management as advised by the European Union**

Waste reduction and reuse of products are the methods of waste prevention. These methods eliminate the production of waste at the source of generation and reduce the demands for large scale treatment and disposal facilities. Methods of waste reduction include manufacturing products with less packaging, encouraging customers to bring their own reusable bags for packaging, encouraging the public to choose reusable products such as: cloth napkins and reusable plastic and glass containers, backyard composting and sharing and donating any unwanted items rather than discarding them. All of the methods of waste prevention mentioned require public participation. In order to get the public on board, training and educational programmes need to be undertaken to educate the public about their role in the process. Also the government may need to regulate the types and amount of packaging used by manufacturers and make the reuse of shopping bags mandatory.

Recycling may generally be considered as a key strategy for alleviating the pressures of the society on the environment. Recycling refers to the removal of items from the waste stream to be used as raw materials in the manufacture of new products. Thus from this definition recycling occurs in three phases: first the waste is sorted and recyclables collected, the recyclables are used to create raw materials. These raw materials are then used in the production of new products. The sorting of recyclables may be done at the source (*i.e.*, within the household or office) for selective collection by the municipality or to be dropped off by the waste producer at a recycling centre. The pre-sorting at the source requires public participation which may not be forthcoming if there are no benefits to be derived. Also a system of selective collection by the government can be costly. It would require more frequent circulation of trucks within a neighborhood or the importation of more vehicles to facilitate the collection. Another option is to mix the recyclables with the general waste stream for collection and then sorting and recovery of the recyclable materials can be performed by the municipality at a suitable site. The sorting by the municipality has the advantage of eliminating the dependence on the public and ensuring that the recycling does occur. The disadvantage however, is that the value of the recyclable materials is reduced since being mixed in and compacted with other garbage can have adverse effects on the quality of the recyclable material (http://www.cyen.org/).

A variety of environmental justifications for recycling exists: recycling processes reduce demand for energy and finite resources, result in less water pollution and air emissions and mitigate the problem of solid waste disposal. Recycling is considered economically beneficial in developing countries. *First,* it provides significant employment opportunities to a large informal sector. The high degree of labour intensity of certain reclamation processes enables numerous people to accrue some kind of income. *Second,* recycling can reduce the costs for raw materials in the production process and thereby may result in an increase in the supply of cheaper products. *Third,* it can reduce dependence on foreign resources, thereby saving expenditure on imports in developing countries. Global paper consumption has reached more than 350 million tons per year and is fast approaching a million tons per day. In 2004, United States citizens on average consumed more than 700 lbs of paper per person. Despite the assumption that the Internet and online reading capabilities would lead to a decline in paper consumption, paper use continues to increase demonstrating the need to address not only the volume but the content of the paper consumed. As national and global populations continue to rise, the implementation and regulation of sustainable paper harvesting, manufacturing and delivery processes gain increasing importance (Callie *et al.* 2011).

The trash throw away by individuals in developed countries include: items such as: packaging, food scraps, grass clippings, sofas, computers, tires, and refrigerators. Municipal solid wastes do not comprise industrial, hazardous, or construction waste. In 2010, Americans recovered almost 65 million tonnes of municipal solid wastes (excluding composting) through recycling. Composting recovered over 20 million tonnes of waste where about 29 million tonnes for energy recovery (about 12%). Figure 3.2 shows the recycling rates of selected products in 2010 in America. In 2010, newspaper/mechanical papers recovery was about 72 per cent (7 million tonnes), and about 58 per cent of yard trimmings were recovered (http://epa.gov/epawaste/conserve).

In particular, recycling of paper has got added significance since it reduces the pressure on natural resources such as: forests (Pieter and Anantha, 1986). Virgin paper production requires substantially more water and generates waste water that has significantly higher levels of major water pollutants

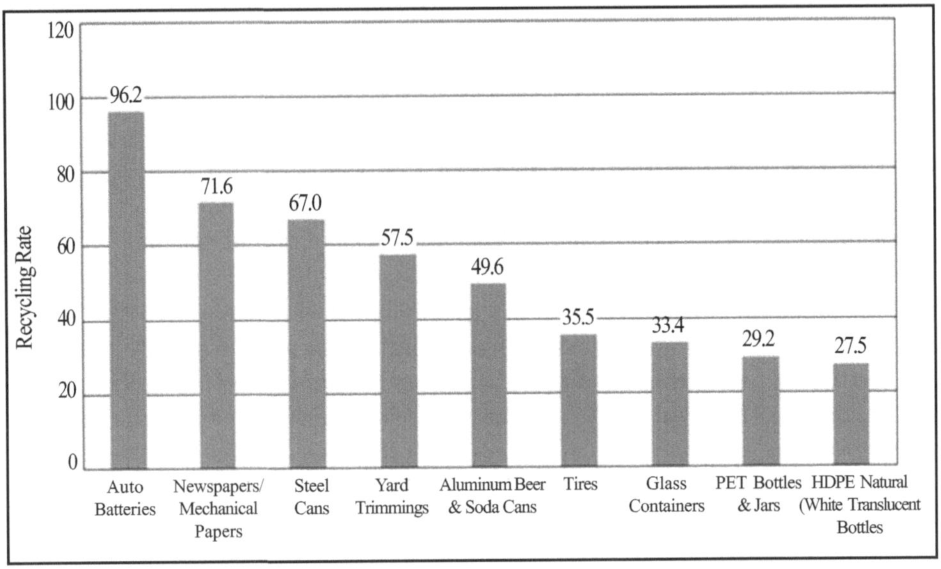

Fig. 3.2: **Recycling rates of selected products in 2010 in America**

Source: (http://epa.gov/epawaste/conserve)

than recycled paper production does. Whenever trees are cut down for paper, much of the carbon they have stored is released. By reducing the demand for virgin fiber, recycling can reduce the frequency at which trees are cut and increase the total stock of carbon in forests. Recycling also helps maintain the stock of carbon stored in paper by reusing it multiple times, instead of allowing it to burning and decomposing in landfills which produces carbon dioxide and methane that are potent greenhouse gases. The problem of accumulation of uncollected solid waste particularly in most of the developing countries has contributed to poor sanitation and low quality of life. In this regard, waste paper is one of the contributors. According to EPA (2008), waste paper is the major contributor by material among the total solid wastes of America in 2008 (Figure 3.3).

MSWDR (1989) reported the following definite environmental benefits from recycling of paper.

- *Saving trees:* By recycling paper, residents in the Metro region saved 8.2 million trees from being harvested – which is equivalent to the number of trees in eight Forest Parks.
- *Saving air quality:* Air quality is improved by recycling. Recycling 437,000 tonnes of paper reduces air emissions equivalent to that produced by 200,238 cars driving one year. The benefit of reduced air emissions due to recycling in the U.S., is equivalent to taking 24 million cars off the road for one year.

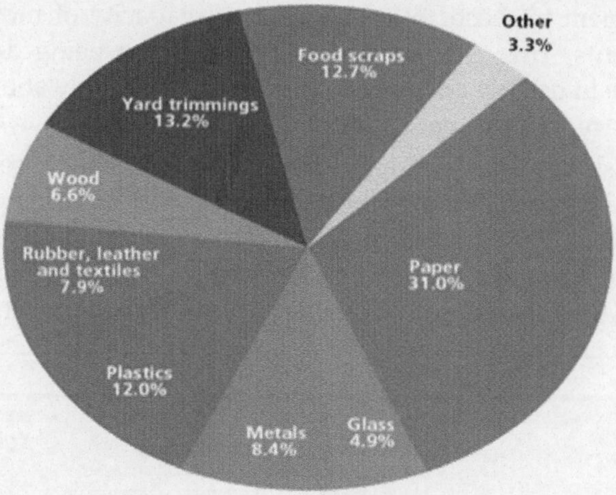

Fig. 3.3: **Total Municipal Solid Waste by material in the United States in 2008**
(*Source* EPA 2008)

- *Saving water:* In 2003, paper recycling efforts in the Metro region saved more than one billion gallons of water that would have been discharged as effluent into the environment. Recycling all U.S. paper would save 114 billion gallons of water per year.
- *Saving energy:* Producing recycled paper requires only 60 per cent of the energy used to make paper from virgin wood pulp. For example, manufacturing one ton of office and computer paper with recycled paper stock can save between 3,000 and 4,000 kilowatt-hours over the same tonne of paper made with virgin wood products.

The typology of wastes generated in Africa from point and non-point sources encompass industrial, agricultural, sewage, domestic, municipal and other wastes including wastes from the medical, nuclear, electrical and electronic industry. These wastes are either non-hazardous or hazardous. Specific data relating to waste generation and characterization in African countries is generally lacking. Household waste in Africa contains food waste (biodegradable/compostable), sand, gravel, paper, plastic, metals (*e.g.*, aluminium) and glass (the last four components are recoverable, reusable and recyclable). Plastic is a major nuisance in municipal solid waste which degrades the environment, clogs drains and causes flooding in the rainy season. Waste management problems in Africa are varied and complex with infrastructure, political, technical, social/economic, organizational/management, regulatory and legal issues and challenges to be addressed. Waste is typically disposed off without consideration for environmental and human health impacts, leading to its accumulation in cities, towns and uncontrolled dumpsites. Co-disposal of non-hazardous and hazardous waste without segregation is common practice. Municipal Solid Waste (MSW) management has continually been an intractable problem in recent times beyond the capacity of most municipal/state governments. This has resulted in refuse heaps being dumped in the urban landscape in heavily populated cities as typically only about 40 to 50 per cent of waste is reportedly being collected.

Figure 3.4 shows the Municipal solid waste collection by selected regions of the world and Figure 3.5 shows the Municipal Solid waste disposal methods by various regions. The figure significantly point to the lowest percentage of collection of solid wastes by the African region. The recycling percentage indicates that Africa stands second lowest after Latin American regions.

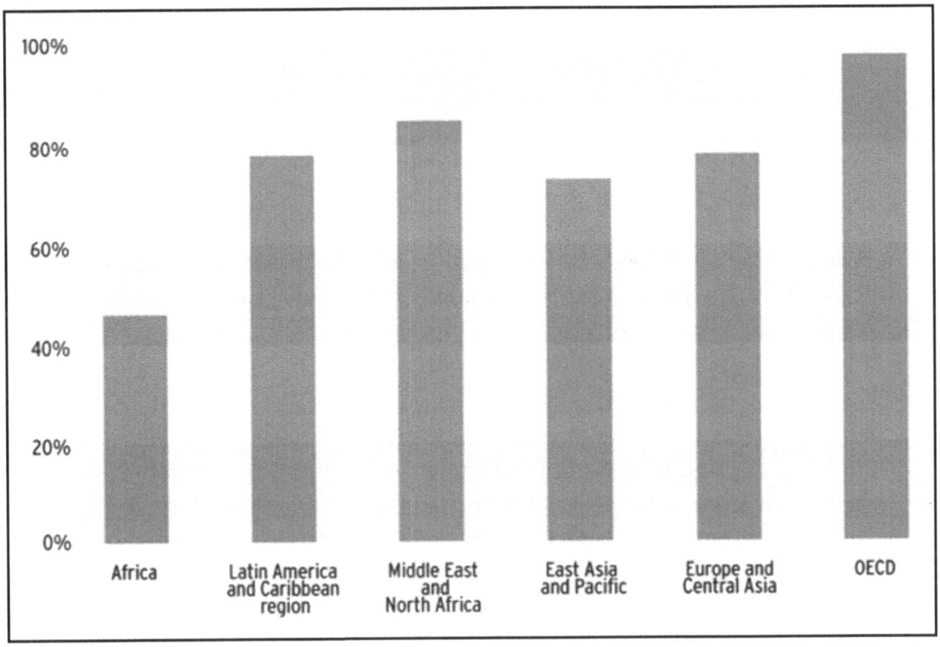

Fig. 3.4: **The solid waste collection status of various regions of the world**

(*Source:* The World Bank, 2012)

According to the Africa Review Report on Waste Management (2009), major trends and issues on waste management in Africa were the following.

- Poor waste management practices, in particular, widespread dumping of waste in water bodies and uncontrolled dump sites, aggravates the problems of generally low sanitation levels across the African continent.
- Urbanization is on the rise in Africa and this trend is expected to continue in the future. Of concern is the inability of infrastructure and land use planning methods (including for waste management) to cope with urban growth, (the highest in the world) at 3.5 per cent annually. This is particularly urgent in slum areas, which constitute a big part of many of the cities and towns in Africa.

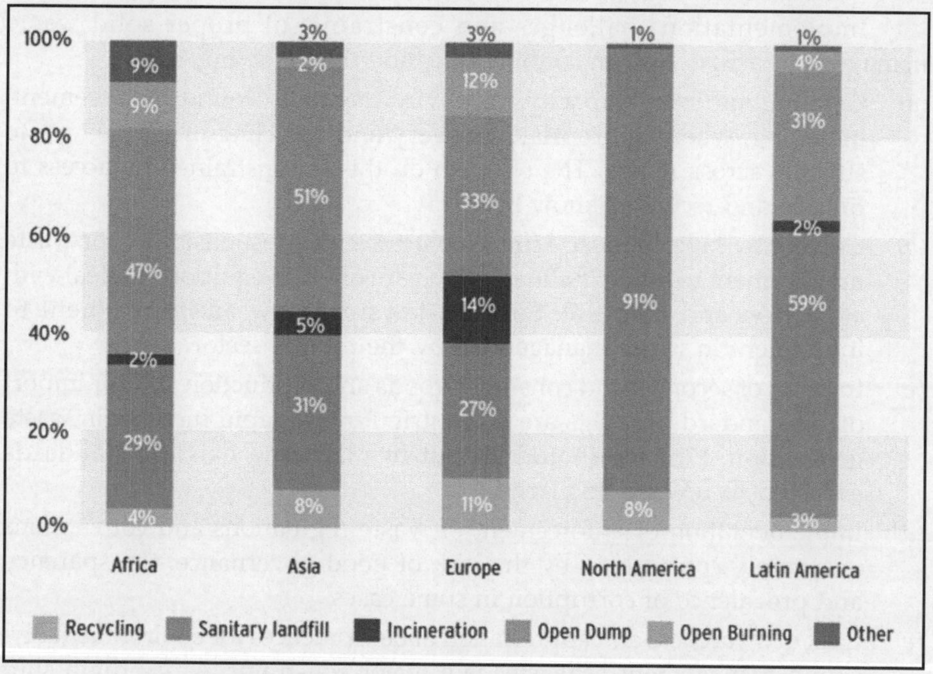

Fig. 3.5: **Municipal solid waste disposal method by various regions**

(Source: The World Bank, 2012)

- Waste management infrastructure is largely non-existent in rural areas of Africa. Improvements in infrastructure are urgently needed to combat the high cost of health services and thereby alleviate poverty and reduce rural-urban migration.
- The gap between waste management policy and legislation and actual waste management practices is widening due to perennial capacity constraints and lack of waste management facilities for various waste streams. Access to major investments and acquiring the technical know-how needed to resolve the capacity constraints remain a tall order.
- Waste generation is expected to increase significantly as a result of industrialization, urbanization and modernization of agriculture in Africa. This will further aggravate current capacity constraints in waste management.
- The fast growing use of ICT and rapid turn-over in technology (particularly computers, mobile phones, etc.,) is creating a growing E-waste stream, for which there is no waste management capacity yet. This leads to disposal of both E-waste and municipal waste in dump sites.
- Changing lifestyles and consumption patterns of the growing urban middle class, in particular, is increasing the complexity and composition of waste streams in Africa (http://www.uncsd2012.org).

Implementation challenges and constraints of proper solid waste management across African continent include the following.

(a) Creating sufficient capacity for environmentally sound management, including, where appropriate recovery and recycling of various waste streams across Africa. The effort to do this is constrained by access to finance and technical know-how.

(b) Current by-laws in most African countries give responsibility for waste management to municipalities, which are often ill-equipped to deal with collection and disposal. Such by-laws are now an impediment to investment in waste management by the private sector.

(c) Imports of second-hand consumer goods and production and/or import of substandard products are all contributing to rapid increase in waste generation. Policies should be put in place and existing standards enforced to reverse this trend.

(d) Implementation or enforcement of waste regulations and conventions is severely constrained by the lack of good governance, transparency and prevalence of corruption in some cases.

(e) Lack of awareness and appreciation of best practices for environmentally-sound management of wastes is a major constraint. A paradigm shift among communities and society at large is needed (http://www.uncsd 2012.org).

Solid waste management is becoming a major public health and environmental concern in urban areas of Ethiopia. In Ethiopia, like: developing countries, increase of solid waste generation is resulted from rapid urbanization and population booming. "The average solid waste generation rate is about 0.221 kg per person per day and it is also estimated that only 2 per cent of the population received solid waste collection services". This shows that the operational condition of MSWM service and efforts made to change the situation are low. As a result, small proportions of the urban dwellers are served and large quantity of solid waste left uncollected. The public sector in Ethiopia is unable to deliver services effectively, as result illegal dumping of solid waste along road sides and open areas is a common practice due to inadequate supply of waste containers and longer distance to these containers. The involvement of private sectors are also very limited, but currently a number of micro and small scale enterprises are emerging to participate in primary solid waste collection *i.e.,* collect garbage at source from households and transport it to the municipal waste containers and transfer points (Solomon, 2011).

Colleges and universities have the ability to foster an atmosphere where their communities think about their ecological responsibilities in this world. Many of these institutions have realized the challenges and rewards that come with the effort to protect natural resources and reduce the ecological footprint created by modern society. College campuses generate a large amount of waste that could be recycled, reused or composted. In addition, college campuses use huge amounts of chlorine-based bleached paper products that have the potential to contaminate the waste stream. By identifying what items are thrown away, it is possible to make inferences and raise questions about the kind of waste the campus is generating, collection practices and the items that should be targeted for diversion. Driven by the wisdom that waste is a wealth if prudently managed, this study earnestly looks into the status of waste paper generation, collection, disposal at Ambo University and the possibility of recycling and the environmental as well as economic merit it can bring in.

Materials and Methods

Description of the Study Area

The study is carried out in Ambo University, Ambo, Ethiopia. Ambo (also known as Hagere Hiwot) is a town in central Ethiopia. The town located 125 km., to the West of Addis Ababa, is the capital of West Shoa Administrative zone of Oromia Regional State (Fig. 3.6). Ambo has a latitude and longitude of 8°592 N 37°51′E/8.983°N 37.85°E/8.983; 37.85 and an elevation of 2101 meters. It is both the largest town and the administrative centre of Ambo woreda.

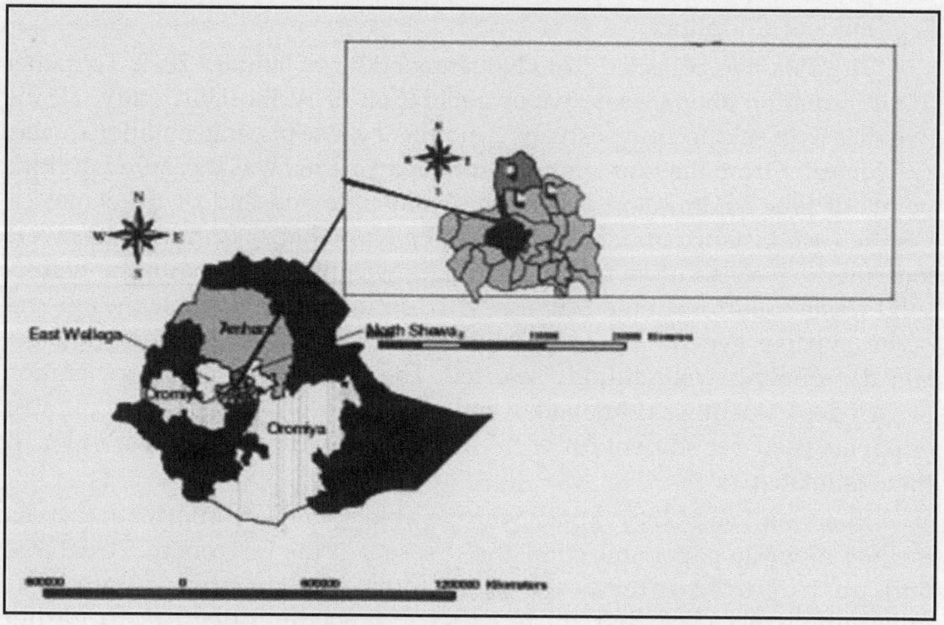

Fig. 3.6: **Ethiopia and West Shewa Zone showing Ambo District**

(*Source*: Hunduma, 2006).

Ambo University is one of the foremost higher learning institutions with significant contributions in the country's overall development by building the capacity of development agents through short, medium and long term trainings in various fields since its establishment in 1939. Moreover, the University recently secured 100 hectares of land to establish another campus for further expansion and buildings of satellite stations in Holeta, Gedo and Woliso. During the study period the University was effectively running 30 undergraduate programmes in various fields and 7 post graduate programmes in Cooperative Management, Cooperative Accounting, Plant Protection, Plant Pathology, Environmental Sciences, Analytical Chemistry and Fisheries and Aquaculture. More than 300 highly competent local as well as expatriate staffs work with Ambo University.

Data Collection Methods

Both qualitative and quantitative data were used to obtain information on the waste paper generation, collection and method of disposal during one semester at Ambo University. The sample collection was constituted through five sites *viz;*

1. Management offices.
2. Library.
3. Departments.
4. Class rooms.
5. Student dormitory.

The data was collected from November 2011 to January 2012. To gather the information about waste paper generation of Ambo University, all the five sites were selected purposively. Amount of waste paper generation during one semester from the four sites (except departments) was measured at three points of time - admission of students, mid time and end of the semester. During each instance of data collection, the waste paper from the sites were measured for consecutive two weeks using weighing scale, with the help of solid waste collectors of the University. To accurately congregate the amount of waste paper generation of departments with enhanced accuracy, colleges and departments were entirely selected. The mean waste paper generation of each department was obtained by gathering information about the number of papers used per student for each course. Weight of waste paper in kg., is then estimated.

Interviews and observations were used to obtain key information about method of waste paper collection and disposal at the University. Structured and unstructured interviews were sources for primary data. The questionnaires were distributed to solid waste collectors to gather information about method of waste paper collection and disposal.

Laboratory experiments were conducted to analyze the pulp quality of waste paper. Laboratory analysis for pulp quality including the following parameters were conducted through standard methods, using digital instruments at the well established laboratory of Anmol Products PLC, a paper recycling factory operating at Ginchi, off Ambo.

- *Consistency*: The parameter used to determine the solid content of pulp during pulp processing. Higher the consistency indicates higher amount of fibers having lesser distance between them. For pulp and paper maker this is the most important process parameters. 4-5 per cent is the standard consistency for the product.
- *Beating degree and dewatering capacity*: These are pulp coarseness quality measurements. To measure beating degree and dewatering capacity, CSF - Canadian Standard Freeness or SR - Schopper-Riegler was used. The standard of Schopper-Riegler (°SR) for the particular product produced from the waste paper is 30-40°SR.
- *Ash*: Ash is the residue left after igniting pulp at 500°C. Ash content in pulp may consist of various chemicals used during pulping/bleaching, mineral matter from wood or metallic matter from pipes and other machinery. This parameter tells the amount of chemicals used in various processes. Standard of ash for paper product produced from printing waste paper is 7-12 GSM (Grams per Square Meter). If ash is 7 and less than 7 GSM the chemical used for that product is insufficient and if it is above 12 GSM chemical is used more than expected.
- *Sizing/Cobb*: Resistance of paper towards the penetration of aqueous solution/water is measured by Sizing or Cobb values. The ability of fluids, both liquid and gaseous, to penetrate the structure of paper becomes a property, highly significant to the use of paper. The standard for water absorption parameter (Cobb) is 22-28 GSM.

Statistical Analysis

The collected data was systematically organized in a manner that facilitates analysis. Descriptive analysis was done for qualitative data. Quantitative data analysis was facilitated by the Microsoft Excel and the SPSS statistical softwares.

Results and Discussion

Waste Paper Generation Rate of Departments in Weight

The total waste paper generation from departments is shown in Table 3.1. Relationship between student's number and waste paper generation in undergraduate regular programme is shown in Table 3.2. Apparently the waste paper generation is increased with the number of students because the correlation coefficient between number of students and waste paper generation becomes 0.95. This implies that the number of students is one of the major factors for the amount of waste paper generation. Hence established is a positive relationship between student's number and waste paper generation.

Table 3.1: Total waste paper generation of departments

Programmes	No. of Students	Waste Paper (kg)
Undergraduate	4510	3120.207
Postgraduate	65	69.154
CEP	1675	863
Special training	240	133.908
Winter	621	343.93
Total	**7111**	**4530.199**

Table 3.2: The relationship between students' number and waste paper generation in under graduate regular programme

Correlations			
		Number of students	Waste paper generation
Number of students	Pearson Correlation	1	.950**
	Sig. (2-tailed)		.001
	N	30	30
Waste paper generation	Pearson Correlation	.950**	1
	Sig. (2-tailed)	.001	
	N	30	30

**. Correlation is significant at the 0.01 level (2-tailed).

The study showed that during the study period the total production of waste paper by the undergraduate students was 3120.27 kg., and their total number was 4510. The total production of waste paper by the 65 post graduate students was only 69.154 kg., which was very meager compared to the waste paper production by the undergraduate students. In case of Continuing Education Programme (CEP), the total number of students were 1675 and the total waste paper production was 863 kg. These values appreciably pointed to the positive relation between the number of students and the waste paper production in the campus during the study period.

College campuses use huge amounts of chlorine-based bleached paper products that have the potential to contaminate the waste stream. By identifying what items are thrown away, it is possible to make inferences and raise questions about the kind of waste the campus generates, type of collection practices and the items that should be targeted for diversion. The most effective way to determine the efficiency of a recycling programme is to 'know your trash' (Crawford, 1996; Smith, 1993).

Percentages of contribution of waste paper generation at the end of the semester, at the mid time and at the beginning of the semester are 73.81 per cent, 22.56 per cent and 3.63 per cent respectively. Waste paper generation at the end semester takes the largest proportion. Figure 3.7 shows these results at the beginning, mid time and end of the semester. Compared to the beginning and mid time, the waste paper production at the end semester was the highest. This might be due to the examinations, submission of assignments and projects in paper at the end of the semester and after evaluation these papers might have reached to the waste paper stream.

The goal of the waste management is to meet the requirement of sustainability as much as possible. In short this is contained in 'reduce, reuse and recycle' which has been frequently used in legislation guidelines, university education, public campaigns and green promotion of producers. It has become a well-recognized slogan for waste management strategy for authorities, institutions and corporations (Gertsakis and Lewis, 2003).

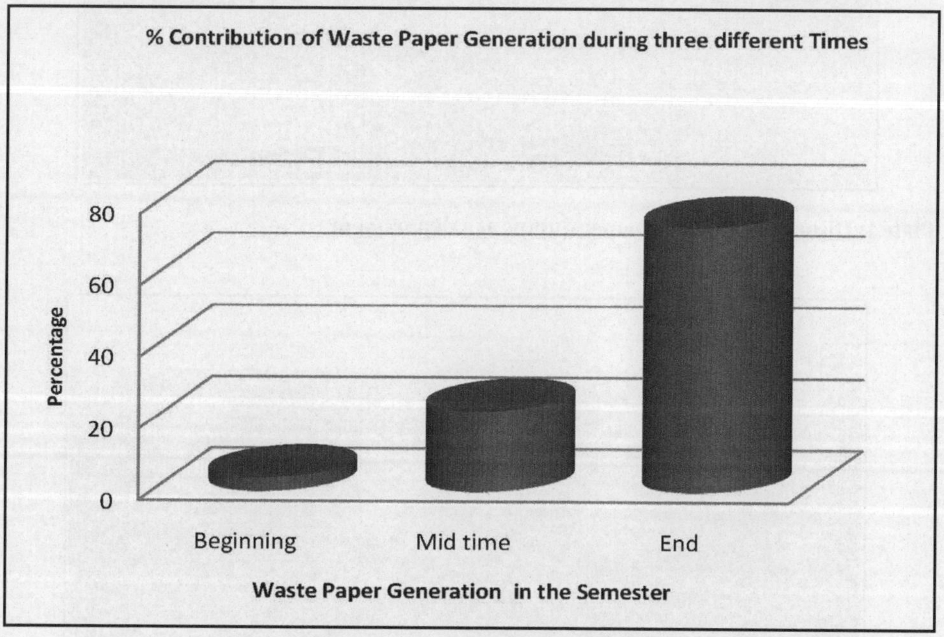

Fig. 3.7: **Per cent contribution of waste paper generation at the beginning, mid time and end of semester**

The researcher observed the disorganized dumps of waste paper at various departments (Plate 1) and haphazard burning of waste papers collected by the solid waste workers at the premises of the University (Plate 2). The disorganized dumps in various departments spoil the working environment of the departments. Houghton *et al.* (2001) reported that burning of solid wastes releases various gases especially the carbon dioxide to the atmosphere and bring in changes to climate patterns. According to Themelis and Nickolas (2003) during complete combustion, nearly all of the carbon content in the waste is emitted as CO_2 to the atmosphere.

Plate 1: Disorganized waste paper dumps at a department

Plate 2: Open burning of the waste paper

Table 3.3 shows the total waste paper generation of all study sites in the study period. Total waste paper generation of Ambo University was 5960.65 kg., in the study period. Among the various study sites, the Departments were contributing the highest percentage of waste paper *i.e.* 76 per cent and libraries were contributing the least percentage *i.e.* 2.05 per cent.

Table 3.3: Total waste paper generation of all study sites

Sl. No.	Sites	Semester Waste Paper Generation in kg	Waste Paper Generation in %
1.	Departments	4,530.199	76.00%
2.	Dormitories	596.368	10.01%
3.	Class rooms	468.48	7.86%
4.	Libraries	122.08	2.05%
5.	Around management offices	243.52	4.08%
	Total	**5960.65**	**100%**

During the study period, the researcher observed that most of the students write and prefer to write on one side of a white paper than using both sides. The students were least aware of the wastage of paper and total waste paper generation out of it. This is also adding to the overall generation of waste paper in the campus.

The University assigned workers to collect solid wastes inside campus. The researcher observed that the workers segregate the generated solid wastes especially papers and they simply burn it on the open ground near the main hall. Detailed interview with the workers indicated that most of the workers were least aware of the environmental implications associated with the burning of paper and they were not using any safety measures like masks or hand gloves while they were engaged in burning. Plate 3 shows a worker engaged in open burning of paper without proper safety measures. Many of the workers were having diseases like: asthma, sinusitis and allergic rashes in their hands. The workers were curious to know about the environmental and health implications associated with the open burning. So the researcher observed a scope for awareness programme about the issue among the workers.

Table 3.4 shows the results of pulp quality analysis of the waste paper collected from Ambo University. The pulp quality analysis was conducted to ensure the scope of recycling of the collected waste paper. Consistency is the parameter used to determine the solid content of pulp during pulp processing. Higher consistency indicates higher amount of fibers having lesser distance between them. 4-5 per cent is the standard consistency for good quality pulp for recycling purpose. Beating degree and dewatering capacity are pulp coarseness quality measurements. To measure beating degree and dewatering

Plate 3: A worker engaged in burning of paper without proper safety measures

capacity, CSF - Canadian Standard Freeness or SR - Schopper-Riegler is used. Ash is the residue left after igniting pulp at 500°C. This parameter tells the amount of chemicals used in various processes. Resistance of paper towards the penetration of aqueous solution or water is measured by Cobb values. The ability of fluids, both liquid and gaseous, to penetrate the structure of paper becomes a property, highly significant to the use of paper. The pulp quality analysis results of the collected waste paper from Ambo University showed that all the analyzed parameters were within the standard range. This implies that the waste paper from Ambo University has got huge scope in the recycling industry. Garner (2002) reported that the paper manufacturing is the third largest user of fossil fuels worldwide. PRF and US EPAR (1996) reported that every ton of recycled paper saves about 17 trees. Thus by sending its 5960.65 kg., of waste paper for recycling Ambo University can indirectly save 102 trees per semester. This figure gives a glaring evidence for the environmental significance of practicing paper recycling in the University campus.

Table 3.4: Pulp quality of waste paper collected from Ambo University

Parameters	Standard	Pulp Quality of Waste Paper
Consistency	4-5%	5%
Beating degree and dewatering capacity	30-40 °SR	34 °SR
Ash	7-12GSM	11 GSM
Cobb	22-28 GSM	24 GSM

Buclet and Godard (2000) reported that most of the countries were trying to formulate policies for identifying success in recycling of paper and paper boards, because it encouraged them in the environmental and economic point of views. An economic feasibility study of Chinese waste recycling industry in 2009 showed big opportunity for waste material recycling business owing to heaping quantities of solid waste, soaring demand for recyclables in a situation where there is a natural resource scarcity and price hike on virgin material (Zhao *et al*. 2010).

Table 3.5 shows the economic significance of the University's waste paper in the recycling market. The results showed that the University could generate 35,763.9 Birr per semester or 71,527.8 Birr annually. Jiayi (2011) recommended a model approach specifying the formulation of a recycling alliance between Government and other responsible bodies to meet a higher recycling rate, incorporating stakeholders such as: municipalities, professional recyclable (recyclable take-back) companies, recyclers, environmental NGOs, producers, media, schools, universities, residential management companies and entire inhabitants in an area. Inside this alliance, every participator has to contribute for a common goal of improving recycling and to achieving individual goals.

Table 3.5: Economic significance of waste paper

Waste Paper (kg.)	Waste Paper Price (birr)
1 kg.	6 birr
5960.65 kg. (One semester waste paper generation)	35,763.9 birr

Conclusion

At Ambo University waste paper is collected separately from other solid wastes. Waste paper is collected separately not for recycling but for burning. Inadequate waste paper management has been observed in some department offices, which lead to uninviting working environment. The total waste paper generation rate per semester of Ambo University during the study period is 5960.65 kg. The study revealed that large amount of waste paper is generated from departments and relatively small amount of waste paper is generated from libraries. Waste paper generation at the end of the semester is the highest compared to its production at the beginning and mid time of the semester. The experimental analyses results revealed that the pulp quality of waste paper collected from Ambo University was within the standard quality for recycling. This shows an enhanced scope of recycling of the waste paper from Ambo University. If Ambo University collects and supplies its waste paper to a recycling company, in addition to environmental conservation, the University will generate 35,763.9 Birr per semester. The study also recommends achieving source reduction by practicing the use of both sides of white paper.

REFERENCES

Buclet, N. and Godard O. (2000): Municipal Waste Management in Europe – A Comparative Study in Building regimes, Kluwer Academic Publishers, The Netherlands.

Callie Brazil, Lauren Frisch, Noah Goldberg, Connor Hedges, Meghan Kiernan, Adam Kobayashi, and Paul Vogelsang (2011): Paper Purchasing and Consumption at Colgate University: An Analysis of Current paper use and Recommendations for the Future, Community-Based Study of Environmental Issues, Colgate University.

Crawford, M. (1996): University waste Characterization using Manual Sorting Methods – A Michigan State University Case Example, Living Planet Press, California.

EPA (2008): Municipal Solid Waste Generation, Recycling, and Disposal in the United States: Facts and Figures for 2008, United States Environmental Protection Agency, Accessed from http://www.epa.gov/osw/nonhaz/municipal/msw99, accessed on 28/01/2013

Garner, J.W. (2002): Energy Conservation Practices Offer Environmental and Cost Benefits - Pulp and Paper, American Forest and Paper Association, Canada.

Gertsakis, J. and Lewis, H. (2003): Sustainability and the Waste Management Hierarchy, Eco Recycle Victoria, A Discussion paper on the Waste Management Hierarchy and its Relationship to Sustainability, available at: http://www.ecorecycle.vic.gov.au/resources/documents/TZW_-_Sustainability_and_the_Waste_Hierarchy_(2003).pdf

Houghton, J. T., Ding, Y. Griggs, D. J., Noguer, M., P. J. Vander Linden and Xiaosu, D. (2001): Climate change: The Scientific Basis, Contribution of Working Group I to the Third Assessment Report of the Intergovernmental Panel on Climate Change (IPCC), Cambridge University Press, Cambridge.

http://epa.gov/epawaste/conserve/tools/warm/index.html, Accessed on 8/10/2014

http://www.uncsd2012.org/content/documents/AfricanReviewReport-onWaste ManagementSummary.pdf, Accessed on 8/10/2014

http://www.cyen.org/, Accessed on 4/10/2014

Hunduma, T. (2006): Local Crop Genetic Resource Utilization and Management in Gindeberet, West central Ethiopia, *Master Thesis*, NORAGRIC Centre for Environment and Development Studies, Norway.

Jiayi Yin, (2011): Dealing with Waste, thinking about Individual – A Conceptual Design to Supporting China's Municipalities to Reach their Target on Waste Separation and Recycling with a Focus on the Social Aspect, *Master thesis*, Industrial Ecology, Norwegian University of Science and Technology.

MSWDRS (Missouri Solid Waste Diversion and Recycling Status) (1989): Reports of Metro Recycling, Department of Natural Resources, Missouri.

Pieter van, B. and Anantha, D. (1996): The Economic and Environmental Impacts of the Waste Paper, Amsterdam, The Netherlands.

PRF and US EPAR (Purdue Research Foundation and US Environmental Protection Agency Report), (1996), Facts about paper and paper waste. From http://www.id2.ca/downloads/eco-design-paper-facts.pdf. Retrieved September 2012.

Smith, A. (1993): Campus Ecology – A Guide to Assessing Environmental Quality and Creating Strategies for Change, Living Planet Press, California.

Solomon Cheru (2011): Assessment of Municipal Solid Waste Management in Dessie Town, *MA Thesis*, Addis Ababa University, Ethiopia.

Themelis and Nickolas, J. (2003): An Overview of the Global Waste-to-Energy Industry. *Waste Management World*, 40: 40-47.

Zhao, W., Leeftinkb, R.B. and Rotterc, V.S. (2010): Evaluation of the Economic Feasibility for the Recycling of Construction and Demolition Waste in China – The Case of Chongqing, Institute of Construction Management and Real Estate, Resources, TU Berlin, *Conservation and Recycling*, 54 (6): 377-389.

Pages: 64-72

WASTE GENERATION AND UTILIZATION
Edited by: **Dr. Priya Bajaj; Dr. B. Tabassum** and **Dr. Pawan Kumar 'Bharti'**
ISBN: 978-93-5056-792-0
Edition: **2016**
Published by: **Discovery Publishing House Pvt. Ltd., New Delhi (India)**

CHAPTER - 4

Solid Waste Disposal and Its Management with Special Reference to Sibsagar Town Area

Case Study

Bristi Dutta Borah

ABSTRACT

Widespread industrial development and unplanned urbanization result in the creation of the ever increasing problem – The solid waste problem, which has been mostly experienced in most of the developing countries including India. The mad rat race among the nations for development, economic eruptions and unlimited exploitation of population result in increased and uncontrolled disposal of solid wastes. These pile up at public places and cause obstruction in daily life. Today, solid waste management has become a serious issue. On the other hand there is lack of advanced and environmentally sound solid waste management technique in our country which results in the production of various pollutants affecting our environment. It is high time to think if there is any management technique we can practice easily, which may reduce the impact of this problem permanently and without affecting the environment and biodiversity.

The study area is Sivasagar town area where I have selected a few solid waste prone areas. Piles of garbage are a familiar sight in these places. However, Sivasagar municipality board uses to collect the garbage and

Department of Zoology, Swahid Peoli Phukan College, Namti, Sivasagar, Assam, India.

dispose in a fixed area. But the way they dispose looked vary unscientific and unhyighgenic. Again in the selected medical areas, it has been noticed that the guide lines provided has not been followed properly or if followed, it is not perfect. Thus my study has aimed in finding the reason behind it and also to find a fruitful solution for this, which must be environmentally sound and easily applicable.

Keywords: Unplanned urbanization, environment, solid waste, bio-degradable waste, garbage.

INTRODUCTION

Rapid and widespread industrial development, unplanned urbanization, regular flow of persons from rural to urban areas and improper and inadequate action of the authorities entrusted with the work of pollution control and environmental protection have largely contributed to unhealthy and degraded environment. Unplanned and alarming rate of urbanization has given rise to many environment related problems. Apart from air and water pollution problems, most gigantic problem which modern cities and industries are facing is the solid waste disposal problem (Ecology environment, Sharma P.D. 1975). The Municipal Solid Wastes Management and Handling Rules, (2000) has defined 'Municipal Solid Waste' as 'commercial and residential wastes generated in a municipal or notified areas in either solid or semi-solid form excluding industrial hazardous wastes but includes treated bio-medical wastes. Solid wastes are the ever increasing problem in most of the developing countries including India. These pile up at public places and cause obstruction in daily life. Solid waste may affect both terrestrial and aquatic life as well. Today, solid waste management has become a serious issue. Solid waste management procedures and practices must be designed to prevent or reduce the discharge of wastes. The municipal authorities have been practicing various techniques for solid waste management. But most of them cannot be considered as permanent solution to get rid of this problem. It is important to ascertain the nature of waste whether it is biodegradable or combustible in handling and disposal of solid waste. Combustion and landfill method of disposal further gives rise to problems like: air, water and land pollution, affecting adversely the health of the man, and flora and fauna. On the other hand there is lack of advanced and environmentally sound solid waste management techniques in our country. Instead of advanced scientific techniques, old methods are used, that leads to the production of various pollutants affecting our environment. Therefore we want a permanent solution for this problem. It is the high time to think if there is any management technique we can practice easily which may reduce the impact of this problem permanently and without affecting the environment and the biodiversity. Keeping all these in view, my present study has been conducted. The goal of my present study is to survey the present status of garbage management and how much safe to the environment. Urban areas are severely affected by solid wastes disposal. Therefore, I have selected the Sivasagar town area that is located nearby, which have made my study easier.

Objectives

1. To collect the solid wastes from various sites, prone to solid waste disposal problem.
2. Assessment of the problems experienced by the local people because of these solid wastes.
3. Surveying the methods practiced by the municipal authority to manage this problem.
4. To discuss if there is any safe and scientific method to be practiced, which are environmentally sound and sustainable.

Methodology

Study Area

The study was conducted in Sivasagar town area, under the Sivasagar district which is located about 150 km., East of the famous Kaziranga National park and 50 km., East from Jorhat in the state of Assam.

Sivasagar is an administrative district of Assam (NE India), situated between 94°25′ and 95°25′ longitude East and 21°45′ and 27°15′ latitude North. It has an elevation of 86.6 meter above the sea level. It carries a pleasant weather throughout the year. The district is characterized by the highly humid climate with abundant rains. The annual rainfall is about 2000-2300 millimeters with nearly 60-80 per cent of the rainfall occurring during the Monsoon months (June - August). After the rainy season, the colder autumn starts from October and real cold weather prevails from the end of November and continues till the middle of February.

The Sivasagar town area considered for the present study is a moderately populated town occupying a total area of 12.55 sq. km. Sivasagar town areas includes 14 wards containing residential and certain areas, four nursing homes. I have selected only a few areas for my present purpose. The selected sites were – Ward No. 9, the Central market, The Pragati nursing home, The Sampreeti nursing home and The Civil hospital. These are proved to be highly solid waste prone areas.

Study Period

The study was carried out for a very short period of time. It was only for 4 Months (June 2010 to September 2010).

Map

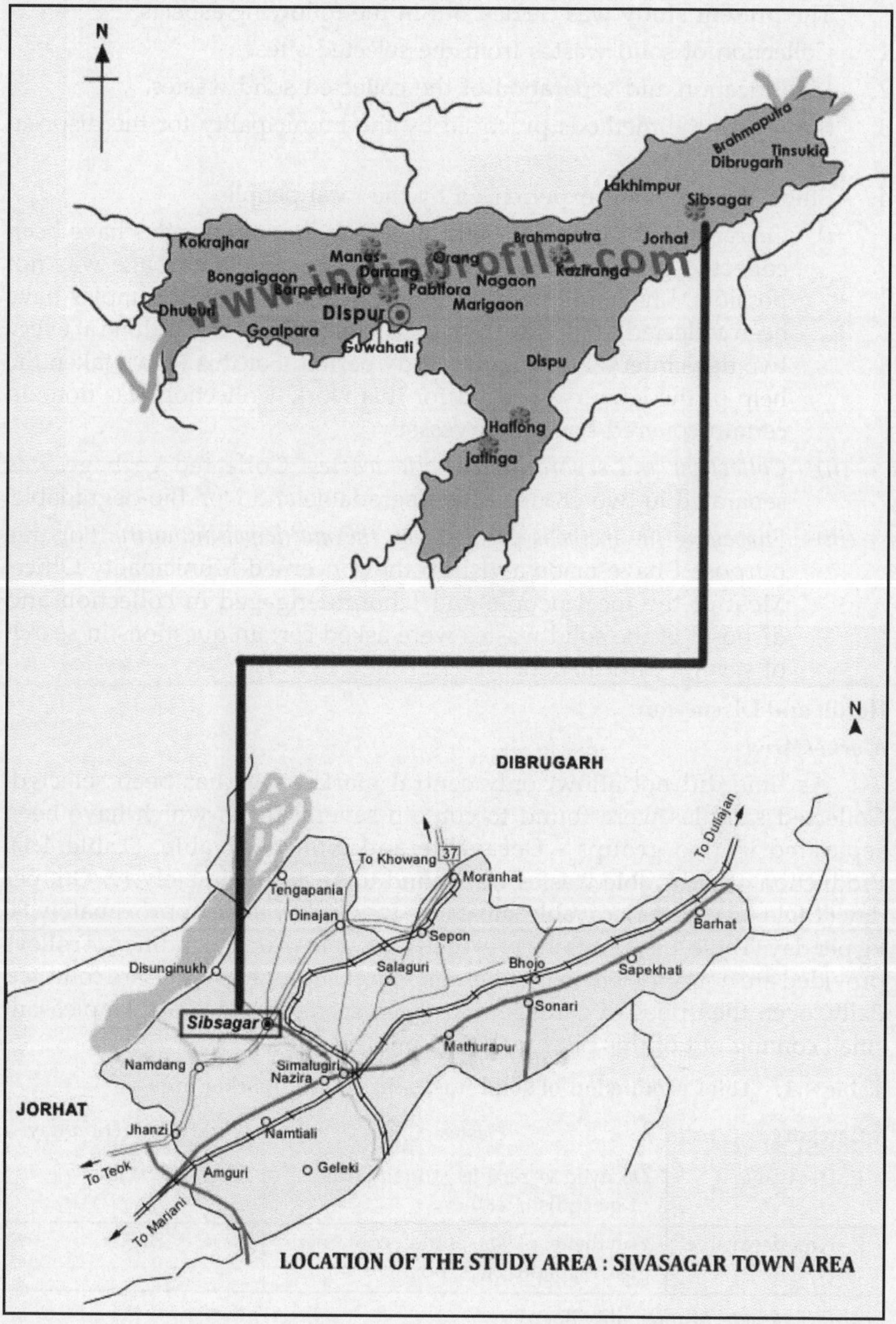

LOCATION OF THE STUDY AREA : SIVASAGAR TOWN AREA

Study Aspects

The present study was carried out in the following aspects:

1. Collection of solid wastes from the selected sites.
2. Identification and separation of the collected solid wastes.
3. Surveying the methods practiced by the municipality for the disposal of these wastes.
4. Study the problems experienced by the local people.
   (i) *Collection of solid wastes*: Solid wastes from various sites have been collected randomly. As collection of the whole garbage was not possible, I have followed sampling method. A lot of samples have been collected randomly from each site. Collection was done at every two days interval during the study period. For this I have taken the help of the labours engaged for this work. Collection was done in certain covered boxes and vessels.
   (ii) *Collection and separation of solid wastes*: Collected garbage was separated in two groups - Bio-degradable and Non Bio-degradable.
   (iii) *Surveying the methods practiced by the municipal authority:* For this purpose I have made a visit to the concerned Municipality Office. Most of the local people and labours engaged in collection and disposal of the solid wastes were asked certain questions in search of several information.

Result and Discussion

Market Area

As time did not allow, only central market area has been selected. Collected samples were found to contain several items which have been separated in two groups - Decayable and Non decayable. (Table 4.1). Production of decayable wastes was found to be approximately 1.5 Qtl. per day (Table 4.1). Non-decayable substance was found to be approximately 80 kg per day (Table 4.1). Dustbins provided are not in proper condition. Trolleys provided are not sufficient in number. Therefore, though garbage are collected daily, even then piles of garbage have been seen at road sides. Unpleasant smell coming out of this piles make the public suffer.

Table 4.1: Total production of solid wastes in central market area

Category	Wastes	Total Production/day
1. Decayable	Decayed vegetables, rotten parts of meat, fish, feathers	1.5 Qtl.
2. Non-decayable	Polythene, plastic bottles, containers, glasses, paper bags, boxes	80 Kg.

Source: Sivasagar Municipality Board.

Residential Area

Collection was done only in Ward No. 9. Collected wastes were grouped in two categories same as that of market wastes (Table 4.2). Decayable wastes were found to be approximately 5 Qtl. Per day and non-decay able were found to be approximately 100 kg per day. Daily collection and disposal of these wastes have been practiced since long, but only 60 per cent can be collected in this way. Then what about the rest 40 per cent. Improper collection and unscientific disposal result in the production of piles of garbage in public places (Photo-1) and unhealthy environment. However, certain garbage are thrown in nearby water bodies and drains which cannot be collected and disposed. As a result, these pile up day after day and leads to water pollution, air pollution and threatening effect to the public. In certain residences they use to burn the garbage without proper knowledge about the harmful affect of this unscientific burning.

Table 4.2: Total production of solid wastes per day in the residential area (Ward No. 9)

Category	Wastes	Total Production/day
1. Decayable	Rotten parts of vegetables, fruits, rice, left off food	5 Qtl.
2. Non-decayable	Glass and plastic containers, paper, paper products (such as: juice packets, oil packets, packing materials), polythene bags, clothes	100 kg

Source: Sivasagar Municipality Board.

Medical Areas

According to the bio-medical waste rules 1998, bio-medical waste means 'any waste which is generated during the diagnosis, treatment or immunizations of human beings or animals or in research activities. As study was conducted in three medical sites, total solid waste production was found to be 30 Kg./day in Sibsagar Civil Hospital, 5-7 Kg./Day in Pragati Nursing Home and 6-9 Kg./Day in Sampreeti Nursing Home (Table 4.3). All collected medical wastes have been grouped in several categories as directed by the Bio-medical waste management and handling rules, 1998 (Table 4.4). It has been found that the Guidelines provided for the disposal of bio-medical wastes has not been followed properly and if followed it is not perfect. However, ETP or Effluent treatment Plant has been transplanted in Pragati Nursing Home for the treatment of liquid wastes, which is seen to be scientific to a large extent. This practice must be encouraged in other nursing homes and medicals. Besides, incinerators have also been provided in the respective nursing homes and the civil hospital. But, work only to a certain extent .On the other hand, the incinerator of the civil hospital has been damaged since last one year, which results in the throwing of the medical wastes without proper treatment (Photo-3). It did not seem to be scientific and environmentally safe.

Table 4.3: Total production of solid wastes per day in the respective medical areas

Hospitals/ Nursing Homes	Total Solid Waste Production/day	Solid Waste Production/annum
Civil Hospital	30 kg.	10950 kg. (apx.)
Pragati	5-7 kg.	1825-2555 kg. (apx.)
Sampreeti	6-9 kg.	2190-3285 kg. (apx.)

Source: The respective hospitals.

Table 4.4: List of the collected Bio-medical wastes from respective sites according to their categories

Category	Treatment of the Wastes		
	Civil Hospital	Pragati Nursing Home	Sampreeti Nursing Home
Human Anatomical Waste: (Human tissues, organs body parts.)	Throw away	Incinerate	Incinerate
Waste sharps: (Needles, syringes, scalpels, blades, glass, etc. that may cause puncture and cuts. This includes both used and unused sharps.) Discarded Medicines and Cytotoxic drugs: (Wastes comprising of outdated, contaminated and discarded medicines.)	Throw away	Disinfect and deep burial	Disinfect and deep burial
Liquid Ash: (Waste generated from laboratory and washing, cleaning, house-keeping and disinfecting activities.)	Throw away	Disinfect and purify	Disinfect and purify
Incineration Ash: (Ash from incineration of any bio-medical waste)	—	Deep burial	Throw away and landfill
Chemical Waste: (Chemicals used in production of biologicals, chemicals used in disinfection, as insecticides, etc.)	Throw away	Chemical treatment and discharge	Chemical treatment
Solid Waste: (Items contaminated with blood, and body fluids including cotton, dressings, soiled plaster casts, lines, beddings, other material contaminated with blood.)	Disinfect and throw away	Autoclave and incinerate	Incinerate
Solid Waste: (Wastes generated from disposable items other than the waste sharp such as: tubings, catheters, intravenous sets, etc.)	Disinfect and throw away	Disinfect	Disinfect

Source: Respective hospitals and nursing homes and the bio-medical waste management and handling rules, 1998

Steps taken by The Sibsagar Municipality

1. They collect the solid wastes from market and residential areas and dispose untreated in Darikapar. It did not seem to be the proper place for disposal. Disposal of untreated wastes has been practiced since last 24 years which results in the production of huge piles and unhealthy condition. (Photo-4). These effect the nearby areas. During rainy season, rain water carrying a large part of these waste drains into the Darika river and cause water pollution.
2. 5 tractors and 7 apes have been provided which are not sufficient for cleaning purpose. On the other hand one tractor does not work properly.
3. A few dustbins have been constructed, but already in broken and damaged condition. Those dustbins have no use.
4. 25 labours and 40 sweepers have been employed for collection and cleaning. But due to irregular payment and lack of strictness of municipal authority, they do not work properly. Unscientific methods of garbage collection influence the health of the concerned people.

Conclusion

Though various laws are available but either they are not well couched to meet such type of exigencies, or are not efficiently and efficaciously implemented. Rather these laws are never made use of to deal with the problem of municipal solid waste. However, the present investigation and study that there is lack of people awareness and scientific technologies regarding solid waste management. Economic strength of the concerned authority may also be a matter. I have come to certain conclusions which are summarized below:

1. Storage facilities or bins should be 'easy to handle'. Vehicles used for the transfer and transportation of wastes must be covered - not visible to public. Storage facilities-bins should be cleaned on daily basis and should not be overflowed. Dustbins which have already broken must be repaired or newly constructed and also be provided with a lid over it.
2. Disposal should be proper and scientific. Before disposal, the municipal authority must take the labour of separating the wastes accordingly, so that recyclable things can be sent for recycling. To encourage recycling of materials, some motivation should be given.
3. Bio-degradable wastes shall be processed by composting, anaerobic digestion or any other appropriate biological processing for stabilization of wastes. On the other hand we can process the bio-degradable wastes at source only. If those wastes are stored in certain properly constructed pits and put there suitable microorganisms which will convert them to compost, then it will be an eco friendly practice.

4. Only non-biodegradable and other wastes which are not suitable either for recycling or for biological processing shall be used for land filling. Before secure landfill' the wastes should treated to make it safe for land and water of the area.
5. Incineration must be proper. There will be no chemical pretreatment before incineration. Chlorinated plastics should not be incinerated.
6. The most important point is the public awareness about solid waste problem. They must be concerned about the danger of unscientific and untreated disposal of solid wastes. In order to ensure community participation in segregation of waste, the municipal authority shall organize awareness programmes through regular meetings of representatives of local residents, welfare associations and non-governmental organization.
7. Efficient laws alone cannot solve the problem, unless we have efficient mechanism to implement, will of the government to implement and attitudinal change among the masses is needed.
8. Bio-medical wastes should not be mixed with other wastes. The workers engaged in cleaning of these bio-medical wastes are ignorant about the waste problem and pollution control. So, it is the duty of pollution control board to make them concern. Skilled people must be invited or employed for their proper training.

REFERENCES

A.K. Dey, (1987): Environmental Chemistry, New Age International Limited Publishers, pp. 100-102.

Environmental Resources Management, (2004): Strategic Planning Guide for Municipal Solid Waste Management.

Kumar, S. and Gaikuad, S.A. (2004): Municipal Solid Waste Management in India Urban Centers. An Approach for Betterment, Urban Development Debates in the New Millennium, edited by K.R. Gupta, Atlantic Publishers and Distributers, New Delhi pp. 100-111.

NEERI Report Strategy paper on Solid Waste Management in India, pp. 1-7.

Sashtri, C. (2008): Solid Waste Management and Indian Legal Profile.

Sharma, P.D. (1975): Ecology and Environment, Rastogi Publication, Gangotri Shivaji Road, Mirat, 250002, India, pp. 243-245.

Pages: 73-90

WASTE GENERATION AND UTILIZATION

Edited by: **Dr. Priya Bajaj; Dr. B. Tabassum** and **Dr. Pawan Kumar 'Bharti'**

ISBN: 978-93-5056-792-0

Edition: **2016**

Published by: **Discovery Publishing House Pvt. Ltd., New Delhi (India)**

CHAPTER - 5

Municipal Solid Waste Management in India with Special Reference to Silchar, A City of North East India

Siddhartha Bhattacharjee and **Susmita Gupta**

ABSTRACT

This chapter described the development of the concept of solid waste management from ancient to pre-independent to post-independent India followed by Municipal Solid Waste Management (MSWM) and MSW (Management and Handling) Rules, 2000. The concept of Integrated Sustainable Waste Management (ISWM) consisting of three dimension of sustainability such as: stakeholders (city council, NGOS, etc.), system elements (waste collection, separation at source etc.,) and aspects (technical, environmental, etc.,) also has been explained. A comparative analysis of the solid waste management of four capital cities of North East India and the city Silchar of South Assam in particular has been made.

The study focused on the nature, biomass and physico-chemical characteristics of the solid waste of Silchar and found that there is larger proportion of organic matter in MSW of Silchar city along with optimum moisture content indicating the desirability of biological processing of waste. The study revealed that poor collection and inadequate

Department of Ecology and Environmental Science, Assam University, Silchar -788 011, Assam, India.

transportation are responsible for the accumulation of MSW at every nook and corner of a city. The difficulties in providing the desired level of public service in the urban centres are often attributed to the poor financial status of the managing municipal corporations. Hence a city specific detailed investigations need to be carried out to evolve an effective SWM system.

Definition of Waste

Solid waste has been defined by the United States Environment protection Agency (EPA, 1972) as 'useless, unwanted, or discarded material with insufficient liquid content to be free flowing'. According to Organization for Economic Co-operation and Development (OCED) waste is "materials generated in production and consumption activities that do not have, in the context in which they are produced, any economic value. TERI (1998) defined Municipal Solid Waste as "all solid wastes generated in a community except industrial and agricultural waste". Though waste from hospitals and nursing homes are required to be collected and treated separately, in most cities and towns such wastes continue to form a part of MSW. The Municipal Solid Waste (Management and Handling) Rules 2000 states that Municipal Solid Waste is commercial and residential waste generated in a municipal or notified areas in either solid or semi-solid form excluding industrial hazardous wastes but including treated bio medical wastes.

Solid Waste Management in Ancient India

Since Vedic time, the prime motto of Indian social life was to live in harmony with nature and in a hygienic environment. *Vedas, Upanishads, Smritis and Dharmashastras* preached for worshiping plants, trees, Mother earth, *Vayumandal* (Sky), water and animals (all living creatures). Thus, polluting air, water or land was regarded as sin as they were to be respected and regarded as God and Goddesses. *Manusmriti* – The first systematic treatment of Hindu law, also prohibited the throwing of garbage, dust, rubbish, pieces of meat etc., on the highway and in water bodies and made it punishable. It emphasised on maintenance of clean, hygienic and unpolluted atmosphere near dwelling houses and around towns and villages. *Kautilya* in his *Arthshastra* has mentioned that maintaining sanitation of habitat is essential. The great epic *Mahabharata* also emphasized the environmental pollution and its harmful impact on the society. The *Charak* – doyen of Ayurveda also emphasised the purity of water and air. Other scripture also cautioned against disposal of civic waste and industrial refuse into rivers as they are considered to be sacred and respectable by the Hindus.

Solid Waste Management in Pre-Independent India

British India followed good hygienic practices for other wastes. Nightsoil from dry latrines was buried in trenches in rotation. Large 'grass farms' outside cities naturally purified sewage through land application.

Domestic waste was collected door-to-door in bullock-carts and sent to the outskirts of town. City Garbage was mostly organic then, and unpolluted. Farmers used it on their fields to return nutrients and micro-nutrients to their soils before synthetic fertilizers became available. So there was no need for large areas for treatment or disposal of MSW. All this changed when urea was subsidized and the Plastic Yug began. The Green Revolution changed the urban environment too (Patel, 2002).

Solid Waste Management in Post Independent India

Solid waste management in India is a part of public health and sanitation, and according to Indian Constitution, it is within the purview of the State list. Since this activity is non-exclusive, non-rivaled and essential, the responsibility for providing the service lies within the public domain. The activity being of local nature is entrusted to the Urban Local Bodies (ULBs). The ULB undertakes the task of solid waste service delivery with its own staff, equipment and funds. In some cases, works are contracted out to private enterprises (CPHEEO, 2000).

Regarding scientific solid waste management initiatives of Government of India began as early as in the 1960s when the Ministry of Food and Agriculture offered soft loans to ULBs for SWM. Further initiative was taken by the Government of India in terms of planned support by providing block grants and loans to state governments for setting up MSW composting facilities under the fourth five-year plan (1969-74). This initiative was taken further in 1974 when the Government of India modified this scheme for specific support to cities above 30 lakhs population. However, a number of reasons led to failure of the above initiatives.

In 1975, the Government of India set up a high-level committee for reviewing the problems of urban waste in India. The committee, in its report made 76 recommendations, covering eight important areas of waste management. Between 1975 and 1980, ten mechanical compost plants were set up in the country. In 1990 Government of India constituted the National Waste Management Council (NWMC). One of the objectives of NWMC was to improve MSW and it provided financial assistance to 22 municipalities to undertake surveys to assist them in improving SWM situation. However, in 1994, the whole India realised the magnitude of problem of urban waste management after outbreak of an epidemic in Surat. Consequently, a high-powered committee was constituted in 1995, under the chairmanship of Prof. J.S. Bajaj. This Committee gave a number of suggestions including need for source segregation, community-based door-to-door collection and transportation to municipal *dhalaos;* charge of user-fees, standardisation of design for municipal vehicles for transportation, need for composting of waste as the most feasible alternative for disposal, and private sector participation in waste management.

Post-Surat scenario saw a burst in SWM related activities at the policy. In 1995, The Ministry of Environment and Forests (MoEF) and the CPCB organized an interaction meet with municipal authorities and other concerned ministries to evolve a strategy for the management of MSW. Since 1995 over 50 waste treatment facilities have been set up across the country, mostly with private sector participation. In this period, increased awareness among urban residents saw a number of public interest litigations being filed. Responding to these, the Hon'ble Supreme Court set up a committee to review the MSW conditions in Class I cities. The Ministry of Environment and Forest (MoEF) meanwhile issued draft rules on Municipal Waste (Management and Handling) Rules. These rules mandated all cities to set up waste treatment facilities by 2001 and specified standards for segregation, collection, storage, transportation and disposal. In 1996, the MNES initiated a pilot programme to promote waste-to-energy projects in India, which may be considered as the birth of the new era of waste-to-energy programmes in India.

The Municipal Waste Rules of 1999 was complemented by a Manual on Municipal Solid Waste Management which was developed by the CPHEEO under aegis of the Ministry of urban development (MoUD). This manual was prepared by an Expert Group and lays down guidelines and procedures for ULB to improve SWM in their cities. Recently, under directions from the Hon'ble Supreme Court, a 'Technology Advisory Group' has been set up to improve SWM in the country and oversee implementation of innovative technologies of waste management in the country.

Municipal Solid Waste Management (MSWM)

Planning and implementation of systems to handle MSW in sustainable manner is known as MSWM. The manual on municipal solid waste management (2000) grouped activities with management of MSW into six functional elements. They are waste generation, waste handling and sorting, storage and processing at source, collection, sorting, processing and transformation, transfer and transport, disposal. This can be broadly classified into three categories, namely: Collection, Transportation and Disposal (CTD).

The management of solid waste is one of the earliest of man's branches of knowledge. In some way it is one of the latest. The reason for this seeming paradox is the success which rewarded the efforts of public health specialists and sanitary engineers in overcoming the abysmally unhygienic conditions into which man has allowed his habitations to degenerate at different times in his history (Wilson, 1977).

MSW (Management and Handling) Rules, 2000

According to MSW Rules, 2000, every municipal authority is responsible for setting up a waste processing and disposal facility, and for preparing an annual report. The State governments and Union Territory Administrations have the overall responsibility for enforcement of the provisions of these rules in the metropolitan cities and within territorial limits of their jurisdiction (MSW Rules, 2000). The Central Pollution Control Board (CPCB), State Boards, and the other committees are required to monitor the compliance of the standards regarding groundwater, ambient air, leachate quality, and compost quality including incineration standards, and they are to examine the proposal taking into consideration the views of other agencies. As per implementation rules, set up of waste processing and disposal facilities are to be done first. These facilities must be monitored once every 6 months. Existing landfill sites must be improved, and identification of landfill sites for future use must be carried out. Waste collection by any method (community bin, house-to-house collection, etc.,) must be conducted by using bell ringing or a musical vehicle to alert citizens without exceeding permissible noise levels. Biomedical and industrial wastes must not be mixed with MSW. Municipal authorities are to establish and maintain MSW storage facilities for avoiding unhygienic conditions in the area. Citizens must be encouraged by the municipal authority to segregate wastes. Vehicles for transportation must be covered and the MSW must be processed to reduce the burden on landfills. Biodegradable wastes are to be processed by composting and anaerobic digestion while landfills are restricted for non-biodegradable waste or inert, or which are not suitable for recycling.

The Concept of Integrated Sustainable Waste Management (ISWM)

Solid waste management includes all activities that seek to minimize the health, environmental and aesthetic impacts of solid wastes. Today the world is looking forward to integrate solid waste management systems for tackling the waste related issues of urban environments.

Integrated Sustainable Waste Management or Integrated Solid Waste Management refers to a waste management system that best suits the society, economy and environment in a given location, a city in most cases. The concept of ISWM not only takes technical or financial-economic sustainability into account, it also includes socio-cultural, environmental, institutional and political aspects that influence overall sustainability of waste management. ISWM also stands for a strategic and long-term approach. The ISWM concept consists of three dimension of sustainability, which needs to be integrated. They are Stakeholders (city council, NGOS, etc.), System elements (waste collection, separation at source etc.,) and Aspects (technical, environmental, etc.) In the case of development projects the ISWM concept can be used as an analysis and assessment tool for all stages of the project cycle: design/ formulation, selection/appraisal, monitoring and evaluation. ISWM can be used as a policy tool and as an assessment/analysis tool (Klundert and Anschiitz, 2000). It minimizes resource use and environmental impact, and conducted in an environmentally conscientious manner that conserves natural resources and recovers waste where appropriate. It also provides incentives for waste minimization, recycling, and resource recovery at source or as near to the source as possible (Zhu *et al.* 2008). There are a number of examples from all over India and around the world where communities have practiced managing their waste locally and set up successful community-based waste management models. The different aspects of ISWM are as follows:

Source Reduction

- Designing products or packaging to reduce the quantity or the toxicity of the materials used, or to make them easy to reuse.
- Manufacturing of products that last as long as possible by the use of durable designs and materials and providing repair services and replacement parts. This facilitates consumers to repair, resell, exchange, or donate unwanted products as much as possible to avoid disposal. Sharing and rental of tools and equipments is also encouraged.
- Reusing existing products or packaging. For example, refillable bottles, reusable pallets and reconditioned barrels and drums.
- Phasing out of products or packaging those are unsafe in production, post consumer use or that produce or release harmful products when disposed.
- Limination of excess packaging and packaging that is difficult to recycle.
- Managing non-product organic wastes (*e.g.*, food scraps and yard trimmings) through on-site composting or other waste management methods.
- Providing incentives to firms for decreased generation of wastes.

Recycling of Waste

- Imparting awareness to discourage the 'throwaway' mentality.
- Governmental regulations and policies that encourage the use of virgin materials through taxes, incentives etc., should be revised to discourage the use of virgin materials.
- The establishment of stable markets for recycled materials is essential.
- Products and packaging materials should be conspicuously labeled to indicate recycled content.
- Uniform governmentally approved standards should be applied to terms commonly used for product labeling and promotion..
- Household and small quantity commercial toxic and hazardous wastes should be segregated, labeled and collected separately.
- Convenient recycling opportunities and sufficient incentives to recycle should be provided to all residents.

Composting

- Composting of kitchen and yard wastes at the household and community level should be encouraged through public education and dissemination of information on composting.

- Organic materials such as: kitchen waste, yard waste and wet or soiled paper that cannot be recycled should be composted to produce a useful product.
- Composting should serve to complement programmes for recycling and reuse rather than substituting for these programmes.
- Standards should be established to set levels of inorganic materials, heavy metals, and organic chemicals in compost appropriate for the use of the compost.
- Wastewater pre-treatment and treatment should be sufficient to make sewage sludge safe as a soil conditioner or for composting with food and plant wastes.

Landfilling

It is regarded as one of the best methods of solid waste disposal. It refers to the scientific dumping of municipal solid wastes using an engineering facility that requires detailed planning and specifications, careful construction and efficient operation. The various categories of municipal solid waste disposal facilities are Sanitary Landfills, Modified Sanitary Landfills and Selected Waste Landfills.

- Sanitary Landfills are defined as disposal facilities which are normally, but not necessarily, located in areas having populations of 5,000 or more and which may accept all types of municipal solid wastes.
- Modified Sanitary Landfills are defined as disposal facilities, which may accept all types of municipal solid wastes.
- Selected Waste Landfills are defined as disposal facilities, which accept selected types of refuse such as: demolition, land clearing and construction (DLC) debris.

Thus Integrated Waste Management encompasses adoption of one or more of above mentioned technologies and or practices, in tune with local conditions. Effective waste management should be based on communities, industries, and individuals taking responsibility for their own wastes.

Solid Waste Management Scenario in North East India and Physico-chemical Composition of the Solid Waste of Silchar City

In Asia, Europe, Africa and USA several studies were made on solid waste management (EPA, 1972; Alter, 1991; Luis *et al.* 1997; UNEP, 2001; Visvanathan and Tränkler, 2003; Zhu, *et al.* 2008; Meidiana and Gamse, 2010; Mensah *et al.* 2010). In major cities of India like: Delhi, Bangalore, Kolkata, Chennai, Pune, Mumbai etc., also several studies on MSW were conducted by several workers and organizations (Planning Commission, 1995; CPCB, 2000; MoEF, 2000; MOUD, 2000; Ingle and Mali, 2000; Union Ministry of Health, 2004; NEERI, 2005 a,b ; Rampal and Kour, 2005; AuS AID, 2006; Sharholy *et al.* 2007; Kumar *et al.* 2009; Ramachandra, 2009). Only a few studies have been conducted on the SWM systems on the cities of North East India (Lalhmingliana, 1999; JNNURM, 2006; GMC, 2006; Shillong MB, 2006; Silchar MB 2006; LAD, Government of Mizoram, 2006; DUDH, DUDA, Government of Arunachal Pradesh, 2006; Goswami and Sharma 2007a, b; NBCC, 2007). Cities of North East India being remote and isolated with a very few industries have shown the sign of poor level of SWM services. Analysis of physical and chemical characteristics of MSW is essential as it provides basic data for planning, design and operation of management system. It provides knowledge for selection of appropriate technology and also helps to decide the amount and type of waste suitable for processing, recovery and recycling. Hence two studies were conducted during 2006-08. One study was on comparison of present status of Municipal Solid Waste management system of some major cities of North East India like: Guwahati (Assam), Shillong (Meghalaya), Silchar (Assam), Aizwal (Mizoram) and Itanagar (Arunachal Pradesh) and another on physico-chemical properties of waste of city Silchar.

Comparative Study of the Five Cities of North – East India

(Bhattacharjee and Gupta, 2009 a)

Among the five cities three are municipal cities and two are non-municipal cities (Fig.5.1).

Municipal City

1. Guwahati City (26° 11′03.66" N Lat, 91° 45′05.58"E long.), Assam.
2. Silchar (24 ° 49′47"N Lat, 92 ° 46′80"E Long.), Assam.
3. Shillong Municipal City (25 ° 34′11.24"N Lat, 92 ° 52′32.91"E Long.), Meghalaya Non-Municipal City.
4. Aizwal City (23 ° 44′00.68"N Lat, 92 ° 42′22.12"E Long.), Mizoram.
5. Itanagar City (27 ° 07′46.27"N Lat, 93 ° 37′07.13"E Long.), Arunachal Pradesh.

Comparative study of the management aspects of the five cities were made by collecting information through limited discussion with concerned officials, preliminary field survey, collection of primary data by direct personal interview (MOUD, 2000), site visits and discussion with stake holders of the respective cities. The data were also collected from secondary sources of information *viz;* Report on City Development Plan (CDP) for Capital Region Aizawl, Shillong, Guwahati and Itanagar, (JNNURM, 2006), Study reports (CPCB, 2000; NEERI, 2005 a,b). Other secondary sources of data *viz;* Census Records, Records of Municipality of Shillong, Guwahati and Silchar, Local Administrative Department, Government of Mizoram, Director of urban Development and Housing, District Urban Development Authority, Government of Arunachal Pradesh and Publications of the different state Government were also consulted (SMB, 2006; Shillong MB, 2006; LAD, 2006).

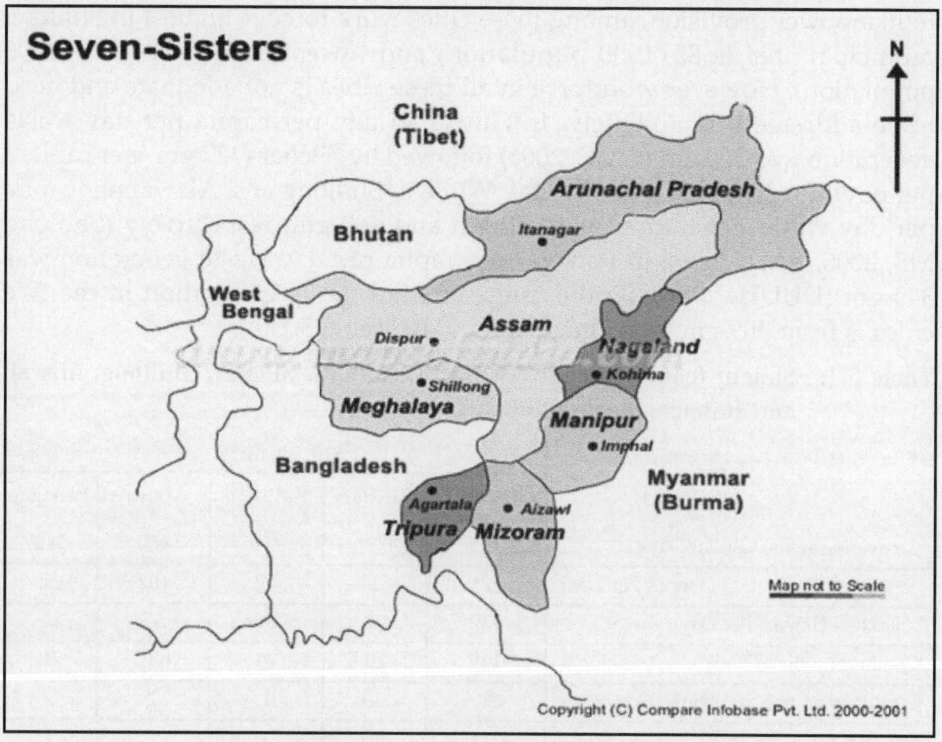

Fig. 5.1: **Map of different states of north-east India**

The study of present status of Municipal Solid Waste management system of five cities of North East India revealed a comparative account of two systems, *viz;* Urban Administrative system (Non Municipal) prevailing in Aizawl (Mizoram), Itanagar (Arunachal Pradesh) and a Municipal system prevailing in Guwahati (Assam), Shillong (Meghalaya) and Silchar (Assam). In Aizawl the Sanitary Wing, Local Administrative Department and Trade and Commerce Department of Government of Mizoram address solid waste management. Guwahati has achieved its Municipal Corporation status in 1974. Silchar is still operating as Silchar Municipal Board. Aizawl city alone shares 51 per cent of the total urban population of the state, which has not been recorded in any other cities of India. Shillong is still operating as Shillong Municipal Board. The density of population of Shillong municipal area is 7.5 times of Aizawl and 3.5 times of Guwahati and 1.5 times of Silchar. The density of population of Silchar is 5.0 times of Aizawl and 2.3 times of Guwahati, which shows that among these cities Shillong municipal area is the most crowded and congested one followed by Silchar. The study revealed that the number of designated high officials involved in the solid waste management of Aizawl city is far less compared to other cities. With respect to manpower provision, among these cities work force is highest in Shillong municipal area (1.85/1000 population) and lowest in Silchar (0.75/1000 population). However workforce in all these cities is not adequate and need to be addressed immediately. In Guwahati city per capita per day waste generation was 309 gm (GMC, 2006) followed by Silchar (477 gm/per capita/ per day) (Present study, 2007 data). While in Shillong and Aizwal per capita per day waste generation was 450 gm and 460 gm, respectively (Shillong MB, 2006, LAD, 2006), in Itanagar per capita per day waste generation was 340 gm (DUDH, 2006). So the range of solid waste generation in the five cities is from 309 gm to 477gm/capita/day (Table 5.1).

Table 5.1: Salient features of the SWM of Guwahati, Silchar, Shillong, Aizwal, and Itanagar during 2006-07

Elements	Site Features				
	Guwahati	Silchar	Shillong	Aizwal	Itanagar
Generation (gms/Capita/Day)	309	477*	450	460	340
Total waste generation (Tonnes Per Day)	321	84*	78	102	22
Collection (Tonnes Per Day)	172	40*	36	51	12
Community Bins (Nos.)	149	40	41	NIL	78
Frequency of transportation (Nos./day)	1	1	1	1	1
Disposal Site (Nos.)	1	1	1	1	1
Distance from City (km)	20	4	18	17	25
Treatment	Spraying of insecticides etc.	No treatment	Compos-ting of biodegrad-able waste	Spraying of insecticides	No treatment etc.
Disposal	Open dumping and burning	Open dumping and burning	Compos-ting of biodegrad-able waste and open dumping	Open dumping and burning	Open dumping and burning

The sources of waste for the study area were households, hotels, restaurants, markets, commercial establishments, street sweeping, drain sleet etc. In these cities, segregation of waste at source had not started. In Guwahati, Silchar, Shillong, Aizwal and Itanagar city, it was observed that the percentage distribution of compostable materials ranged from 52.02 per cent to 62.54 per cent and for recyclable materials the range was 17.24 per cent to 25.30 per cent (Fig. 5.2). Efficiency ratio of Guwahati, Silchar, Shillong, Aizwal and Itanagar were 53 per cent, 48 per cent, 46 per cent, 50 per cent, and 54 per cent, respectively in the year 2006 (Fig. 5.3).

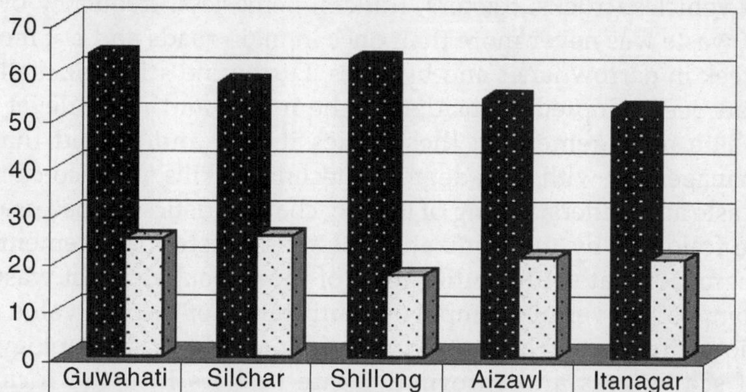

	Guwahati	Silchar	Shillong	Aizawl	Itanagar
■ Compost able	63.44	57.31	62.54	54.24	52.02
□ Recyclable	24.53	25.3	17.24	20.97	20.57

Fig. 5.2: **Percentage distribution of compostable and recyclable materials (%) in the solid waste of Guwahati, Silchar, Shillong, Aizwal and Itanagar**

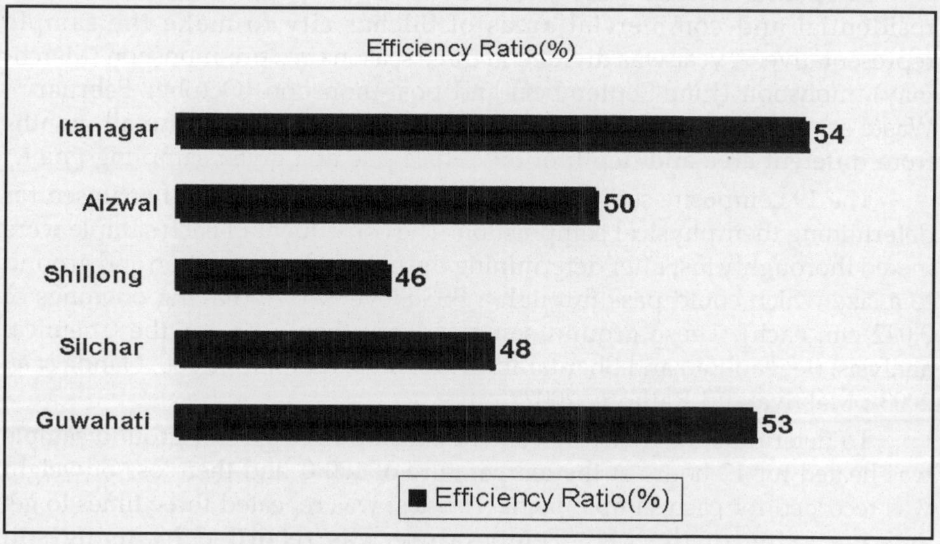

Fig. 5.3: **Efficiency Ratio of Solid Waste Management in Guwahati, Silchar, Shillong, Aizwal and Itanagar**

It was observed that regarding transportation and disposal, Guwahati was more organized compared to other three cities. In all the five places transportation was done through uncovered old trucks, mini trucks, tractors and handcarts/trolleys for narrow lanes and by lanes where loading and unloading was done manually and sanitary workers were handling the solid waste without protective gears *viz*; musk, gum boot, gloves etc. The number of vehicles (trucks, tractors, trailers) being less, frequency of transportation of waste was never more than once in main roads and not more than twice a week in narrow lanes and by lanes. Further no scientific method of disposal had been adopted. Considering the macro and micro level issues of solid waste management in these cities it was understood that the effective management with high degree of technical skills, physico-chemical nature of waste and understanding of the city characteristics are necessary. This should be followed by modernization of solid waste management like complete segregation at source, utilization of nutritional value of waste by microbial composting, vermin composting, utilization of the fuel value of the waste by bio-methanisation and introduction of new plasma technology. Incorporation of scavengers and informal waste pickers into the formal sector and encouraging the private sector participation in solid waste management could be another important step in mitigating the problems of solid waste management.

Physico-chemical Characteristics of the Solid Waste of Silchar Town
(Bhattaracharjee and Gupta 2009 b)

Altogether 19 sites were selected for covering all the 28 wards of the residential and commercial areas of Silchar city to make the sample representative. A year was divided in three seasons *viz;* pre-monsoon (March-may), monsoon (June-September) and post-monsoon (October February). Waste samples were collected for all the three seasons covering all months from different area and depth of the refuse pile at a given sampling point.

The 19 composite samples were physically sorted out and analysed for determining their physical composition. The constituent of each sample were mixed thoroughly just after determining the physical composition and ground to a size which could pass through a BSS Sieve No. 40 (having openings of 0.042 cm. each). These ground samples were then used for the Chemical analysis. (Jeevan Rao and Shantaram, 1993; Ingle and Mali, 2000; Nanda *et al.* 2003 ; Malviya and Rathore, 2007).

To determine the moisture content of samples 50 gms of ground sample was heated for 12 hours at the temperature of 100°C and then loss of weight was recorded for each sample point. This test was repeated three times to get average value of the MC. Temperature was recorded by using soil Thermometer. The recording of temperature was repeated three times for each sample to get average value of the temperature. Carbon content was calculated by using Walkley and Black method (modified). Nitrogen content was determined by using well known Kjeldahl's method. C/N ratio was calculated from the obtained value of C and N. For potassium Flame photometry was used and phosphorus spectrometry was used for Phosphorous (Trivedi and Goel, 1985). The concentration level of Heavy metals (Pb, Cu and Zn) was determined by using standard Atomic Absorption Spectrometry (AAS) analyzer. Samples were also collected from 3 sample points of landfill site.

The physical characteristics of waste of the Silchar city revealed that the organic matter of waste ranged from 49.88 to 66.33 per cent, and other recyclable material (wood, bamboo, old cane furniture, cutting branches of tree etc.,) ranged from 17.16 to 27.89 per cent. While the range of inert and miscellaneous content of waste was 15.09 to 19.52 per cent, the range of paper, plastic, textile, glass and metal was far less ranging from 1.14 to 4.60 per cent, 0.30 to 1.51 per cent, 0.12 to 1.12 per cent, 0.28 to 0.44 per cent and 0.18 to 0.34 per cent, respectively.

Table 5.2: Spatial distribution of physical composition (%) of Silchar MSW

Site	Paper	Textiles	Organics	Metal	Glass	Plastic	Ash	Recyclables
1.	3.09±0.26	0.37±0.1	52.24±1.7	0.21±0.1	0.37±0.1	1.45±0.2	16.43±3.5	25.82±2.90
2.	4.60±0.42	1.12±0.2	55.7±2.63	0.28±0.2	0.29±0.2	1.44±0.1	19.36±2.3	17.16±2.65
3.	1.25±0.11	0.32±0.1	58.89±2.3	0.22±0.1	0.43±0.2	1.51±0.2	15.19±3.1	22.21±4.74
4.	2.52±0.10	0.87±0.1	57.20±2.0	0.29±0.2	0.41±0.2	1.45±0.1	18.99±1.7	18.27±2.03
5.	1.69±0.21	0.43±0.1	49.88±3.5	0.21±0.1	0.43±0.2	0.70±0.5	19.33±4.8	27.32±3.01
6.	2.80±0.21	0.97±0.2	55.34±2.5	0.29±0.2	0.41±0.2	1.05±0.6	19.95±2.7	19.19±1.77
7.	1.89±0.12	0.47±0.1	51.04±3.6	0.18±0.0	0.40±0.2	0.91±0.6	18.14±3.5	26.96±3.26
8.	1.20±0.18	0.32±0.1	53.90±4.4	0.30±0.2	0.44±0.2	0.93±0.6	21.58±1.	21.33±2.78
9.	1.03±0.08	0.28±0.1	50.73±3.3	0.22±0.1	0.30±0.0	0.93±0.6	18.62±5.2	27.89±2.34
10.	1.14±0.06	0.33±0.1	59.36±1.5	0.32±0.2	0.37±0.2	0.91±.62	19.49±1.7	18.08±2.03
11.	1.75±0.12	0.27±0.0	58.65±1.6	0.17±0.0	0.30±0.1	0.79±0.6	16.20±4.0	21.86±5.06
12.	1.55±0.13	0.29±0.1	58.77±1.5	0.20±0.1	0.28±0.1	0.30±.09	17.99±2.4	20.38±2.43
13.	1.91±0.36	0.20±0.0	66.33±2.1	0.33±0.2	0.28±0.1	0.32±0.1	15.27±2.3	15.15±1.37
14.	2.77±0.23	0.41±0.0	61.81±4.1	0.18±0.0	0.34±0.0	0.34±0.1	15.09±2.7	18.61±2.41
15.	2.12±0.17	0.56±0.1	58.08±2.6	0.34±0.2	0.36±0.1	0.31±0.1	18.39±2.3	19.61±1.70
16.	1.43±0.12	0.12±0.0	62.79±0.6	0.22±0.1	0.31±0.0	0.30±0.1	17.15±2.3	17.45±2.34
17.	1.25±0.05	0.25±0.0	57.97±2.3	0.19±0.1	0.37±0.1	0.30±0.1	16.04±3.7	23.39±3.55
18.	1.85±0.12	0.28±0.0	57.99±2.0	0.30±0.2	0.28±0.0	0.34±0.1	19.51±2.1	18.99±1.36
19.	1.58±0.32	0.22±0.1	59.55±2.1	0.19±0.1	0.32±0.0	0.66±0. 6	17.99±1.8	19.51±1.49
Total	**1.97±0.9**	**0.42±0.3**	**57.17±4.9**	**0.25±0.2**	**0.35±0.2**	**0.79±0.6**	**17.93±3.3**	**21.01±4.48**

Table 5.3: Seasonal variation in physical composition of Silchar MSW in percentage

Season	Paper	Textile	Organics	Metal	Glass	Plastic	Ash and Dust	Recyclable Waste
PREM	1.96±0.87	0.41±0.27	55.40±6.96	0.25±0.16	0.39 ±0.17	1.20±0.48	15.50±3.89	25.01±4.49
MON	1.94±0.84	0.42±0.28	54.64±6.84	0.24±0.15	0.38 ±0.17	1.22 ±0.47	15.16±3.80	25.50±4.64
POM	1.98±0.96	0.43±0.29	55.53±7.10	0.26±0.15	0.38±0.18	1.24 ±0.48	15.76±3.96	24.78±4.72
($\tilde{Y} \pm \delta$)	1.96±0.89	0.42±0.28	55.19±6.93	0.25±0.15	0.38 ±0.17	1.22±0.47	15.48±3.87	25.10±4.60

The physico-chemical analyses of the waste revealed that waste temperature varied between 39.20 to 44.97°C and moisture content ranged between 46.14 to 49.53 per cent. The implication of this level of moisture is that samples are not suitable for incineration but are ideal for composting. About 60 per cent of the waste was biodegradable, mostly comprising of high wet weight and high moisture content kitchen wastes. On the other hand, the outstanding 40 per cent of the waste comprised mostly of non-biodegradable out of which 25 per cent was found to be recyclable materials such as: glass, metals, plastic, electrical and electronic equipment, cutting branches of tree, old furniture (plastic, cane, wood, iron) etc. Organic carbon, organic nitrogen and pH of waste varied between 3.95 to 6.37 per cent, 0.22 to 0.31 per cent and 6.64 to 6.98 respectively. C/N ratio ranged from 15.53 to 23.9. Seasonal variation was recorded in Carbon/Nitrogen ratio. Highest was in monsoon and lowest in premonsoon.

Table 5.4: Spatial distribution of waste temperature, moisture content, pH, organic carbon, nitrogen and C/N ratio of Silchar MSW

Sample Site	Waste Temperature (Degree Celsius)	Moisture Content (%)	pH Carbon	Organic	Nitrogen Ratio	C/N
1.	39.60±5.62	47.43±8.04	6.77±0.1	4.27±1.16	0.22±0.01	19.41±1.98
2.	39.46±5.20	46.16±8.66	6.77±0.1	4.03±0.23	0.24±0.02	16.79±3.45
3.	42.60±4.02	47.66±7.47	6.77±0.1	4.88±0.99	0.23±0.01	21.22±0.78
4.	42.16±2.60	47.63±7.87	6.64±0.2	5.15±1.55	0.24±0.07	21.46±0.97
5.	40.46±6.52	46.39±7.41	6.67±0.2	4.92±0.65	0.30±0.04	16.40±3.33
6.	42.36±4.30	46.14±9.06	6.68±0.1	4.35±0.48	0.28±0.04	15.54±6.49
7.	39.20±4.68	48.13±9.74	6.72±0.1	4.51±0.82	0.22±0.02	20.50±5.32
8.	40.60±6.85	48.73±8.36	6.72±0.1	4.72±1.70	0.23±0.01	20.52±1.38
9.	39.56±6.59	48.03±8.30	6.72±0.2	4.52±0.62	0.23±0.02	19.65±2.42
10.	39.90±5.41	48.13±5.67	6.83±0.2	3.95±0.21	0.24±0.06	16.46±4.53
11.	40.30±5.17	45.87±5.77	6.80±0.1	4.74±0.29	0.25±0.05	18.96±6.76
12.	39.50±6.35	46.73±8.83	6.94±0.0	4.73±1.10	0.25±0.02	18.92±3.23
13.	40.11±4.78	49.53±8.92	6.98±0.3	4.45±0.65	0.24±0.02	18.54±2.87
14.	43.13±2.41	47.97±8.22	6.93±0.2	5.16±1.07	0.31±0.02	16.65±3.98
15.	44.30±3.16	46.50±7.43	6.84±0.2	4.92±0.96	0.27±0.04	18.22±4.38
16.	43.03±4.05	47.80±9.24	6.87±0.2	5.56±0.85	0.30±0.03	18.53±3.54
17.	43.43±3.83	48.76±8.98	6.95±0.2	5.53±0.94	0.23±0.02	24.04±1.91
18.	43.93±3.90	48.04±8.28	6.77±0.1	5.36±0.65	0.24±.03	22.33±4.39
19.	44.97±3.73	46.83±8.77	6.77±0.1	6.37±1.60	0.28±.04	22.75±2.12
($\tilde{Y} \pm \delta$)	41.51±4.80	47.50±7.87	6.80±0.2	4.85±1.08	0.25±.04	19.40±3.02

The concentration of Heavy metals (Cu, Pb and Zn) in Silchar municipality waste showed that Copper (Cu) concentration ranged from 0.09 to 0.19 ppm, Lead (Pb) from 0.04 to 0.18 ppm and Zinc (Zn) ranged from 1.04 to 1.38 ppm. Seasonal variation of the concentration of these metals showed that while Cu concentration was highest in pre monsoon and monsoon, lead was highest in postmonsoon. Zinc concentration was found to be highest in monsoon and lowest in postmonsoon. So no specific pattern could be discerned.

Table 5.5: Seasonal variation in concentration of heavy metals (Cu, Pb and Zn) in ppm in Silchar MSW

Seasons	Cu	Pb	Zn
PREM	0.16±0.08	0.07±0.05	0.66±0.06
MON	0.16±0.03	0.07±0.05	2.56±0.28
POM	0.08±0.05	0.13±0.07	0.42±0.07
($\bar{Y}$± δ)	0.13±0.07	0.09±0.06	1.21±0.98

Since the city extended and developed in a totally unorganized manner there is no clear demarcation in the municipal solid waste composition and characteristics between market area and residential area. The composition dictates the technology needed for waste processing prior to disposal. In the city Silchar the larger proportion of organic matter in MSW and more or less optimum moisture content indicated the desirability of biological processing of waste.

Conclusions

Poor collection and inadequate transportation are responsible for the accumulation of MSW at every nook and corner. The management of MSW is going through a critical phase, due to the unavailability of suitable facilities to treat and dispose of the larger amount of MSW generated daily. The difficulties in providing the desired level of public service in the urban centres are often attributed to the poor financial status of the managing municipal corporations. A city specific detailed investigations need to be carried out to evolve an effective SWM system.

REFERENCES

Alter, H. (1991): The Future Course of Solid Waste Management in the US., *Waste Management and Research*, 9(1): 3-20.

AuS AID (2006): North Eastern Region Urban Development Project – "City Report: Shillong (2006). Final Report" Assisted by Asian Development Bank, Sanitation Project – Shillong Water and Sanitation Project – "Strategy Plan for Management of Solid Waste Collection" Jan' 2006.

Bhattaracharjee, S. and Gupta, S. (2009 a); Urban Solid Waste of some North East Indian Cities – Management Scenario, *Pollution Research*, 28 (3):1-7.

Bhattaracharjee, S. and Gupta, S. (2009b): Physical Composition and Characteristics of Municipal Solid Waste of Silchar City, Assam, North East India, *Pollution Research*, 28 (2): 203-206.

CPHEEO (2000): Manual on Municipal Solid Waste Management, Central Public Health and Environmental Engineering Organization, Ministry of Urban Development, New Delhi.

CPCB, (2000): Central Pollution Control Board. Report from Member Secretary on Management of Municipal Solid Waste.

DUDA - Distrct Urban Development Authority, Arunachal Pradesh.

DUDH (2006): Department of Urban Development and Housing Report, Itanagar.

EPA (1972): Environmental Protection Agency, USA, Report - 1972.

GMC (2006): Guwahati Municipal Corporation. Study Report on Municipal Solid Waste.

Goswami, U. and Sarma, H.P. (2007a): Study of Ground Water Contamination due to Municipal Solid Waste Dumping in Guwahati city. *Poll Res.* 26 (2): 211-214.

Goswami, U. and Sarma, H.P. (2007b): Physico-chemical Characteristics of Bio-degradable Solid Wastes in Guwahati City, India. *Poll Res.* 26 (2):267-269.

Ingle, S.T. and Mali, D.S. (2000): Solid Waste Management System for Kolhapur City, Maharastra, *Poll. Res.* 19(2): 185.

Jeevan Rao. K. and Shantaram. M.V (1993): Characteristics of Garbage – A Review, Agril *Rev.* 14(2):102-108.

JNNURM (2006): Jawaharlal Nehru National Urban Renewal Mission (2006). Report on City Development Plan (CDP) for Capital Region Aizawl, Shillong, Guwahati and Itanagar.

Klundert, A. van de. and Anschiitz, J.M. (2000). The Sustainability of Alliances between Stakeholders in Waste-using the Concept of Integrated Sustainable Waste Management – Working paper for UWEP/CWG, 30 May 2000.

Kumar, S., Bhattacharyya, J.K., Vaidya, A.N., Chakrabarti, T., Devotta, S., Akolkar, A.B., (2009): Assessment of the Status of Municipal Solid Waste Management in Metro Cities, State Capitals, Class I Cities, and Class II Towns in India: An insight, *Waste Management* 29: 883-895.

LAD (2006). Directorate of Local Administrative Department, Sanitary Cell, Aizawl, Report on Urban Solid Waste.

Lalhmingliana, F. (1999): Retrospect of Urban Planning and Administration – A Case Study of Aizawl city. In G. Kumar (eds). *Urbanisation in Mizoram-Retrospect and Prospect*, Linkman Publications, Titagarh, West Bengal, India.

Luis F.D., George M.S. and Linda L.E. (1997): Managing Solid Wastes in Developing Countries, *Journal of Waste Management*,: 43-45.

MOEF (2000): Ministry of Environment and Forest, Government of India; Municipal Solid Waste Management and Handling Rules 2000.

MOUD (2000): Ministry of Urban Development, Government of India. Report of the Technology Advisory Group on Solid Waste Management, CPHEEO, Ministry of Urban Development, Poverty Alleviation, New Delhi.

Malviya, P. and Rathore, V.S. (2007): Seasonal Variations in different Physico-chemical Parameters of the Effluents of Century Paper and Pulp Mill, Lal Kuan Uttarakhand. *J.Environ. Bio.* 3 28(2): 219-224.

Meidiana.C. and Gamse, T. (2010). Development of Waste Management Practices in Indonesia, *European Journal of Scientific Research.* 40(2):199-210.

Mensah; Acquah and Abel (2010): Physico-chemical Characteristics of Solid Waste for Treatment Options – A Case Study of Kumai, Ghana http://hdl.handle.net 123456789/1767

Nanda, S.N., Mishra, B. and Tiwari, T.N. (2003). Municipal Solid Wastes in Hirakud Town (Orissa); (I) Preliminary Survey, *Poll. Res.* 22 (2): 289-292.

NBCC (2007): National Building Construction Corporation, Nov., 2007. Detailed. Project Report, Solid Waste Management Project Under Centrally Sponsored Scheme for Mitigation of Bird - Hit menace for IAF Aircrafts at Tezpur (Assam) NPC (2005) - National Productivity Council Report, 2005.

NEERI (2005 a): National Environment of Engineering Research Institute "Municipal Solid Waste Management Training Programme (2005) sponsored by CPCB".

NEERI Report (2005b): Assessment of Status of Municipal Solid Waste Management in Metro Cities, State Capitals, Class I Cities and Class II Towns.

NIUA (1999): National Institute of Urban Affairs, Solid Waste Management: Improvement Initiatives in Selected Cities of India, Research Study Series No. 75, New Delhi.

OCED-Organization for Economic Co-operation and Development.

OECD (1997): OECD Environmental Data: Compendium 1997, OECD, Paris, France.

Patel, A. H. (2002): Urban Solid Waste Management: Progress and Prospects for Social, Technical and Policy Improvement. [Keynote Address for Bangalore University, 12.11.2002] Member, Supreme Court Committee for Solid Waste Management in Class 1 Cities.

Planning Commision (1995): Report on Urban Solid Waste.

Ramachandra, T.V. (2009): Management of Municipal Sold Waste. ISBN: 978-81-7993187-5. TERI Press, The Energy and Resources Institute, Darbari Seth Block, IHC Complex, Lodhi Road, New Delhi - 110 003, India.

Rampal, R.K. and Kour, J. (2005). Solid Waste Generation in Residential Areas of Jammu City (J&K), India. *Pollution Research* 24(2): 285-292.

SMB (2006). Silchar Municipal Board; Study report on Urban Solid Waste.

Shillong MB (2006). Shillong Municipal Board; Report on Urban Solid Waste.

Sharholy, M.; Ahmad, K.; Vaishya, R.; Gupta, R., (2007): Municipal Solid Waste Characteristics and Management in Allahabad, India. *Waste Management* 27 (4):490:-496.

TERI (1998). Tata Energy Research Institute Report 1998.

Trivedi, R.K. and Goel, P.K.(1985): *Analysis of Soils and Aquatic Sediments. Chemical and Biological Methods for Water Pollution Studies*, chapter-3. Environmental Publications, Post Box 60, Karad - 415 110.

UNEP (2001): United Nations Environment Programme (UNEP). State of the Environment, South Asia 2001, ISBN: 92-807-2037-2.

Union Health Ministry Report (2004): www.agapeindia.com/ india_population.htm>

Visvanathan, C. and Tränkler, J. (2003): Municipal Solid Waste Management in Asia – A Comparative Analysis; *Workshop on Sustainable Landfill Management,* 3-5, Chennai, India, pp. 3-15.

Wilson, D.G. (1977): History of Solid Waste Management. Handbook of Solid Waste Management. Ed. David Gordon Wilson, Massachusetts Institute of Technology. Van Nostrand Reinhold Company, New York. ISBN-0-442-29550-2.

Zhu, D.; Asnani, P.U.; Zurbrügg, C.; Anapolsky and Mani, S. (2008): Improving Municipal Solid Waste Management in India. A Sourcebook for Policy Makers and Practitioners. WBI Development Studies, The International Bank for Reconstruction and Development/The World Bank Washington, DC.

Pages: 91-113

WASTE GENERATION AND UTILIZATION

Edited by: **Dr. Priya Bajaj; Dr. B. Tabassum** and **Dr. Pawan Kumar 'Bharti'**

ISBN: 978-93-5056-792-0

Edition: **2016**

Published by: **Discovery Publishing House Pvt. Ltd., New Delhi (India)**

CHAPTER – 6

Practices and Concerns of Electronic Waste in India

Harveen Kaur and **Sushma Goel**

ABSTRACT

Electronic waste is an escalating problem as well as profitable opportunity, given the volumes of E-waste quantity being generated worldwide and the content of both toxic and valuable materials found in them. It is treated as any other waste and scrap and not disposed off in a non environment friendly way. In India, E-waste (Management and Handling) Rules, 2011 have been introduced recently (*i.e.,* on 1st May, 2012) to deal with issues pertaining electronic equipments and electronic waste. However the scenario of India has not changed as it was expected to change even after the introduction of rules in place. The existing management practices related to Electronic waste in developing countries like: India are reasonably substandard and have the potential to risk both human health and the environment. This paper attempts to study the practices followed by consumers and users of electronics in India that are responsible for this menace. The paper also assesses suggestive measures to regulate the management of E-waste at stakeholder levels and possible techno-political remedies for effective implementation of E-waste (Handling and Management) Rules, 2011.

Keywords: E-waste, practices of stakeholders, legislative framework.

Department of Resource Management and Design Applications (RMDA), Lady Irwin College, University of Delhi, India.

INTRODUCTION

Developing countries are facing enormous challenges related to the generation and management of E-waste which are either internally generated or imported illegally; India is no exception to it (Hicks *et.al.* 2005). However, the existing management practices related to E-waste in India are reasonably poor and have the potential to risk both human health and the environment. The menace of electronic waste (E-waste) in India has been increasing at fast pace. Earlier, India had no dedicated E-waste laws and we were taking care of this crucial issue through guidelines and directions. But growing problem of E-waste issue cannot be taken lightly and casually. Although the environment law jurisprudence is very strong and mature yet implementation of stringent E-waste related legislations in India is still missing.

The use of electronic devices has proliferated in recent decades, and proportionately, the quantity of electronic devices, such as: PCs, laptops, mobile phones, ACs and other entertainment electronics that are disposed of, is growing rapidly throughout the world. Rapid obsolescence of electronics goods, compounded by dumping from developed countries, has brought the E-waste problem in India to the brink of spilling over into an acute crisis (Matthews, 1997). The communities that are affected by the toxics in E-waste need not necessarily be those that are creating the waste. The unethical export of E-waste by industrialised nations to developing countries is shifting the onus of development to communities ill-equipped to deal with such waste. A lot of these materials are being sent to developing nations under the guise of reuse – to bridge the digital divide. A 2009 report from the United Nations Environment Programme, Recycling-From E-waste to Resources, offers several considerations of the hidden environmental impact of electronic devices.

In this context, it is important to understand the existing E-waste scenario with respect to legislative framework and its evolution. E-waste is an emerging problem as well as a business opportunity of increasing significance, given the volumes of E-waste being generated and the content of both toxic and valuable materials in them. Over the last decades the electronics industry has revolutionized the world. Electrical and electronic products have become ubiquitous of today's life around the planet. Without these products, modern life would not be possible in (post) industrialized and industrializing countries. These products serve in such areas as: medicine, mobility, education, health, food supply, communication, security, environmental protection and culture. Such appliances include many domestic devices like refrigerators, washing machines, mobile phones, personal computers, printers, toys and TVs (UNEP, 2009).

Objectives

The main purpose of this study was to investigate the practices followed my consumers and users of electronic products in India and the legislations pertaining E-waste management in India and other countries. More specifically, the study aims to achieve the following specific research objectives:

- To study practices concerning E-waste.
- To investigate the awareness and knowledge level of young population.
- To examine the reasons for non compliance of rules and regulations.
- To provide suggestive measures to minimize electronic waste.

Research Approach

The study was conducted to understand the practices and concerns of E-waste in India. The study involved collection of information regarding E-waste through survey method from various people living in Delhi. Various consumers were approached as per their convenience living in RWA's. Sample was randomly selected. Care was taken to include both working and non working users as practices followed by them are almost similar. Both genders were interviewed to obtain gender based variations. Only one member per house will be interviewed to avoid repetitive responses. For the purpose of study only those electronic products erer selected which are used by most of people in their day-to-day life viz-a-viz mobiles, laptops, refrigerator and ACs.

Various secondary sources like: journals content, government reports and websites of DPCC MoEF, Toxics link, CSE etc., were also referred to collect relevant information . In addition, lot of information related to E-waste scenario has also been gathered from Department of Environment, Government of NCT Delhi, Delhi Pollution Control Board and Central Pollution Control Board which involved discussions with Senior Scientific Officers who are facilitating all the work related to E-waste management at State level.

To study the practices and concerns following aspects were studied:

- Types of electronics possessed.
- Life of electronic products.
- Problems faced with electronic products.
- Frequency of replacement of electronic products.
- Usable and serviceable life of product.
- Reasons for buying new products.
- Disposal method adopted.
- Legislative framework.

Definitions E-waste

- *Electronic waste or E-waste* for short is an umbrella term embracing various forms of electric and electronic equipment that have close down to be of any value to their owners. There is no standard definition of E-waste as such still an attempt has been made to define the term from various forms through selection of selected definitions which are as follows.

- "Electrical or electronic equipment which is waste including all components, sub-assemblies and consumables, which are part of the product at the time of discarding." Directive 75/442/EEC, Article 1(a) defines E-waste "as any substance or object which the holder disposes of or is required to dispose of pursuant to the provisions of national law in force" (EU WEEE Directive, 2002).
- E-waste encompasses a broad and growing range of electronic devices ranging from large household devices such as: refrigerators, air conditioners, cell phones, personal stereos, and consumer electronics to computers which have been discarded by their users. (Puckett and Smith, 2002).
- Any appliance using an electric power supply that has reached its end of-life (OECD, 2001).
- "An electrically powered appliance that no longer satisfies the current owner for its original purpose (Sinha, 2004).
- E-waste refers to "the reverse supply chain which collects products no longer desired by a given consumer and refurbishes for other consumers, recycles, or otherwise processes wastes" (StEP, 2005).

Key E-waste Policies

The Ministry of Environment and Forest has issued a number of notifications related to the safe disposal of hazardous waste, as follows:

- Hazardous Wastes (Management and Handling) Rules, 1998/2000/2002/2003.
- MoEF guidelines for Management and Handling of Hazardous Wastes, 1991.
- Guidelines for Safe Road Transport of Hazardous Chemicals, 1995.
- The Public Liability Act, 1991.
- Batteries (Management and Handling) Rules, 2001.
- The National Environmental Tribunal Act, 1995.
- Bio-medical Wastes (Management and Handling) Rules, 1998.
- Municipal Solid Wastes (Management and Handling) Rules, 2000 and 2002.
- Guidelines for Environmentally Sound Management of E-waste 2008.
- E-waste (Management and Handling) Rules 2011.

Regulatory Legislative Measures in India Regarding E-waste

S. No.	Initiatives/Drafted Policies and Acts Concerning E-waste	Ministry/ Department	Year
1.	The Environment Protection Act 1986 (23rd of May)	MoEF	1986
2.	Hazardous Wastes (Management and Handling) Rules, (Amended in 2000 and 2003)	MoEF	1989
3.	Municipal Solid Wastes management and Handling Rules 2000	MoEF	2000
4.	Batteries (Management and Handling) Rules, 2001	MoEF	2001
5.	National Environment Policy, 2006 (18th of May)	MoEF	2006
6.	The Hazardous Wastes Management, Handling and Trans-boundary Movement Rules 2008 (1998 Amended Act)	MoEF	2008
7.	Guidelines for Environmentally sound management of E-waste 2008 (12th of March)	Central Pollution Control Board	2008
8.	Municipal Councilors Initiated Proposal on E-waste Management, December	Municipal Corporation	2008
9.	The National Green Tribunal Bill 2009 (31st July)	MoEF	2009
10.	Processing of safe re-use of E-waste and awareness programmes in collaboration with the Swiss Federal laboratories and central pollution control board of India, May	Karnataka Government	2009
11.	Initiatives of Financial assistance and involvement of rag pickers in E-waste management.	Department of Environment, Government of Delhi	2010
12.	Creation of awareness and training programme on the threat of E-waste and its proper management	Municipal Corporation of Goa	2010
13.	Collaborative initiatives with the Japan Government for proper management of E-waste, March	Gujrat Government	2010
14.	Launch of 'CRYSTAL' pilot project and bringing of informal recyclers into mainstream to manage E-waste	Karnataka Government	2010
15.	Flying Squads (initiative taken by minister of state for environment Sachin Ahir to check the proper disposal of E-waste in the state)	Maharashtra, India	2010
16.	Creating awareness on E-waste through workshops Government of Odisha, India 2010	Government of Odisha	2010
17.	Minimization of E-waste generation, utilization of E-waste through green technology, and sound disposal of E-waste (E-waste Policy 2010)	Government of Tamilnadu	2010
18.	Community Based collection of E-waste	Government of Tamilnadu	2010
19.	E-waste (management and handling) Rules, 2011	MoEF	2012

Source: CPCB and DPCC website, Report on ICTs and Environmental Sustainability, 2012.

Realizing the growing concern over E-waste, the Government of India (GOI) has been supporting several initiatives. Of particular importance is the assessment conducted by the Central Pollution Control Board (CPCB) on the management and handling of E-waste leading to the preparation of "Guidelines for Environmentally Sound Management of E-waste" in May, 2008 and the recent 'E-waste (Management and Handling) Rules, 2011' enforced on 1st May, 2012.

Options available for material recovery from end of life (EoL) electronics

S.No.	Options Available	Explanation
1.	Repair	Original product used after fixing or replacing broken or faulty parts.
2.	Refurbishing	Original product quality restored after disassembly to a certain level and repairing/replacing the faulty or broken
3.	Remanufacturing	'New' product is manufactured from old (recovered from disassembly of old devices) and new components. Technological (software) upgrading may also be carried out.
4.	Cannibalization	Reusable parts and modules are recovered from used products, to be used in any of the three operations mentioned above.
5.	Recycling	Materials recovered from used products and parts by vigorous separation processes (without conserving any product structure).
6.	Energy recovery	High calorific value components (*e.g.*, plastics) could be incinerated in modern waste-to-energy plants for electricity generation or in smelters and cement kilns as source of energy.

Source: Nnorom and Osibanjo (2010).

Results and Discussion

Age Group

85 per cent of the respondents interviewed falls in the category of 15-25 years of age group whereas 20 per cent of the respondents were found to be in the age group of 26-35 years which is comparatively less. Reason for same is that most of the young people were found to be aware of various aspects related to electronics such as: new models, knowledge about warranty and guarantee of products and their keen interest in latest technology etc., people in age group above 40+ were found to be very less aware.

Gender of Respondents

Most of the respondents interviewed were males *i.e.* 60 per cent as compared to 40 per cent of female respondents. Reason for same is more interest of male respondents in electronics and gadgets. Also, it was found that it is the male members in the family who are responsible for taking decisions with respect to purchase, service or maintenance of electronic items such as: laptop, air conditioner, refrigerator etc. Female members were found to be more aware regarding usage and life of electronic items.

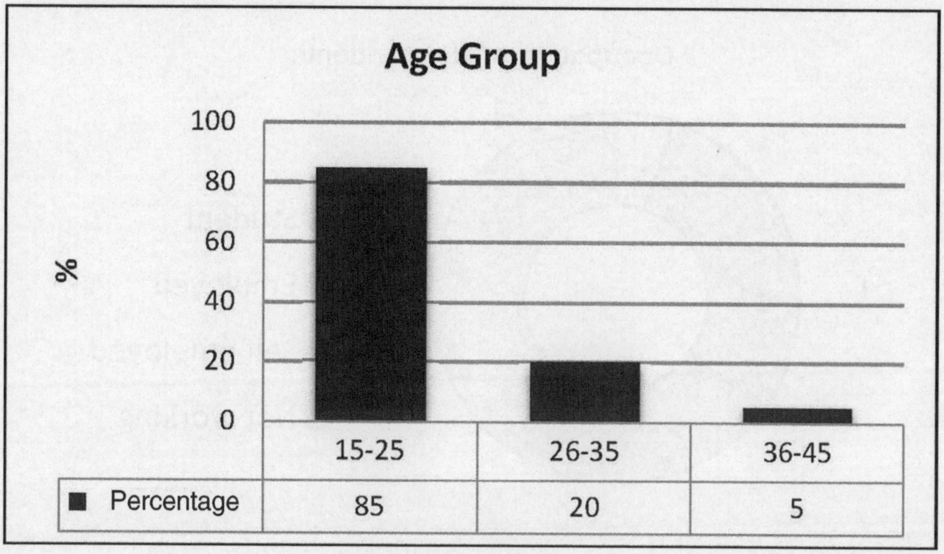

Fig. 6.1: **Age group**

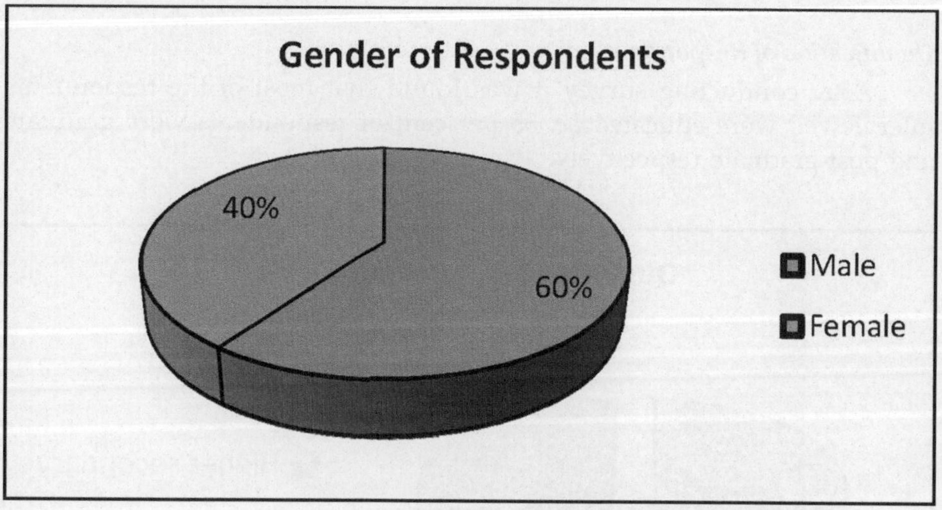

Fig. 6.2: **Gender of respondents**

Occupation of Respondents

Most of the respondents interviewed were students *i.e.* 65 per cent. Only 20 per cent and 10 per cent of the respondents were found to be working and self-employed respectively. Very less percentage of respondents were found to be non-working.

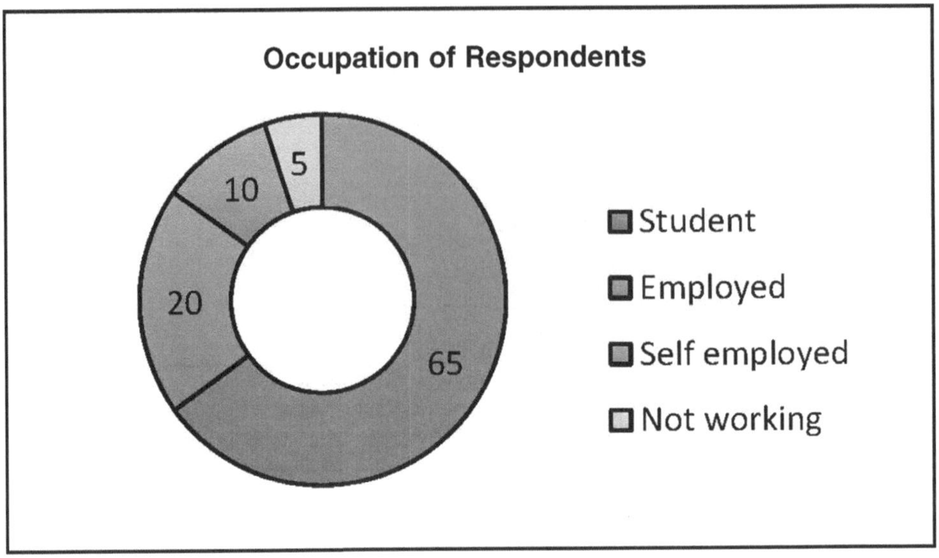

Fig. 6.3: **Occupation of respondents**

Qualification of Respondents

After conducting survey it was found that most of the respondents interviewed were educated *i.e.* 35 per cent of respondents were graduate and post graduate respectively.

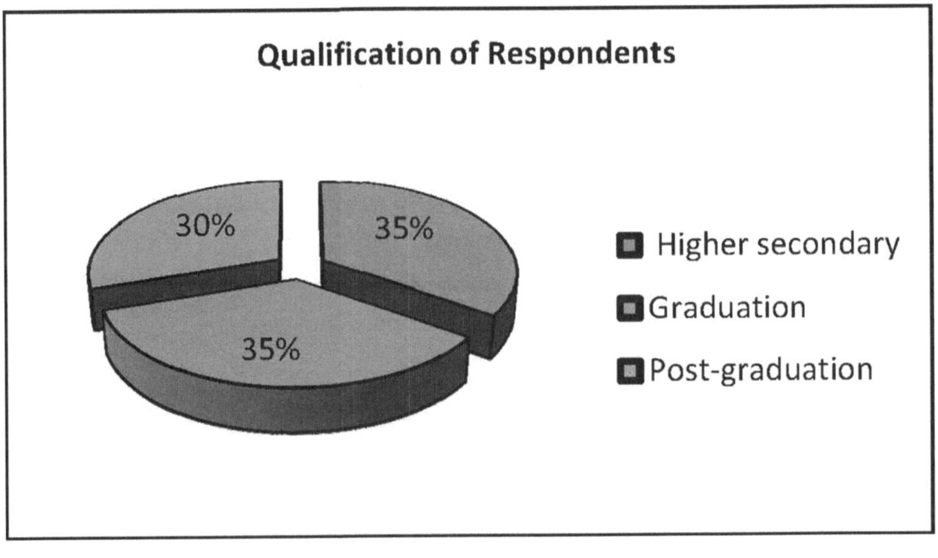

Fig. 6.4: **Qualification of respondents**

Annual Income of Respondents

As most of the respondents were found to be educated they were earning quite well *i.e.* about 25 per cent of all the respondents were found to be earning above 5,00,000 whereas 50 per cent of the respondents are earning between 50,000-1,00,000. This shows that the purchasing power of most of the respondents living in Delhi is quite good and they prefer buying latest electronic gadgets and devices.

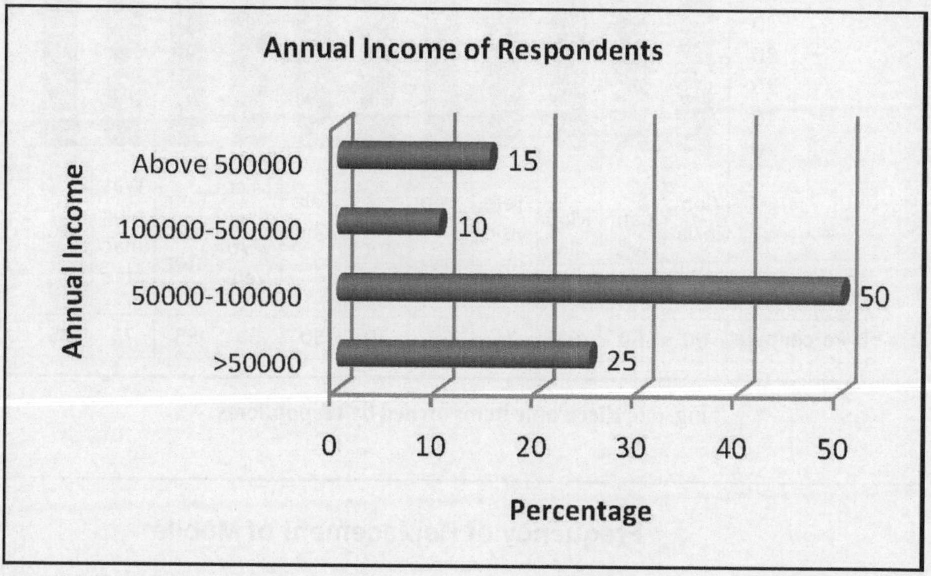

Fig. 6.5: **Annual income of respondents**

Electronic Items Owned by Respondents

The findings of the survey revealed that maximum no. of respondents have mobile phones (95%), refrigerators (95%), computer/laptop (90%) television (75%) and washing machine (75%). This shows that most of the respondents had electronic items and devices that are required in day-to-day life for accomplishing basic needs and requirements. It was also seen that very less no. of respondents had printer (50%) and telephone (50%).

Frequency of Replacement of Mobile

Most of the respondents interviewed (at least 50%) reported that they replaced their mobile phones after a period of 1 year due to reasons like: manufacturing defect, damage because of poor handling, phone being stolen or being bored of existing mobile. 35 per cent of the respondents were found to replace their phones within the period of 3-6 years due to issues like hanging problems, issues with battery life, damage etc.

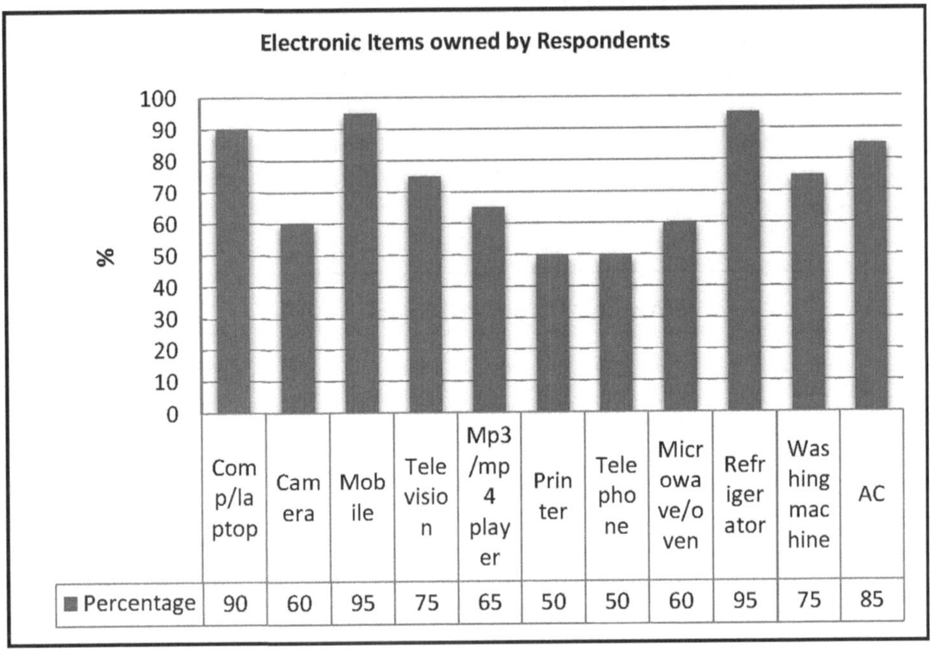

Fig. 6.6: **Electronic items owned by respondents**

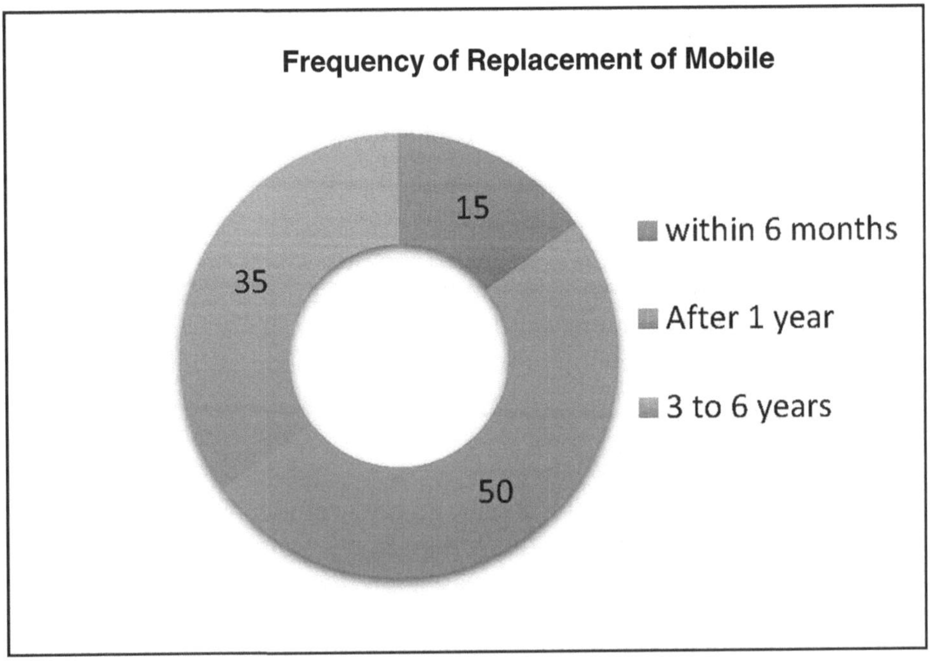

Fig. 6.7: **Frequency of replacement of Mobile**

Frequency of Replacement of AC

In case of air conditioner it was reported by most of the respondents *i.e.* 65 per cent replaced their air conditioner after a period of 6 years or more due to issues like: poor performance, issues of gas leak, manufacturing defect, poor service etc., whereas 30 per cent of the respondents reported that they replaced their air conditioner within a period of 3-6 years.

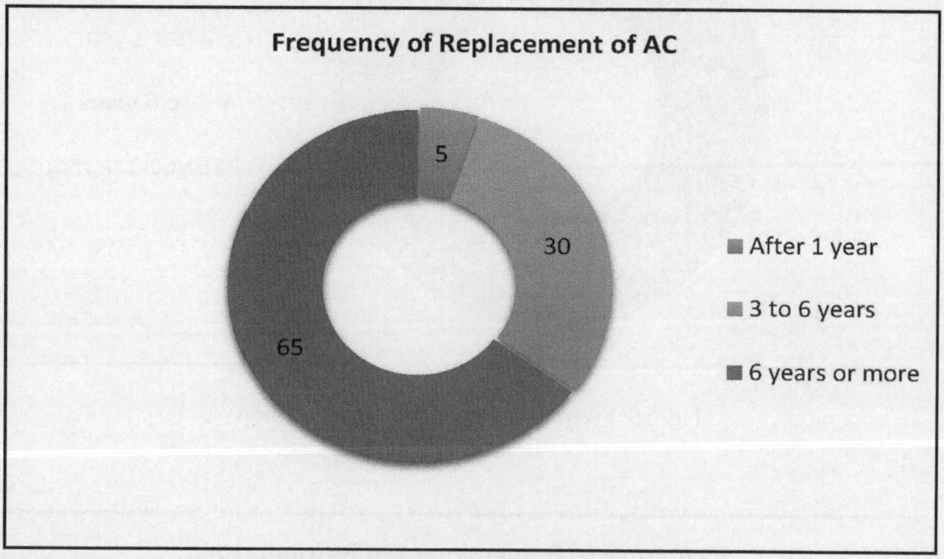

Fig. 6.8: **Frequency of replacement of AC**

Frequency of Replacement of Laptop

In case of laptops it was seen that most of the people replaced it after period of 6 years or more *i.e.* 60 per cent of the respondents. As incase of laptop one gets extended warranty for a period of atleast 2 years excluding one year manufacturer warranty. So, incase of laptops after service provided by manufacturers is quite good which leads to better customer satisfaction and they retain it for a longer period. 30 per cent of the respondents were found to replace their laptops within a period of 3-6 years due to reasons like: non-availability of extended warranty, problem with the touch screen of laptop, issues with touch pad and virus issues.

Frequency of Replacement of Refrigerator

Incase of refrigerators maximum respondents *i.e.* 65 per cent were found to replace them after 10 years or more as refrigerators are quite expensive and they work for longer duration as compared to other electronic items like mobiles and laptops. Only 25 per cent of the respondents replaced it within a period of 6-9 years due to issues like problem with condenser, manufacturing defect, poor service, poor performance and less efficiency with respect to consumption of electricity etc.

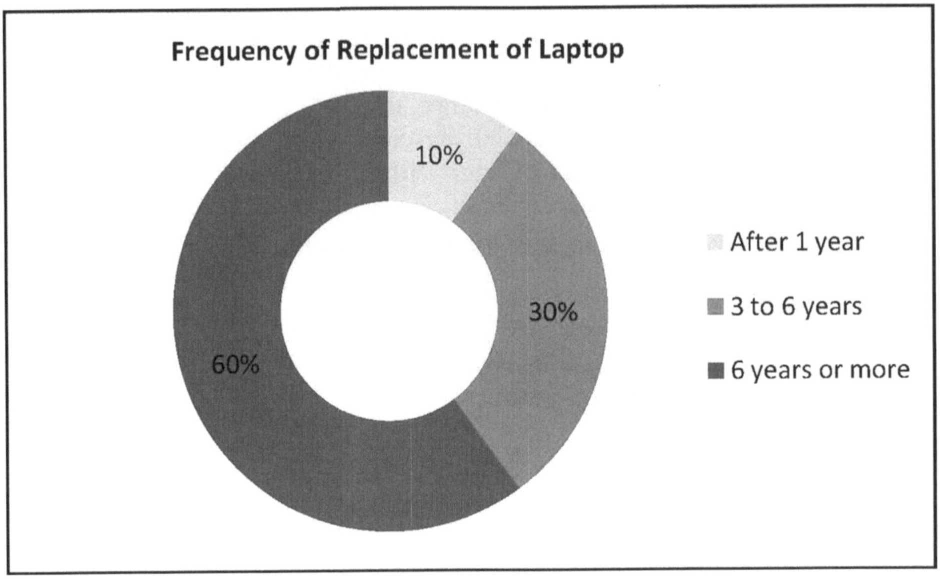

Fig. 6.9: **Frequency of replacement of Laptop**

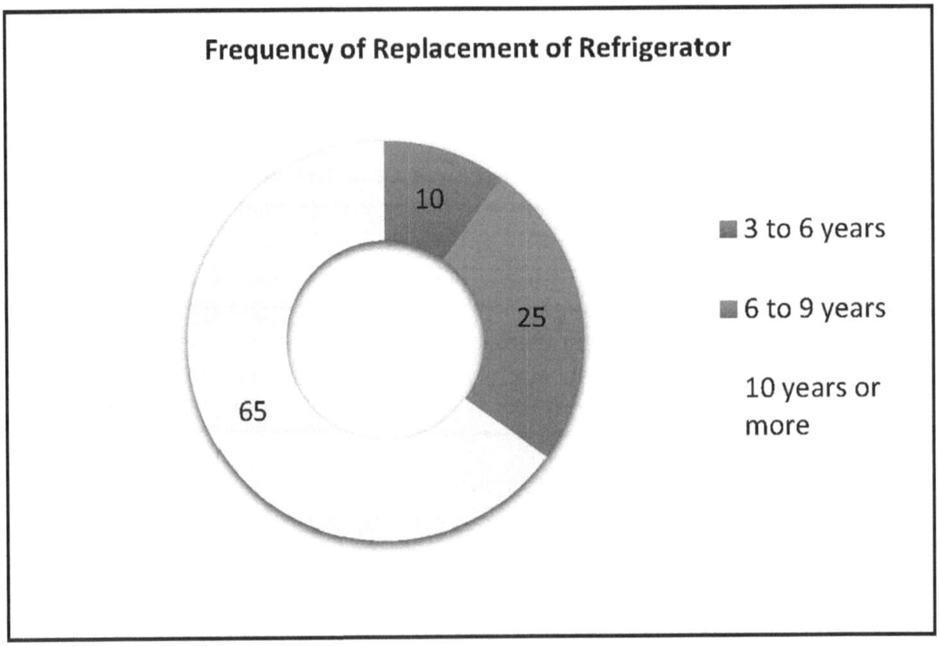

Fig. 6.10: **Frequency of replacement of Refrigerator**

Factors that Influence for Purchase of E-goods

Figure 6.11 shows various factors that influence the respondents regarding purchase of E-goods. It was seen that 55 per cent of the respondents purchased new electronics because of advanced technology and upgraded features. Most of the respondents (40%) purchased new electronic items because of influence from friends and peer pressure. TV commercials equally influenced them for the purchase *i.e.* 40 per cent. However, 20 per cent of the respondents also said that all the above factors influence them equally with respect to purchase of any E-item.

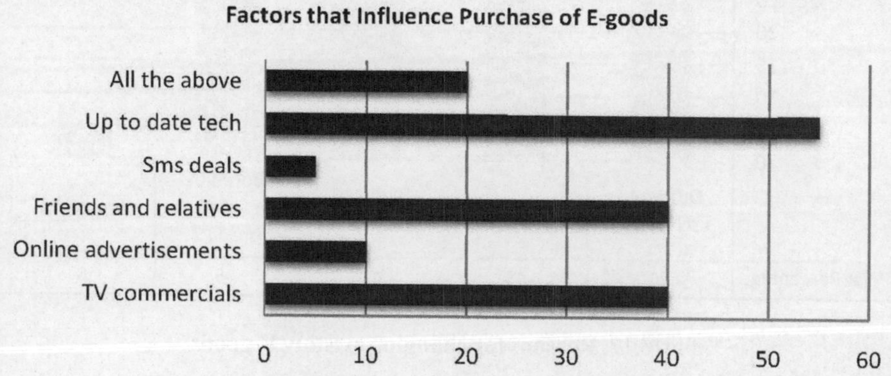

	TV commercials	Online advertisements	Friends and relatives	Sms deals	Up to date tech	All the above
■ Percentage	40	10	40	5	55	20

Fig. 6.11: **Factors that influence purchase of E-goods**

Reasons for Changing Existing E-goods

When asked regarding reasons for changing or replacing their existing E-goods most of the respondents stated that they changed it because the product was damaged beyond repair (45%) and its's functioning (40%) also reduced with time. No. of respondents also stated that they switched to new items as they were bored of existing items and wanted to have some change.

Awareness About E-waste Concept

Figure 6.13 shows the awareness level of respondents regarding E-waste. When interviewed it was found that most of the respondents *i.e.* 70 per cent consider old items not in use at present as E-waste whereas 35 per cent consider items not working at present as E-waste. 20 per cent considered items beyond repair as E-waste. It was seen that respondents had very less knowledge regarding E-waste concept and they were quite confused while stating responses.

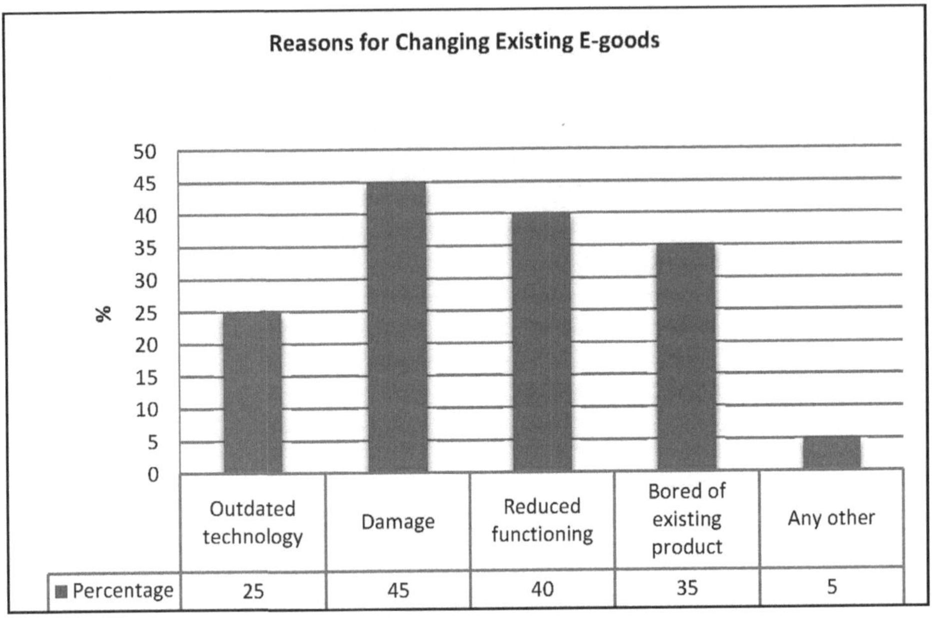

Fig. 6.12: **Reasons for changing existing E-goods**

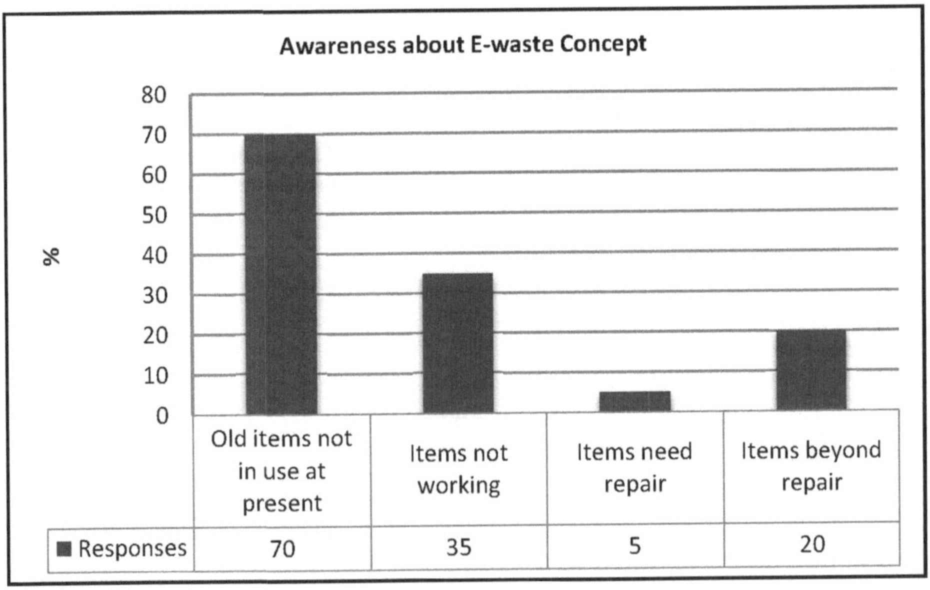

Fig. 6.13: **Awareness about E-waste concept**

Awareness Regarding Concern of Vol of E-waste Generated

Most of the respondents interviewed had very little knowledge regarding volume of E-waste generated by them and its generation in the country. 60 per cent of the respondents among all had very little idea whereas 20 per cent had no idea at all. This shows that there is an urgent need to create awareness regarding E-waste problem and to educate people regarding how to reduce the volume of E-waste generated by them.

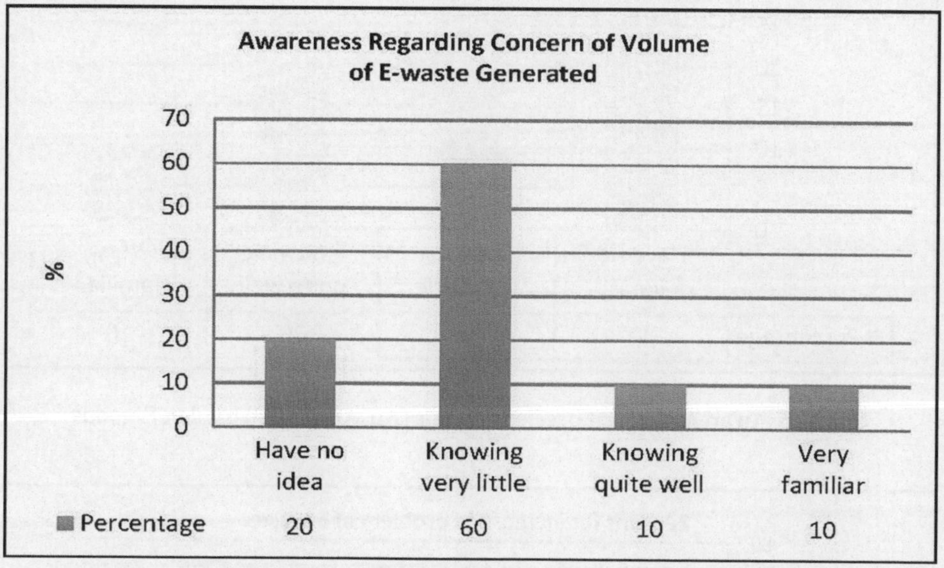

Fig. 6.14: **Awareness regarding concern of vol of E-waste generated**

Awareness about Precious Metals (Au, Ag, Cu, Al) Used in E-goods

It was seen that 40 per cent of the respondents interviewed had no idea at all regarding precious metals that are used in E-goods at the time of manufacturing. 30 per cent of respondents had very little awareness. 20 per cent were knowing quite well as they were working in MNC's and were found to be aware of manufacturing processes. Only 10 per cent of the respondents were very familiar and had quite good knowledge.

Reason for Increase in Problem of E-waste

Figure 6.16 shows that majority of respondents believe that increase in problem of E-waste is due to multiple factors *i.e.* 70 per cent of the respondents stated that all the above factors are equally accountable. 50 per cent of the respondents stated that awareness regarding environmental issues in our country is quite less whereas 40 per cent of the respondents believe that due to technological advancement people tend to buy more electronics. Other reasons include increase in population (35%), absence of sound recycling system (30%) and poor governance (10%).

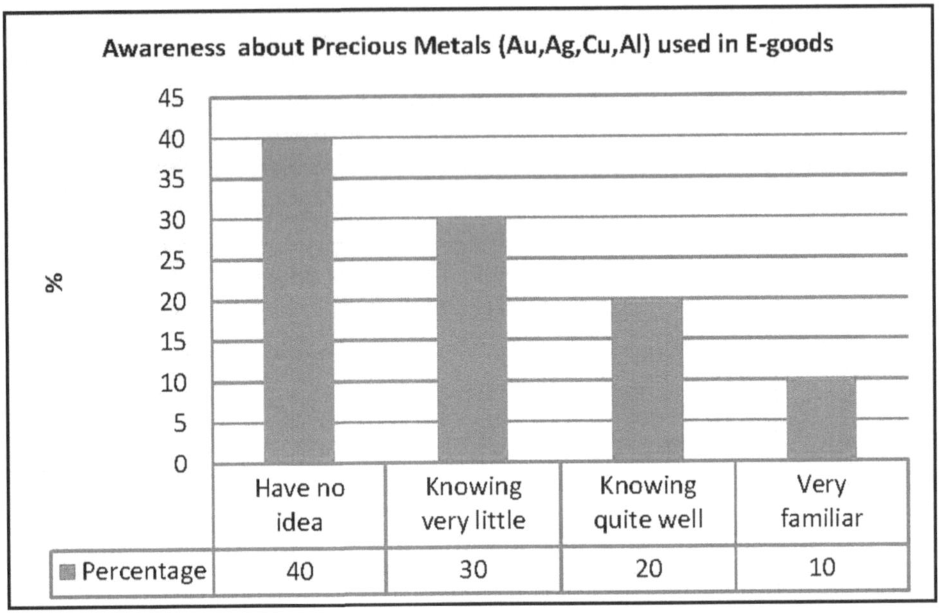

Fig. 6.15: **Awareness about precious metals (Au, Ag, Cu, Al) used in E-goods**

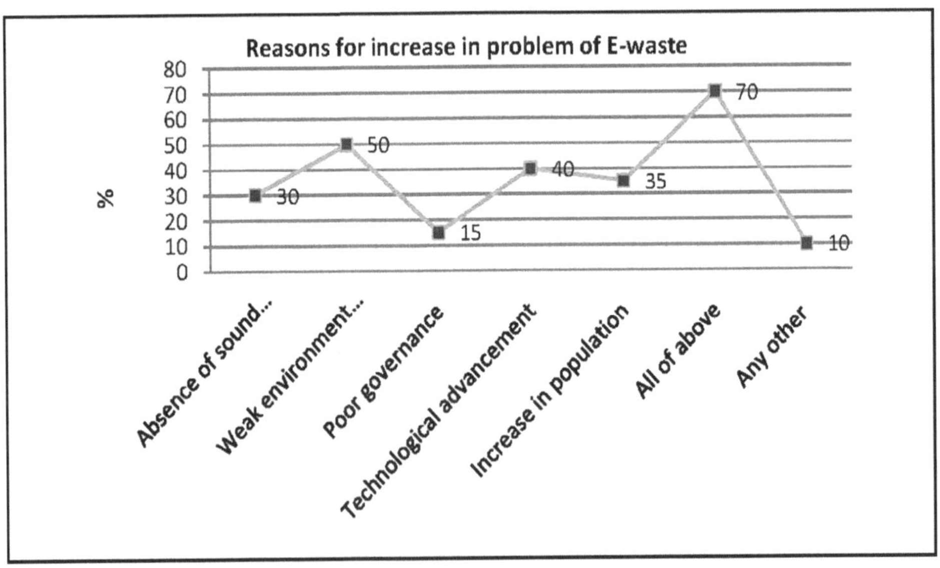

Fig. 6.16: **Reasons for increase in problem of E-waste**

Awareness Regarding Health Hazards Associated with E-waste

It was found that awareness regarding health hazards associated with E-waste was very less as 55 per cent of the respondents were found to be knowing very little and only 25 per cent of the respondents were found to be quite familiar. 10 per cent of the respondents had no idea at all.

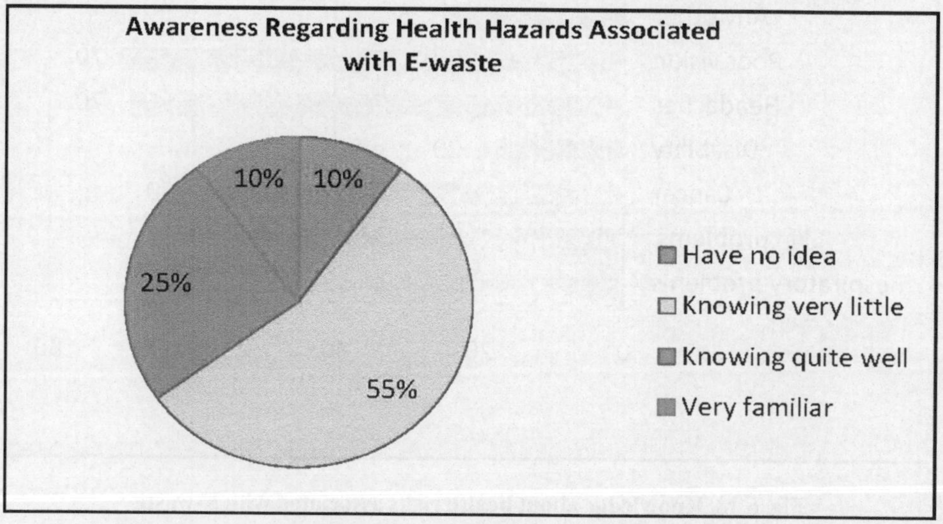

Fig.6.17: **Awareness regarding health hazards associated with E-waste**

Knowledge About Health Risks Associated with E-waste

Most of the respondents (70%) reported that headaches and poor vision are the health risks associated with E-waste respectively whereas 60 per cent of the respondents stated that cancer which is an acute health problem is also associated with E-waste. These problems people mainly related with usage of day to electronic items such as: mobile phones, laptop and TV.

Awareness Regarding Threats of E-waste to Environment

Most of the respondents were found to be relatively concerned about environment and were found to have little idea of threats of E-waste to environment *i.e.* 50 per cent. 25 per cent of respondents had quite good knowledge about threats of E-waste to environment. Very less percentage was found to be very familiar *i.e.* 5 per cent.

Knowledge about National and International Regulations

Majority of the respondents *i.e.* 60 per cent had no idea about National and International regulations concerning E-waste management. 25 per cent of the respondents were knowing little regarding environmental regulations and believed that some regulations must be there on E-waste as well. Some of the respondents were knowing quite well regarding international E-waste management system *i.e.* 10 per cent as they have been abroad or have relatives or friends living there who are source of information for them.

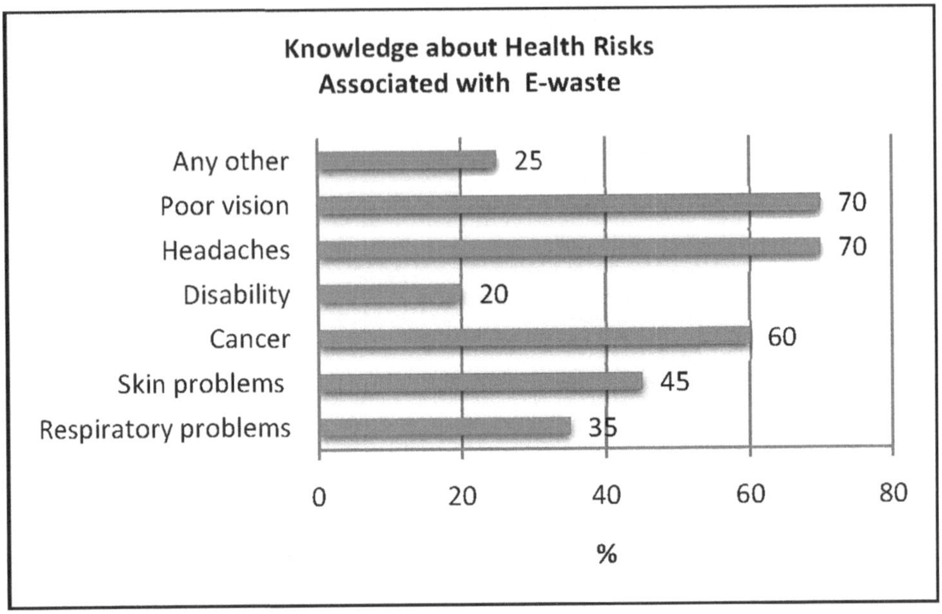

Fig. 6.18: **Knowledge about health risks associated with E-waste**

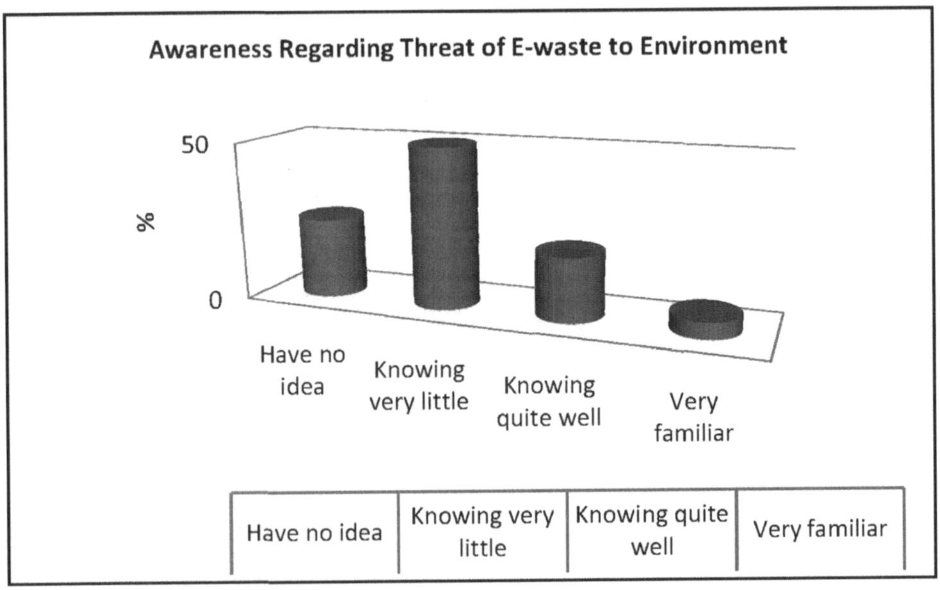

Fig. 6.19: **Awareness regarding threat of E-waste to environment**

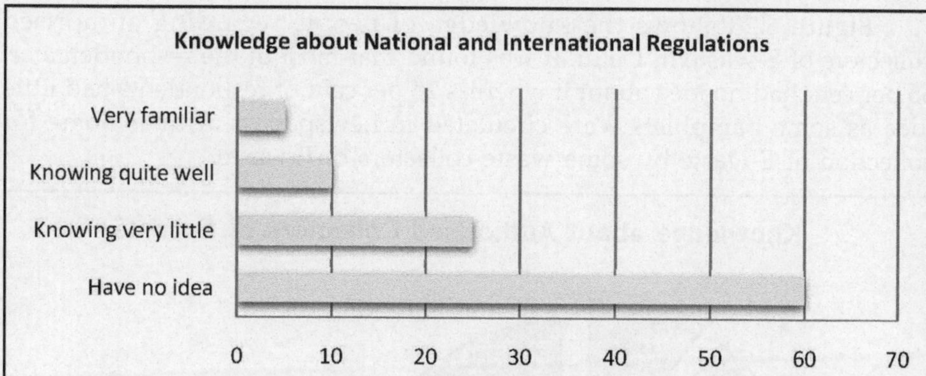

	Have no idea	Knowing very little	Knowing quite well	Very familiar
Percentage	60	25	10	5

Fig. 6.20: **Knowledge about National and International regulations**

Awareness Regarding EPR Concept

It was noticed that majority of people (85%) had no idea about EPR concept and they had heard it for the first time. Only 10 per cent stated that they know little. This shows that people are hardly aware of responsibility of manufacturers with respect to processing, collection and disposal of old or not in use E-waste items. This concept is very new to them.

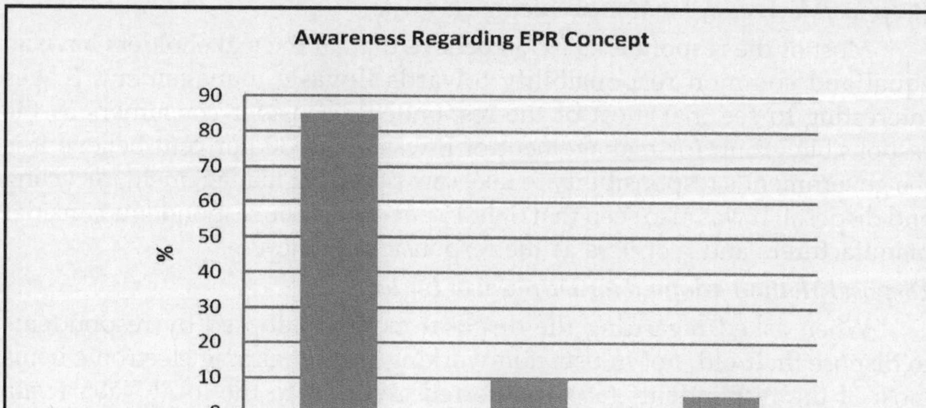

	Have no idea	Knowing very little	Knowing quite well
Percentage	85	10	5

Fig. 6.21: **Awareness regarding EPR concept**

Knowledge About Authorized Collectors of E-waste

Figure 6.23 shows the knowledge of people regarding authorised collectors of E-waste in Delhi. It was found that most of the respondents *i.e.* 65 per cent had no idea about it whereas 25 per cent of respondents had little idea as some pamphlets were circulated in newspapers at their home for collection of E-waste by some waste collectors of E-waste.

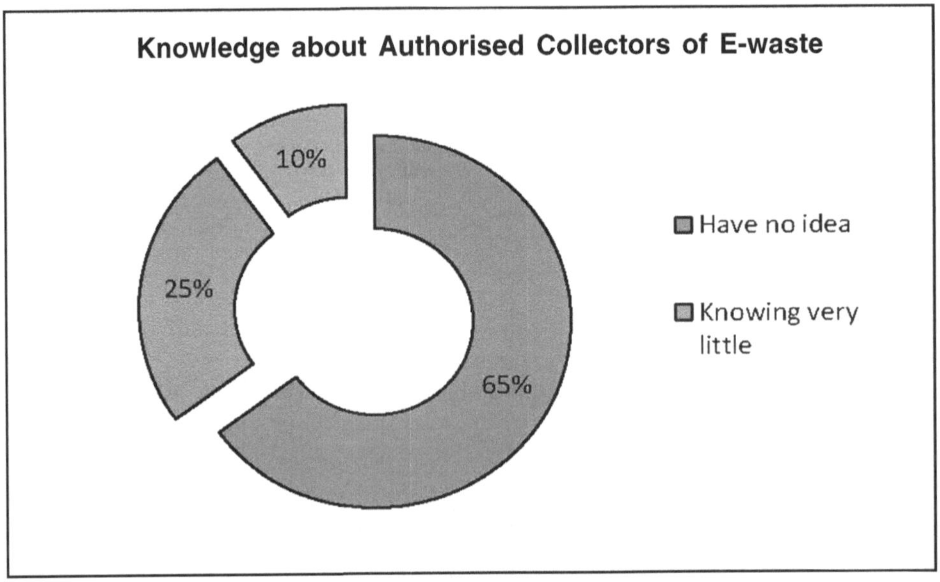

Fig. 6.22: **Knowledge about authorised collectors of E-waste**

Responsible Agency for Management of E-waste

Most of the respondents (85%) believe that all the stakeholders have an equal and common responsibility towards E-waste management. It was interesting to see that most of the respondents consider consumers as the responsible group for management of E-waste and 30 per cent believe it is the government's responsibility to take care of proper management, recycling and disposal. It was also seen that only 15 per cent of the respondents consider manufacturers and recyclers as the responsible agency.

Disposal Method Adopted for Disposal of E-waste

When asked regarding the disposal method adopted by respondents to dispose their old, not in use, non-working and repairable electronic items most of the respondents (65%) preferred giving it to the local Kabariwala because of ease of accessibility and had very less knowledge regarding authorised collectors. 25 per cent also reported that they either throw them in dustbin for collection by sweeper or give them to their relatives for reuse whereas 10 per cent hardly bothers how and in what manner shall they dispose it off.

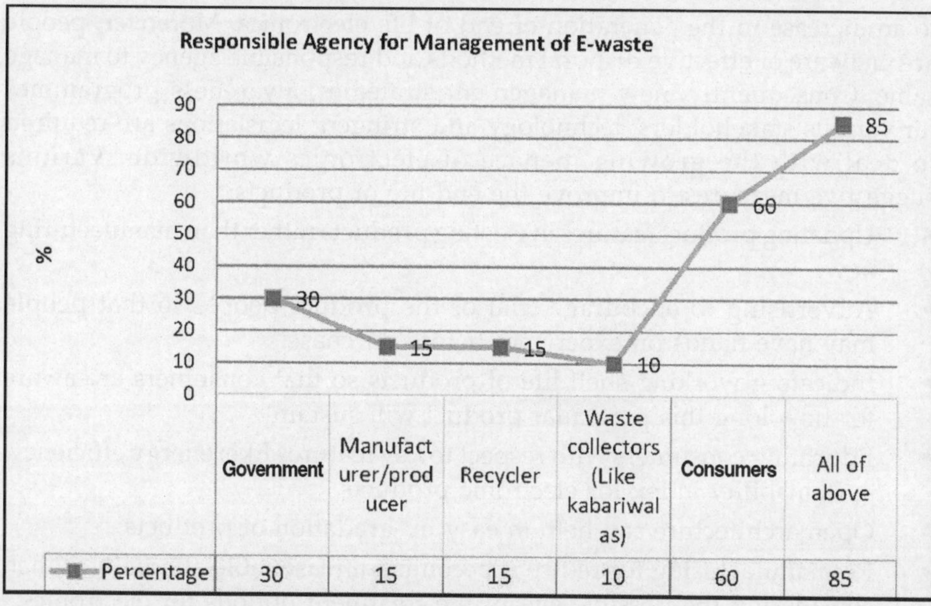

Fig. 6.23: **Responsible agency for management of E-waste**

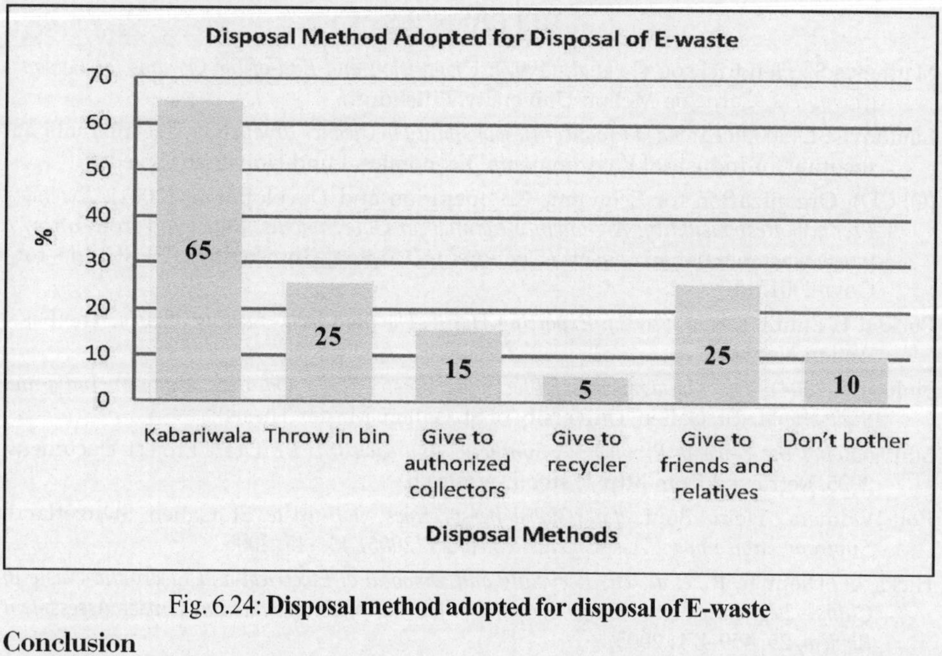

Fig. 6.24: **Disposal method adopted for disposal of E-waste**

Conclusion

The management practices have not advanced at the same pace as the manufacturing of electronics is advancing posing environmental challenges and health hazards. The functional life of electronic products has become moderately short because of fast changes in the technological aspects leading to an increase in the generation of end of life electronics. Moreover, people are unaware of effective disposal methods and responsible agency to manage same. Consequently, new management strategies, awareness programmes for various stakeholders, technology and stringent legislations are required to deal with the growing menace of electronics worldwide. Various suggestive measures to improve the end life of products:

- Updating product features in existing products rather than manufacturing new.
- Advertising to encourage trial of the product people so that people may have hands on experience before purchase.
- Indicating working shelf life of products so that consumers are aware for how long this particular product will sustain.
- Educating consumers with respect to key features like: energy efficiency, sustainability index for electronic products.
- Open architecture can help in easy up-gradation of products.
- Re-manufacturing for re-use is becoming a reasonable alternative when considering the possible end of life treatment options for electronics.
- Building capacity for sustainable management of used electronics.

REFERENCES

Matthews S., Hendrickson C., *et.al.* (1997): *Disposition and End-of-life Options for Personal Computers*. Carnegie Mellon University, Pittsburgh.

Lindhqvist T. (2000): *Extended Producer Responsibility in Cleaner Production*. The International Institute for Industrial Environmental Economics. Lund University, Sweden.

(OECD), Organization for Economic Co-operation and Development (2001): *Extended Producer Responsibility: A Guidance Manual for Governments*. Retrieved from http://www.wastenet.net.au/Assets/Documents/Content/Information/EPRGuide_for_Govt-2001.pdf

Puckett J., Smith T, *et.al.* (2002): *Exporting Harm: The high-tech Trashing of Asia*. The Basel Action Network.

Sinha D. (2004): *The Management of Electronic Waste: A Comparative Study on India and Switzerland*. (St. Gallen, University of St. Gallen. Master Thesis).

StEP, *Solving the E-waste Problem: A Synthetic Approach (StEP)*, Draft Project Document; 2005. Retrieved from http://step.E-waste.ch

Rolf Widmera., Heinz Boni. *et.al. Global Perspectives on E-waste*. St. Gallen, Switzerland, *Environmental Impact Assessment Review 25 (2005)* 436-45; 2005.

Hicks, C., Dietmar, R., *et al. The Recycling and Disposal of Electrical and Electronic Waste in China - Legislative and Market Responses. Journal of Environmental Impact Assessment Review*, 25, 459-471; 2005.

Maharashtra Pollution Control Board, *Report on Assessment of Electronic Wastes in Mumbai-Pune Area*; March 2007, Mumbai. Retrieved from http://mpcb.mah.nic.in

United Nations Environment Programme (UNEP), *Report: Recycling-From E-waste to Resources*; July, 2009.

Editorial, "Growing E-waste Causing Concern", *The Hindu*, February 28, 2009, Retrieved from http://www.thehindu.com/todays-paper/tp-national/tp-newdelhi/growing-ewaste-causing-concern/article364266.ece

Sushant B. Wath., P. S. Dutt. *et al. E-waste scenario in India, its Management and Implications*. National Environmental Engineering Research Institute (NEERI), Nehru Marg, Nagpur, Maharashtra, India; 2010.

Goel *et al*. (2015): *Sustainability Audit Criteria for Electronic Products* (unpublished report).

Nnorom and Osibanjo (2010): *Overview of Prospects in Adopting Remanufacturing of end-of-life Electronic Products in the Developing Countries. International Journal of Innovation*, Management and Technology, Vol. 1, No. 3, ISSN: 2010-0248.

Alejandra Sepúlveda. (2010): *et.al. A Review of the Environmental Fate and Effects of Hazardous Substances Released from Electrical and Electronic Equipments during Recycling: Examples from China and India*. Environmental Impact Assessment Review 30 (2010) 28-41.

Murali, (2010): *'Tackling E-waste'*; Retrieved from http://www.giswatch.org/thematic-report/sustainability-E-waste/tackling-E-waste.

Manzar and Das (2010): *Report on ICTs and Environmental Sustainability*. Retrieved from http://www.giswatch.org/sites/default/files/gisw2010countryindia_en.pdf

Editorial, "E-waste draft Regulations Ignore the Unorganised Sector" *The Hindu*, May 19, 2010. Retrieved from http://www.thehindu.com/news/cities/Delhi/article433742.ece

E-waste (Handling and Management) Rules (2011): Available on website of Ministry of Environment and Forests, envfor.nic.in/

Research Unit (Larrdis), Rajya Sabha, *Report on E-waste in India* (2011). Retrieved from http://rajyasabha.nic.in/rsnew/publication_electronic/E-Waste_in_india.pdf

Kazi and Menon (2011): *Report on ICTs and Environmental Sustainability*. Digital Empowerment Foundation, Kalu Sarai, New Delhi, India. Retrieved from http://defindia.net/files/2012/01/India-Baseline-Study.pdf

Borthakur and Singh, (2012): *Electronic Waste in India: Problems and Policies. International Journal of Environmental Sciences*, Volume 3, No. 1.

Borthakur and Sinha (2013): Generation of Electronic Waste in India: Current Scenario, Dilemmas and Stakeholders. *African Journal of Environmental Science and Technology*, Vol. 7(9), pp. 899-910.

Kissling, R., Coughlan, D., Fitzpatrick, C. *et al*. (2013): *Success Factors and Barriers Identified*; 2013. Retrieved from http://www.aluproireland.ie/E-waste-re-use:-success-factors-and-barriers-identified-news5171.html

Pages: 114-138

WASTE GENERATION AND UTILIZATION

Edited by: **Dr. Priya Bajaj; Dr. B. Tabassum** and **Dr. Pawan Kumar 'Bharti'**

ISBN: 978-93-5056-792-0

Edition: **2016**

Published by: **Discovery Publishing House Pvt. Ltd., New Delhi (India)**

CHAPTER - 7

Decontamination of Wastewater and Smudged Soil Employing Bioremediation Technologies

Bina Rani; M.M. Abid Ali Khan[1]; Vikram Singh Chauhan[2]; Murtaza Abid[3] and **Raaz K. Maheshwari[4]**

ABSTRACT

Bioremediation is an ecologically sound and state-of-the-art technique that employs natural biological processes employing microorganisms, fungi, green plants or their enzymes to return the natural environment altered by contaminants to its original condition and to completely eliminate toxic contaminants occurring in sludges, and groundwater contaminated with petroleum hydrocarbons, solvents, pesticides, wood preservatives, non-halogenated SVOCs, BTEX and other organic chemicals, especially effective for remediating low level residual contamination in conjunction with source removal. Compared with other technologies, such as: thermal desorption and incineration (which require excavation and heating), thermally enhanced recovery (which requires heating), chemical treatment (which may require relatively expensive chemical reagents), and in situ soil flushing (which may

Department of Engineering Chemistry and Environmental Engineering, PCE, Sitapura, Jaipur, Rajasthan, India.

1. Department of Botany, Shia P.G. College, Lucknow U.P., India.
2. Department of Botany, SBRM Government PG College, Nagaur, Rajasthan, India.
3. Department of Biochemistry, King George's Medical University, Lucknow, U.P., India.
4. Department of Chemistry, SBRM Government PG College, Nagaur, Rajasthan, India.

require further management of the flushing water), bioremediation may enjoy a cost advantage. Not all contaminants, however, are easily treated by bioremediation using microorganisms. For example, heavy metals such as: Cd and Pb aren't easily absorbed or captured by organisms. The assimilation of metals such as: Hg into the food chain may worsen matters. While bioremediation (nor any other remediation technology) can't degrade inorganic contaminants, can be used to change the valence state of inorganics and cause adsorption, immobilization onto soil particulates, precipitation, uptake, accumulation, and concentration of inorganics in micro or macroorganisms. These techniques, while still largely experimental, show considerable promise of stabilizing or removing inorganics from soil. This manuscript delineates the general processes of bioremediation within the soil environment, factors of bioremediation strategies, genetic engineering approaches, monitoring bioremediation, and further, the pros and cons of the technique, limitations and potential of both *ex situ* and *in situ* bioremediation as viable alternatives to conventional remediation are explained and addressed.

Keywords: Groundwater; hazardous substances; Radionuclide; Phytoremediation; Recalcitrant molecules; Methylotrophs; SDS; Bioreactors; BTEX; VOC; PAH; SVOC; Heavy metals and GEM.

INTRODUCTION

Enormous quantities of organic and inorganic compounds are released into the environment each year as a result of human activities. In some cases, these releases are deliberate and well regulated (*e.g.*, industrial emissions) while in other cases they are accidental (*e.g.*, chemical or oil spills). Many of these compounds are both toxic and persistent in terrestrial and aquatic environments. The contamination of soil, surface and groundwater is simply the result of the accumulation of these toxic compounds in excess of permissible levels. The quality of life on earth is linked inextricably to overall quality of the environment. In early times, we believed that we had an unlimited abundance of land and resources; today[1], however, the resources in the world show, in greater or lesser degree, our carelessness and negligence in using them. The problems associated with contaminated sites now assume increasing prominence in many countries. Contaminated lands generally result from past industrial activities when awareness of the health and environmental effects connected with the production, use and disposal of hazardous substances were less well recognized than today. The problem is worldwide, and the estimated number of contaminated sites is significant. It is now well recognized that contaminated land is a potential threat to human health, and is continual discovery over recent years has led to international efforts to remedy many of these sites, either as response to the risk of adverse health on environmental effects caused by contamination or to enable the site to be redeveloped for use[2].

The conventional techniques used for remediation have been to dig up contaminated soil and remove it to a landfill, or to cap and contain the contaminated areas of a site. The methods have some drawbacks. The first method simply moves the contamination elsewhere and may create significant risks in the excavation, handling and transport of hazardous material. Additionally, it is very difficult and increasingly expensive to find new landfill sites for the final disposal of material. The cap and contain method is only an interim solution since the contamination remains on site, requiring monitoring and maintenance of the isolation barriers long into the future, with all the associated costs and potential liability. A better approach than these traditional methods is to completely destroy the pollutants if possible, or at least to transform them to innocuous substances. Some technologies that have been used are high-temperature incineration and various types of chemical decomposition (*e.g.*, base-catalyzed dechlorination, UV oxidation). They can be very effective in reducing levels of a range of contaminants, but have several drawbacks, principally their technologies complexity, the cost for small-scale application, and the lack of public acceptance, especially for incineration that may increase the exposure to contaminants that may increase the exposure to contaminants for both the workers at the site and nearby residents.

BTEX is the term used for benzene, toluene, ethylbenzene, and xylene - (VMAOCs) volatile, monocyclic aromatic compounds present in coal tar, petroleum products, and various organic chemical product formulations. These are the most soluble of the major gasoline compounds and, therefore, are common indicators of gasoline contamination.

Bioremediation is an option that offers the possibility to destroy or render harmless various contaminants using natural biological activity. As such, it uses relatively low-cost, low-technology techniques, which generally have a high public acceptance and can often be carried out on site. It will not always be suitable. However, as the range of contaminants on which it is effective is limited, the same time scales involved are relatively long, and the residual contaminant levels achievable may not always be appropriate.

Although the methodologies employed are not technically complex, considerable experience and expertise may be required to design and implement a successful bioremediation programme, due to the need to thoroughly assess a site for suitability and to optimize conditions to achieve a satisfactory result. Because bioremediation seems to be a good alternative to conventional clean-up technologies research in this field, especially in the US is rapidly increasing. Bioremediation of pollutants is a new technology that has emerged as an important tool. This process is focused on destroying or immobilizing toxic waste materials in eco-friendly manner pesticides are a common hazard around the world, as these chemicals are leaching into

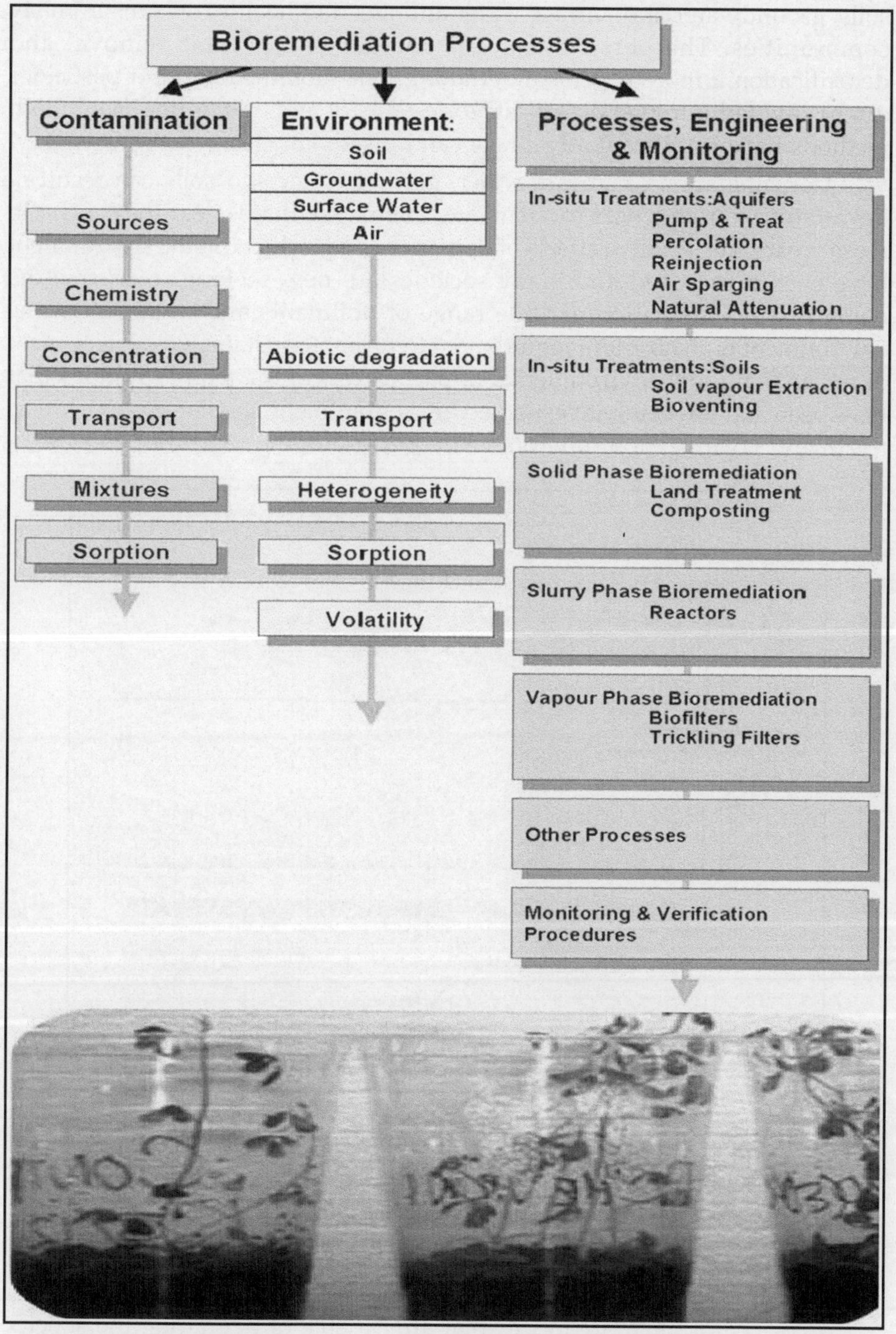

Fig. 7.1a: **Pictorial representation various processes of bioremediation**

soils, groundwater and surface water and creating health concerns in many communities. The persistence of pesticides makes their removal and detoxification a more urgent undertaking. The bioremediation of pesticides can be divided into two broad categories: *in-situ* and *ex-situ* treatment. Both methods have significant advantages and disadvantages.

Contamination of surface water, ground water and soils can result in devastating consequences for plant and animal life that is near the source. In recent years, the negative effects of human waste products on the environment have been recognized and many societies are now seeking to reverse the damage. The elimination of wide range of pollutants and wastes from the environment is an absolute requirement to promote sustainable development of society with low environmental impact. A few of the many solutions that have been and are being investigated are containment, incineration, chemical treatment, volatilization, phytoremediation and bioremediation.

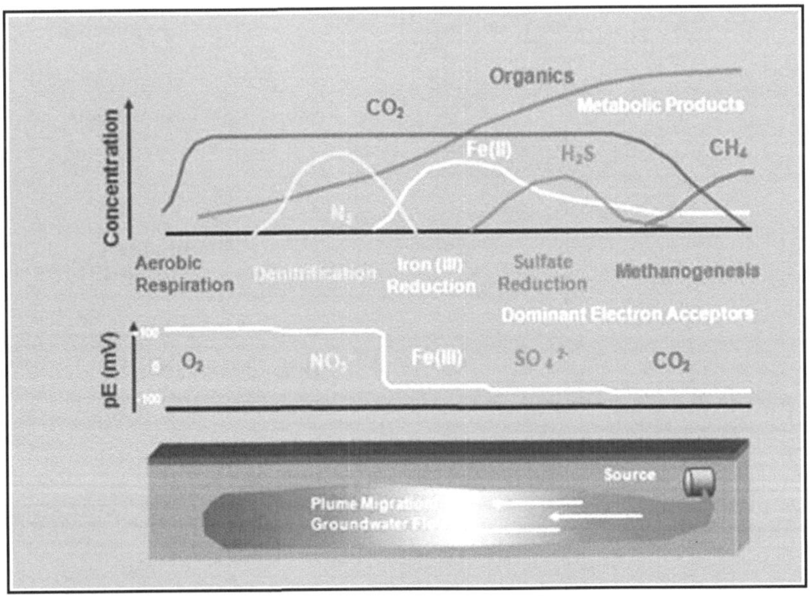

Fig. 7.1b: **Microorganisms *vs.* degrading the specific contaminant**

This paper focuses on bioremediation as a solution to the worldwide contamination problem.

Three primary ingredients for bioremediation are:

1. Presence of a contaminant.
2. An electron acceptor.
3. Presence of microorganisms that are capable of degrading the specific contaminant (Figure 7.2).

Generally, a contaminant is more easily and quickly degraded if it is a naturally occurring compound in the environment, or chemically similar to a naturally occurring compound, because microorganisms capable of its biodegradation are more likely to have evolved. Petroleum hydrocarbons are naturally occurring chemicals; therefore, microorganisms which are capable of attenuating or degrading hydrocarbons exist in the environment. Development of biodegradation technologies of synthetic chemicals such DDT is dependent on outcomes of research that searches for natural or genetically improved strains of microorganisms to degrade such contaminants into less toxic forms. Microorganisms have limits of tolerance for particular environmental conditions, as well as optimal conditions for pinnacle performance. Factors that affect success and rate of microbial biodegradation are nutrient availability, moisture content, pH, and temperature of the soil matrix. Inorganic nutrients including, but not limited to, N and P are necessary for microbial activity and cell growth.

Fig. 7.2: **Intrinsic biodegradation processes**

It has been shown that treating petroleum-contaminated soil with nitrogen can increase cell growth rate, decrease the microbial lag phase, help to maintain microbial populations at high activity levels, and increase the rate of hydrocarbon degradation[4].

All soil microorganisms require moisture for cell growth and function. Availability of water affects diffusion of water and soluble nutrients into and out of microorganism cells. However, excess moisture, such as: in saturated soil, is undesirable because it reduces the amount of available oxygen for aerobic respiration. Anaerobic respiration, which produces less energy for microorganisms (than aerobic respiration) and slows the rate of biodegradation, becomes the predominant process. Soil pH is important because most microbial species can survive only within a certain pH range. Furthermore, soil pH can affect availability of nutrients. Biodegradation of petroleum hydrocarbons is optimal at a pH 7 (neutral); the acceptable range is pH 6-8. Temperature influences rate of biodegradation by controlling rate of enzymatic reactions within microorganisms. Generally, speed of enzymatic reactions in the cell ~ doubles for each 10°C rise in temperature. There is an upper limit to the temperature that microorganisms can withstand. Most bacteria found in soil, including many bacteria that degrade petroleum hydrocarbons, are mesophiles which have an optimum temperature ranging from 25°C to 45°C. Thermophilic bacteria (those which survive and thrive at relatively high temperatures) which are normally found in hot springs and compost heaps exist indigenously in cool soil environments and can be activated to degrade hydrocarbons with an increase in temperature to 60°C. This finding suggested an intrinsic potential for natural attenuation in cool soils through thermally enhanced bioremediation techniques[5].

Contaminants can adsorb to soil particles, rendering some contaminants unavailable to microorganisms for biodegradation. Thus, in some circumstances, bioavailability of contaminants depends not only on the nature of the contaminant but also on soil type. Hydrophobic contaminants, like: petroleum hydrocarbons, have low solubility in water and tend to adsorb strongly in soil with high organic matter content. In such cases, surfactants are utilized as part of the bioremediation process to increase solubility and mobility of these contaminants. Additional research findings of the existence of thermophilic bacteria in cool soil also suggest that high temperatures enhance the rate of biodegradation by increasing the bioavailability of contaminants. It is suggested that contaminants adsorbed to soil particles are mobilized and their solubility increased by high temperatures. If the challenges of bioremediation, particularly of *in situ* techniques, can be overcome, bioremediation has potential to provide a low cost, non-intrusive, natural method to render toxic substances in soil less harmful or harmless over time.. On a broader scope, much research has been and continues to be developed enhance understanding of the essence of microbial behaviour as microbes interact with various toxic contaminants. Additional research continues to evaluate conditions for successful introduction of exogenic and GEMs a contaminated environment, and how to translate success in the laboratory to success in the field (Figure 7.3)[6].

Fig. 7.3: **Field bioremediation test and microbiological screening**

Approach of Bioremediation

Bioremediation is a waste management technique that involves the use of organisms to remove or neutralize pollutants from a contaminated site. According to the EPA, bioremediation is a "treatment that uses naturally occurring organisms to break down hazardous substances into less toxic or non toxic substances". Technologies can be generally classified as *in situ* or *ex situ*. *In situ* bioremediation involves treating the contaminated material at the site, while *ex situ* involves the removal of the contaminated material to be treated elsewhere). Bioremediation may occur on its own (natural attenuation or intrinsic bioremediation) or may only effectively occur through the addition of fertilizers, oxygen, etc., that help encourage the growth of the pollution-eating microbes within the medium (biostimulation). Depleted soil nitrogen status may encourage biodegradation of some nitrogenous organic chemicals, and soil materials with a high capacity to adsorb pollutants may slow down biodegradation owing to limited bioavailability of the chemicals to microbes[6-8].

Recent advancements have also proven successful via the addition of matched microbe strains to the medium to enhance the resident microbe population's ability to break down contaminants. Microorganisms used to perform the function of bioremediation are known as bioremediators. However, not all contaminants are easily treated by bioremediation using microorganisms. For example, heavy metals such as: Cd and Pb are not readily absorbed or captured by microorganisms. A recent experiment, however, suggests that fish bones have some success absorbing lead from contaminated soil. Bone char has been shown to bioremediate small amounts of Cd, Cu and Zn. The assimilation of metals such as: mercury into the food chain may worsen matters. Phytoremediation[#] is useful in these circumstances because natural plants or transgenic plants are able to bioaccumulate these toxins in their above-ground parts, which are then harvested for removal. The heavy metals in the harvested biomass may be further concentrated by incineration or even recycled for industrial use[9]. Some damaged artifacts at museums contain microbes which could be specified as bio remediating agents. The elimination of a wide range of pollutants and wastes from the environment requires increasing our understanding of the relative importance of different pathways and regulatory networks to carbon flux in particular environments and for particular compounds, and they will certainly accelerate the development of bioremediation technologies and biotransformation processes[10].

#Phytoremediation consists of mitigating pollutant concentrations in contaminated soils, water, or air, with plants able to contain, degrade, or eliminate metals, pesticides, solvents, explosives, crude oil and its derivatives, and various other contaminants from the media that contain them. Phytoremediation may be applied wherever the soil or static water environment has become polluted or is suffering ongoing chronic pollution. Examples where phytoremediation has been used successfully include the restoration of abandoned metal mine workings, reducing the impact of contaminants in soils, water, or air. Contaminants such as: metals, pesticides, solvents, explosives, and crude oil and its derivatives, have been mitigated in phytoremediation projects worldwide. Many plants such as: mustard plants, alpine pennycress, hemp, and pigweed have proven to be successful at hyperaccumulating contaminants at toxic waste sites. Over the past 20 years, this technology has become increasingly popular and has been employed at sites with soils contaminated with lead, uranium, and arsenic. While it has the advantage that environmental concerns may be treated in situ; one major disadvantage of phytoremediation is that it requires a long-term commitment, as the process is dependent on a plant's ability to grow and thrive in an environment that is not ideal for normal plant growth. Phytoremediation may be applied wherever the soil or static water environment has become polluted or is suffering ongoing chronic pollution (Figure 7.3).

Examples where phytoremediation has been used successfully include the restoration of abandoned metal-mine workings, reducing the impact of sites where polychlorinated biphenyls have been dumped during manufacture and mitigation of ongoing coal mine discharges. Phytoremediation refers to the natural ability of certain plants called hyperaccumulators to bioaccumulate, degrade, or render harmless contaminants in soils, water, or air. Breeding programmes and genetic engineering are powerful methods for enhancing natural phytoremediation capabilities, or for introducing new capabilities into plants. Genes for phytoremediation may originate from a microorganism or may be transferred from one plant to another variety better adapted to the environmental conditions at the cleanup site. For example, genes encoding a nitroreductase from a bacterium were inserted into tobacco and showed faster removal of TNT and enhanced resistance to the toxic effects of TNT. Researchers have also discovered a mechanism in plants that allows them to grow even when the pollution concentration in the soil is lethal for non-treated plants. Some natural, biodegradable compounds, such as: exogenous polyamines, allow the plants to tolerate concentrations of pollutants 500 times higher than untreated plants, and to absorb more pollutants[1-3].

By definition, bioremediation is the use of living organisms, primarily microorganisms, to degrade the environmental contaminants into less toxic forms. It uses naturally occurring bacteria and fungi or plants (algal biomass) to degrade or detoxify substances hazardous to human health and/or environment (Figure 7.4 a&b). The microorganisms may be indigenous to a contaminated area or they may be isolated from elsewhere and brought to the contaminated sites. Contaminant compounds are transformed by living organisms through reactions that take place as a part of their metabolic processes. Biodegradation of a compound is often a result of the actions of multiple organisms. When microorganisms are imported to a contaminated site to enhance degradation we have process known as bioaugmentation[11]. For bioaugmentation to be effective, microorganisms must enzymatically attack the pollutant and convert them to harmless products. A bioremediation can be effective only where environmental conditions permit microbial growth and activity, its application often involves the manipulation of environmental parameters to allow microbial growth and degradation to proceed at a faster rate. Like other technologies, bioremediation has its limitations[12].

Fig. 7.4a & b: **Fungi and algae in bioremediation**

Some contaminants, such as: chlorinated organic or high aromatic hydrocarbons, are resistant to microbial attack. They are degraded either slowly or not at all, hence it is not easy to predict the rates of clean-up for a remediation; there are no rules to predict if a contaminant can be degraded. Bioremediation techniques are typically more economical than traditional methods such as: incineration, and some pollutants can be treated on site, thus reducing exposure risks for clean-up personnel, or potentially wider exposure as result of transportation accidents. Since bioremediation is based on natural attenuation the public considers it more accepted than other technologies. Most remediation systems are run under aerobic conditions, but running a system under anaerobic conditions may permit microbial organisms to degrade otherwise recalcitrant molecules[13].

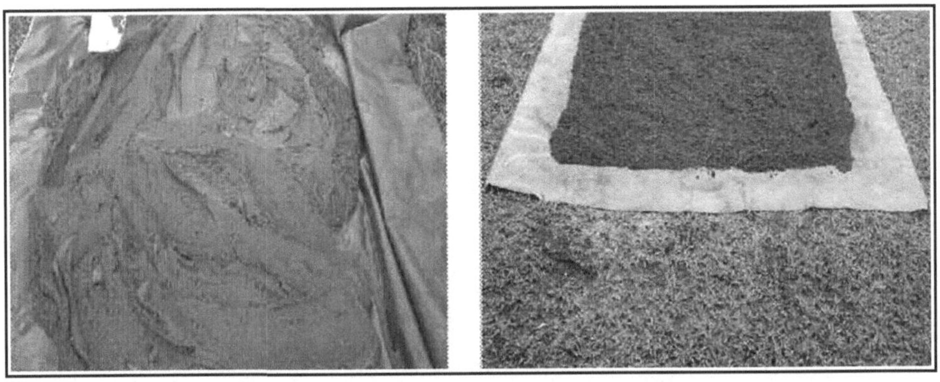

Fig. 7.5: **Soil before and after Bioremediation**

Fig. 7.6: **Farming in Fertile Soil**

Inimitability for Remediation

The control and optimization of bioremediation processes is a complex system of many factors. These factors include: the existence of a microbial population capable of degrading the pollutants; the availability of contaminants to the microbial population; the environment factors (type of soil, temperature, pH, the presence of oxygen or other electron acceptors, and nutrients)[14].

Microbial Population for Bioremediation Processes

Microorganisms can be isolated from almost any environmental conditions. Microbes will adapt and grow at subzero temperatures, as well as extreme heat, desert conditions, in water, with excess of oxygen, and in anaerobic conditions, with the presence of hazardous compounds or any waste stream. The main requirements are an energy source and a carbon source. Because of the adaptability of microbes and other biological systems, these can be used to degrade or remediate environmental hazards[15-17]. We can subdivide these microorganisms in Table 7.1.

Table 7.1: Some contaminants potentially suitable for Bioremediation

Class of Contaminants	Specific Examples	Aerobic	Anaerobic Sources	More Potential
Chlorinated solvents	Trychloroethylene Perchloroethylene		+	Drycleaners
Polychlorinated biphenyls	4-Chlorobiphenyl4, 4-Dichlorobiphenyl		+	Electrical manufacturing Power station
Chlorinated phenol 'BTEX'	Pentachlorophenol Benzene, Toluene, Ethylbenzene, Xylene	+	++	Timber treatment Landfills, Oil production and storage gas work sites, Airport Paint manufacture, Port facilities, Railway yards, Chemical manufacture
Polyarmatic hydrocarbons (PAHs)	Naphthalene, Anthracene Bezopyrene	+		Oil production and storage Gas work sites, Coke plant Engine works landfill
Pesticides	Atrazine Carbaryl Carbofuran Diazine Glycophosphate Parathion Propham 2,4-D	+	+	Agriculture Timber treatment plants, Pesticide manufacture Recreational areas Landfills

Aerobic

Number of bacteria *viz; Pseudomonas, Alcaligenes, Sphingomonas, Rhodococcus,* and *Mycobacterium* are examples of aerobic bacteria recognized for their degradative abilities. These microbes have often been reported to degrade pesticides and hydrocarbons, both alkanes amd polyaromatic compounds. Many of these bacteria use the contaminant as the sole source of carbon and energy.

Anaerobic

Anaerobic bacteria are not as frequently used as aerobic bacteria. There is an increasing interest in anaerobic bacteria used for bioremediation of polychlorinated biphenyls (PCBs) in river sediments, dechlorination of the solvent trichloroethylene (TCE) and chloroform.

Liginolytic fungi

Fungi such as: white rot fungus *Phanaerochaete chrysoporium* have the ability to degrade an extremely diverse range of persistent or toxic environmental toxicants. Common substrates used include straw, saw dust, or corn cobs.

Methylotrophs

Aerobic bacteria that grow utilizing methane for carbon and energy. The initial enzyme in the pathway for anaerobic degradation, methane monooxygenase, has a broad substrate range and is active against a wide range of compounds, including the chlorinated aliphatics trichloroethylene and 1,2-dichloroethane. For degradation it is necessary that bacteria and the contaminants be in contact. This is not easily achieved, as neither the microbes nor contaminants are uniformly spread in the soil. Some bacteria are mobile and exhibit a chemotactic response, sensing the contaminant and moving toward it. Other microbes such as: fungi grow in a filamentous form toward the contaminant. It is possible to enhance the mobilization of the contaminant utilizing some surfactants such as: sodium dodesyl sulphate (SDS)O.

Environmental Requirements

Microbial growth and activity are readily affected by pH, temperature and moisture. Although microorganisms have been also isolated in extreme condition, most of them grow optimally over a narrow range, so that it is important to achieve optimal conditions. If the soil has too much acid it is possible to rinse the pH by adding lime. Temperature affects bio-chemical reactions rates, and the rates of many of them double for each 10°C rise in temperature. Above a certain temperature however, the cells die. Plastic covering can be used to enhance solar warming in the late spring, summer and autumn[18]. Available water is essential for all the living organisms and irrigation is needed to achieve the optimum moisture level. Soil structure controls the effective delivery of air, water, and nutrients. To improve soil structure, materials such as: gypsum or organic matter can be applied. Low soil permeability can impede movement of water, nutrients, and oxygen; hence, soil with low permeability may not be appropriate for *in situ* clean-up techniques. Although the microorganisms are present in contaminated soil, they can't necessarily be there in the numbers required for bioremediation of the site. Their growth and activity must be stimulated. Biostimulation usually involves the addition of nutrients and oxygen to help indigenous microorganisms. These nutrients are the basic building blocks of life and allow microbes to create necessary enzymes to break down the contaminants. All of them will need C, N and P (Table 7.2). C is the most basic element of living forms and is needed in greater quantities than other elements. In addition to H, O and N, it constitutes about 95 per cent of the weight of cells. P and S contribute with 70 per cent of the remainders[19-21]. The nutritional requirement of C to N is 10:1 and C to P is 30:1.

Table 7.2: Composition of a microbial cell

Element	Percentage	Element	Percentage
Carbon (C)	15	Sodium (Na)	1
Nitrogen (N)	14	Calcium (Ca)	0.5
Oxygen (O)	20	Magnesium (Mg)	0.5
Hydrogen (H)	8	Chloride (Cl)	0,5
Phosphorus (P)	3	Iron (Fe)	0.2
Sulphur (S)	1	All others	0.3
Potassium (K)	1		

Basic Types of Bioremediation Techniques

Biostimulation provides nutrients and suitable physiological conditions for the growth of the indigenous microbial populations. This promotes increased metabolic activity, which then degrades the contaminants. Bioaugmentation means introduction of specific blends of laboratory-cultivated microorganisms into a contaminated environment or into a bioreactor to initiate the bioremediation process. Optimum environmental conditions for the degradation of contaminants are reported in Table 7.3. The process of developing bioremediation techniques may involve the following steps[22]:

- Isolating and characterizing naturally-occurring microorganisms with bioremediation potential.
- Laboratory cultivation to develop viable populations.
- Studying the catabolic activity of these microorganisms in contaminated material through bench scale experiments.
- Monitoring and measuring the progress of bioremediation through chemical analysis and toxicity testing in chemically-contaminated media.

Field applications of bioremediation techniques using either/both steps: *(i)* in-situ stimulation of microbial activity by the addition of microorganisms and nutrients and the optimization of environmental factors at the contaminated site itself. *(ii)* Ex-situ restoration of contaminated material in specifically designated areas by land-forming and composting methods.

Table 7.3: Environmental conditions affected degradation

Parameters	Condition Required for Microbial Activity	Optimum Value for an Oil Degradation
Soil moisture	25-28% of water holding capacity	30-90%
Soil pH	5.5-8.8	6.5-8.0
Oxygen content	Aerobic. Minimum air-filled pore space of 10%	10-40%
Nutrient content	N and P for microbial growth	C:N:P = 100:10:1
Temperature°C	15-45	20-30
Contaminants	Not too toxic	Hydrocarbon 5-10% of dry weight of soil
Heavy metals	Total content 2000ppm	700ppm
Type of soil	Low clay or silt content	

Bioremediation Strategies

Different techniques are employed depending on the degree of saturation and aeration of an area. *In situ* techniques are defined as those that are applied to soil and groundwater at the site with minimal disturbance. Ex situ techniques are those that are applied to soil and groundwater at the site which has been removed from the site via excavation (soil) or pumping (water). Bioaugmentation techniques involve the addition of microorganisms with the ability to degrade pollutants. It frequently involves the addition of microorganisms indigenous or exogenous to contaminated sites. Two factors limit the use of added microbial cultures in a land treatment unit.

1. Non-indigenous cultures rarely compete well enough with an indigenous population to develop and sustain useful population levels.
2. Most soils with long-term exposure to biodegradable waste have indigenous microorganisms that are effective degrades if the land treatment unit is well managed.

- *In situ* bioremediation is generally the most desirable options due to lower cost and fewer disturbances since they provide the treatment in place avoiding exaction and transport of contaminants. *In situ* treatment is limited by the depth of the soil that can be effectively treated in some cases[23-29].
- *Bioventing* is the most common *in situ* treatment and involves supplying nutrients through wells to contaminated soil to stimulate the indigenous bacteria. Bioventing employs low air flow rates and provides only the amount of oxygen necessary for the biodegradation while minimizing volatilization and release of contaminants to the atmosphere. It works for simple hydrocarbons and can be used where the contamination is deep under the surface. In situ biodegradation involves supplying

oxygen and nutrients by circulation aqueous solutions through contaminated soils to stimulate naturally occurring bacteria to degrade organic contaminants. It can be used for soil and groundwater. Generally, this technique includes conditions such as: the infiltration of water-containing nutrients and oxygen or other electron acceptors for groundwater treatment.

- *Biosparging* involves the injection of air under pressure below the water table to increase groundwater oxygen concentrations and enhance the rate of biological degradation of contaminants by naturally occurring bacteria. Biosparging increases the mixing in the saturated zone and thereby increases the contact between soil and groundwater. The ease and low cost installing small-diameter air injection points allows considerable flexibility in the design and construction of the system[30].
- *Ex situ* Bioremediation: This technique involves the excavation or removal of contaminated soil from ground. Land farming is a simple technique in which contaminated soil is excavated and spread over a prepared bed and periodically tilled until pollutants are degraded. The goal is to stimulate indigenous biodegradative microorganisms and facilitate their aerobic degradation of contaminants. In general, the practice is limited to the treatment of superficial 10-35 cm in soil. Since landfarming has the potential ti reduce monitoring and maintenance costs, as well as clean-up liabilities, it has received much attention as a disposal alternative. Composting is a technique that involves combining contaminated soil with nonhazardous organic amendments such as: manure or agricultural wastes. The presence of these organic materials supports the development of a rich microbial population and elevated temperature characteristics of composting. Biopiles are a hybrid of land farming and composting[31-35].

Essentially, engineered cells are constructed as aerated composted piles. Typically used for treatment of surface contamination with petroleum hydrocarbons they are a refined version of landfarming that tend to control physical losses of the contaminants by leaching and volatilization. Biopiles provide a favorable environment for indigenous aerobic microorganisms. Bioreactors-slurry reactors or aqueous reactors are used for ex situ treatment of contaminated soil and water pumped up from a contaminated plume. Bioremediation in reactors involves the processing of contaminated solid material (soil, sediment, sludge) or water through an engineered containment system. A slurry bioreactor mat be defined as a containment vessel and apparatus used to create a three-phase (solid, liquid and gas) mixing condition to increase the bioremediation rate of soil bound and water soluble pollutants as a water slurry of the contaminated soil and biomass (usually indigenous microorganism) capable of degrading target contaminants. In general, the rate and extent of biodegradable are greater in a bioreactor system than in situ or in solid-phase systems because the contained environment is more manageable and hence more controllable and predicable. Despite the advantages of reactors systems, there are some disadvantages. The contaminated soils require pre treatment (*e.g.*, excavation) or alternatively the contaminant can be stripped from the soil via soil washing or physical extraction (*e.g.*, vacuum extraction) before being placed in a bioreactor[36-38].

- *Genetic Engineering Approaches:* The use of genetic engineering to create organisms specifically designed for bioremediation has great potential. The bacterium *Deinococcus radiodurans* (the most radioresistant organism known) has been modified to consume and digest toluene and ionic mercury from highly radioactive nuclear waste. Most commonly, the process is misunderstood. The microbes are ever-present in any given context generally referred to as 'normal microbial flora'. During bioremediation (biodegradation) processes, fertilizers/nutrients supplementation is introduced to the environments, in efforts to maximize growth and production potential. Common misbelieve is that microbes are transported and dispersed into an unadulterated environment. *Micoremediation* is a form of bioremediation in which fungi are used to decontaminate the area. One of the primary roles of fungi in the ecosystem is decomposition, which is performed by mycelium. The mycelium secretes extra cellular enzymes and acids that break down lignin and cellulose, the two main building blocks of plant fibre. These are organic compounds composed of long chain of carbon and hydrogen, structurally similar to many organic pollutants[39-41].

Table 7.4: Reactions and Redox Potentials of some processes

Processes	Reactions	Redox Potentials (Eh in mV)
Aerobic	$O_2 + 4e^- + 4H^+ \rightarrow 2H_2O$	600 ~400
Anaerobic		
Denitrification	$2NO_3^- + 10e^- + 12H^+ \rightarrow N_2 + 6H_2O$	500 ~ 200
Manganese IV reduction	$MnO_2 + 2e^- + 4H^+ \rightarrow Mn^{2+} + 2H_2O$	400 ~ 200
Iron III reduction	$Fe(OH)_3 + 3e^- + H^+ \rightarrow Fe^{2+} + 3H_2O$	300 ~ 100
Sulphate reduction	$SO_4^{--} + 8e^- + 10H^+ \rightarrow H_2S + 4H_2O$	0 ~ 150
Fermentation	$2CH_2O \rightarrow CO_2 + CH_4$	-150 ~ -220

- *Monitoring Bioremediation*: The process of bioremediation can be monitored indirectly by measuring the Oxidation Reduction Potential or redox in soil and groundwater, together with pH, temperature, oxygen content, electron receptor/donor concentrations and concentration of breakdown products *e.g.*, CO_2 (Table 7.4).

Bioremediation of Pesticides in Soil

The process of biologically degrading wastes can be applied to many different types of wastes such as: wastewater, petroleum wastes, solvents, and pesticides. Bioremediation as a whole is focused on accomplishing the following objectives, regardless of the waste to be degraded:

- Oxidation of organic contaminants.
- Biotransformation of organic chemicals into smaller, less toxic constituents.

Reduction of highly electrophilic halo - and nitro - groups by transferring electrons from the contaminant (termed the electron donor) to an electron acceptor to gain energy.

EPA defines a pesticide as any substance or mixture of substances intended for preventing, destroying, repelling or mitigating any pest. Pesticides can be broken into subcategories of herbicides, insecticides, fungicides, virucides, and others according to the targeted pest. Pesticides can be classified by their sources. These classifications include: chemical pesticides, biopesticides, antimicrobials, and pest control devices. Biopesticides contain naturally occurring materials such as: plants, animals, bacteria, and minerals.

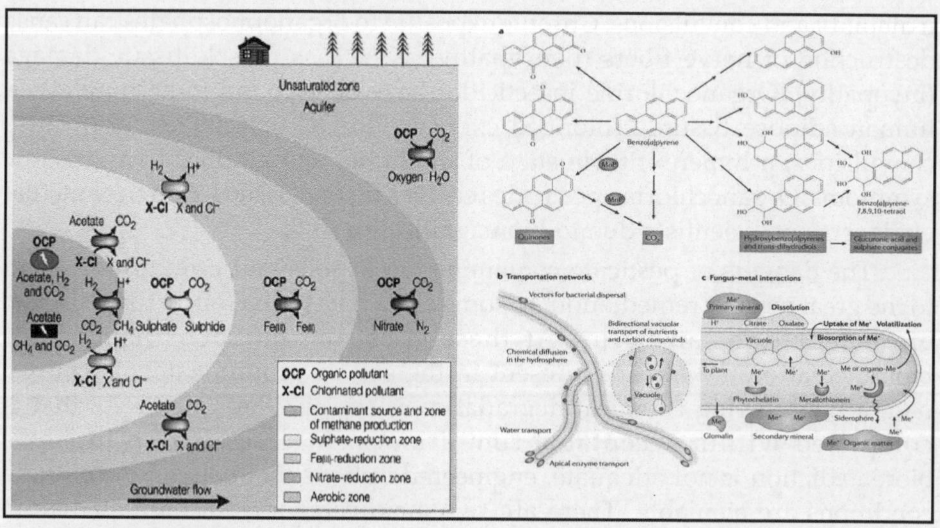

Antimicrobials are pesticides that are used to destroy harmful microorganisms. The final category, pest control devices, includes instruments intended for trapping, destroying, repelling, or mitigating any pest through only physical or mechanical means.). Pesticides are classified by structure. These structural classifications include: organochlorine (OC), organophosphorus (OP), carbamate, cyclodiens and nitrogen-based pesticides, among others. Table 7.5 shows these categories of pesticides and some examples of each category.

Table 7.5: Types of pesticides and examples

Insecticide OP, Carbamate OC, Cyclodienes	Diazinon, dichlorvos, dimethoate, malathion, parathion Carbaryl, propoxur, Aldicarb methiocarb DDT, methoxychlor, toxaphene, mirex, KeponeAldrin, chlordane, dieldrin, endrin, endosulfan, heptachlor.
Herbicides Nitrogen-based Organophosphates	Chlorophenoxy acids, hexachlorobenzene (HCB) Picloram, Atrazine, diquat, paraquat Glyphosate (Roundup).
Fungicide Nitrogen-containing Wood preservatives	Triazines, dicarboximides, phthalimide Creosote, hexachlorobenzene.
Antimicrobial	Chlorine, quaternary alcohols.
Botanicals	Perethrin, permethrine.

Pesticide Concerns

Pesticides are toxic to many organisms and pose a threat to the safety of ground and surface water. The contamination of surface and ground water with pesticides produces many adverse effects on the surrounding ecosystem. Many insecticides function by impeding normal nervous system functions. OC and OP compounds stimulate the nervous system and cause tremors, irritability and convulsions. Chronic exposure to organophosphates can cause destruction of nerve fibers (neuropathy) as well as muscle tissue damage (myopathy). Organochlorine insecticides have been found to accumulate in human adipose tissue. Prolonged exposure to OC insecticides also cause convulsions, a hyperexcitable state of the brain, and cardiac arrhythmiatic symptoms. Organochlorine pesticides create a distinct issue for environmental engineers and scientists due to biomagnifications[34-37].

The dangers of pesticide contamination in soils and groundwater lead to the great need of remediation. In some cases it has been found that intrinsic bioremediation can occur. At these sites, the microbes needed for bioremediation are already present in the soil or groundwater. However, naturally occurring chemical degradation is typically not a process that is completed within acceptable time frames. In cases where intrinsic bioremediation is not adequate, engineered options that better control these conditions are available. There are two main categories of bioremediation methods: *ex-situ* and *in-situ* treatment. In some cases, contaminated soils and water are best treated after being removed from the contamination site. This act of removing and then treating is known as *ex-situ* treatment. The most common processes of *ex-situ* treatment are pump-and-treat, biopile treatment and land farming. The pump-and-treat process is specifically designed to remediate contaminated groundwater. In this process, the contaminated water is removed from the ground and sent to an engineered treatment system. The treatment can occur via activated sludge, a trickling filter, rotating biological contactors, and ion exchange, among other possible systems. Landfarming, as other *ex-situ* treatment methods, involves the excavation and relocation of the contaminated media. The soil is tilled periodically to aerate the waste and remix the active microbes. In this process, several soil conditions are monitored to ensure a high rate of degradation. These criteria include, but are not limited to, moisture content, aeration and pH[36-41].

Throughout the bioremediation process, moisture and nutrients may be added to the soil as needed, and the pH can be controlled by adding crushed limestone or lime. *Ex-situ* bioremediation generally requires a shorter amount of time to be completed than in-situ treatment. Furthermore, ex-situ treatment is easier to control due to the possibility of continuous mixing during treatment. On the other hand, the ex-situ method also requires excavation and a possible increase in labour costs. Some limitations of ex-situ bioremediation drastically affect the feasibility of using this technology. In all *ex-situ* treatments discussed, a large amount of space is required for treatment. In urban areas, this is a viable concern. Volatile contaminants must be either contained or pretreated, as they may volatilize into the air if not monitored, and may cause air pollution. *In-situ,* or in place, treatment can be conducted through several different mediums. One of these mediums is fungi as a degrader of pesticides. The application of white rot fungi for use in pesticide bioremediation has been extensively studied in recent years. In its natural environment, white rot fungi lives on woody tissues that contain lignin, a recalcitrant compound. The white rot fungi contain enzymes necessary to degrade lignin, as well as other toxic and recalcitrant compounds[41-44].

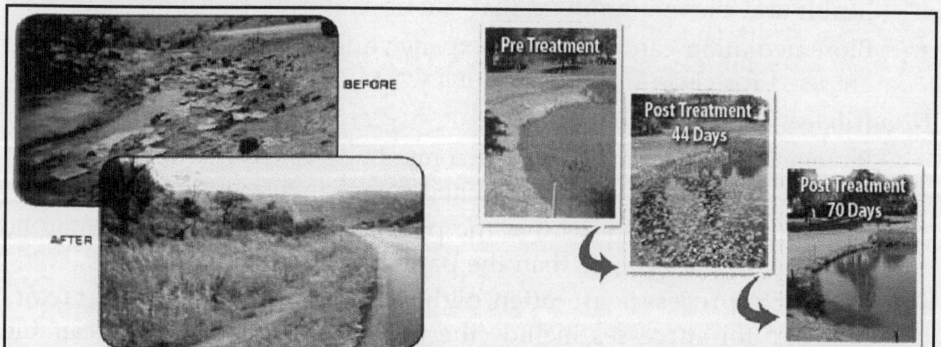

In lab testing, it has been found that this fungi is capable of degrading certain pesticides 45-75 per cent more effectively than control samples. Bioventing is another *in-situ* treatment method for the biodegradation of pesticides. For this method of treatment, injection wells are constructed at the location of contamination. In bioventing, air is injected at a low rate, to supply just enough oxygen to maintain bioremediation. Nutrients and water are generally provided to replace microbial losses throughout the remediation process. N and P are 2 commonly added nutrients. Due to the complex structure of pesticides, they are not as readily biodegraded as some other compounds. Further research needs to be conducted to improve current biodegradation methods. Bioremediation of pesticides are also limited by water and oxygen availability, due to the aerobic nature of the discussed methods[41-46].

Advantages of Bioremediation

Bioremediation is natural process and is therefore perceived by the public as an acceptable waste treatment process for contaminated material such as: soil. Microbes able to degrade the contaminants increase in numbers when the contaminant is present; when the contaminant is degraded, the biodegradative population declines. The residues for the treatment are usually harmless products and include: carbon dioxide, water and cell biomass.

Theoretically, bioremediation is useful for the complete destruction of a wide variety of contaminants.

Many compounds that are legally considered to be hazardous can be transformed to harmless products. This eliminates the chance of future liability associated with treatment and disposal of contaminated material. Instead of transferring contaminants from one environmental medium to another, for example from land to water or air, the complete destruction of target pollutants is possible.

- Bioremediation can often be carried out on site, often without causing a major disruption or normal activities. This also eliminates the need to transport quantities of waste off site and the potential threats to human health and the environment that can arise during transportation.
- Bioremediation can prove less expensive than other technologies that are used for clean-up of hazardous waste.

Disadvatages of Bioremediation

Bioremediation is limited to those compounds that are biodegradable, not all compounds are susceptible to rapid and complete degradation (Table 7.6).

- There are some concerns that the products of biodegradation may be more persistent or toxic than the parent compound.
- Biological processes are often highly specific. Important site factors required for successes include the presence of metabolically capable microbial populations, suitable environmental growth conditions, and appropriate levels of nutrients and contaminants.
- It is difficult to extrapolate from bench and pilot scale studies to full-scale field operations.
- Research is needed to develop and engineer bioremediation technologies that are appropriate for sites with complex mixtures of contaminants that are not evenly dispersed in the environment. Contaminants may be present as solids, liquids and gases.

- Bioremediation often takes longer time than other treatment options, such as: excavation and removal of soil or incineration.
- Regulatory uncertainty remains regarding acceptable performance criteria for bioremediation. There is no accepted definition of 'clean', evaluating performance of bioremediation is difficult, and there are no acceptable endpoints for bioremediation treatments.

Table 7.6: Pros and Cons of Bioremediation

Technology	Examples	Benefits	Limitations	Factors to Consider
In situ	Bioremediation Biosparging Bioventing Bioaugmentation	Most efficient Non-invasive Relatively passive Natural attenuation Process treats soil and water	Environmental constraints Extended treatment time difficulties	Biodegradative abilities of indigenous microorganism Presence of metals and other inorganics Environmental parameters Biodegradability of pollutants Chemical solubility Geological factors Distribution of pollutants
Ex situ	Land farming Composting Biopiles	Cost-efficient Low cost, can be done on site	Space requirements Extended treatment time Need to control abiotic loss Mass transfer problem Bioavailability limitation	As above
Bioreactors	Slurry reactors Aqueous reactors	Rapid degradation Kinetic optimized environmental parameters Enhances mass transfer effective use of inoculants and surfactants	Soil requires excavation Relatively high cost capital Relatively high operating cost	Toxicity of amendments Toxic concentrations of contaminants

Conclusion

The emerging of recent studies in molecular biology and ecology offer opportunities for more efficient biological processes to detoxify contaminants. Notable accomplishments of these studies include the clean-up of polluted water and land areas. Bioremediation is far less expensive than other technologies that are often used to clean up hazardous waste. There are a number of cost or efficiency advantages to bioremediation which can be employed in areas that are inaccessible without excavation. Bioremediation is an option that offers the possibility to destroy or render harmless various contaminants using natural biological activity. As such, it uses relatively low-cost, low-technology techniques, which generally have a high public acceptance and can often be carried out on site. It will not always be suitable. However, as the range of contaminants on which it is effective is limited, the same time scales involved are relatively long, and the residual contaminant levels achievable may not always be appropriate. Bioremediation technology exploits various naturally occurring mitigation processes: natural attenuation, biostimulation, and bioaugmentation. Bioremediation which occurs without human intervention other than monitoring is often called natural attenuation. This natural attenuation relies on natural conditions and behaviour of soil microorganisms that are indigenous to soil.

Although the methodologies employed are not technically complex, considerable experience and expertise may be required to design and implement a successful bioremediation programme, due to the need to thoroughly assess a site for suitability and to optimize conditions to achieve a satisfactory result. Because bioremediation seems to be a good alternative to conventional clean-up technologies research in this field is to be explored with advanced innovations. Furthermore, bioremediation has some disadvantages that are important to investigate. In biodegradation, partial degradation which may result in toxic and potentially volatile products is possible. As with any process that utilizes the natural environment, all conditions cannot be strictly regulated, and these treatment methods results are variable with differing environmental conditions. To ensure acceptable results, extensive monitoring is required throughout the process. Finally, bioremediation of pesticides requires a longer treatment time than other possible detoxifying processes.

REFERENCES

1. Rani, B., Kumar, D., Yadav, R. and Maheshwari R. (2010): *Advances in Applied Biotechnologyand Microbiology*, Chapter No. 19, pp. 117-123.
2. Kensa, V.M. (2011): *Journal of Industrial Pollution Control,* 27 (2):161-168.
3. Rani, B., Choopera, S.L., and Maheshwari, R. (2007): *Journal of Water Land Use Management,* 7 (1):71-81.
4. Singh, P., Rani, B., Chauhan, A.K., Maheshwari, R. and Vyas, M. (2012): *International Journal of Life Sciences Biotechnology and Pharma Research,* 1 (1):32-46.
5. Sims, G.K. (2006): *Soil Biology and Biochemistry* 38:2478-2480.
6. O'Loughlin, E.J., Traina, S.J. and Sims GK. (2000): *Environment Toxicolology and Chemistry* 19:2168-2174.
7. Meagher, R.B. (2000): *Current Opinion in Plant Biology* 3 (2): 153-162.
8. Lovley, D.R. (2003): *Nature Reviews Microbiology* 1 (1): 35-44.
9. Brim, H., McFarlan, S.C., Fredrickson, J.K., Minton, K.W., Zhai, M., Wackett, L.P. and Daly, M.J. (2000): *Nature Biotechnology* 18 (1): 85-90.
10. Tong, A., Peake, B. and Braund, R. (2011): *Environment International* 37: 292-298.
11. Segura, P.A., Francois, M., Gagnon, C. and Sauve, S. (2005): *Environmental Health Perspectives* 117 (5): 675-684.
12. Siegrist, H., Ternes, T.A. and Joss A. (2004): *Journal of Environmental Science and Technology*: 392A-399A.

13. Zheng, W., Yates, S.R. and Bradford, S.A. (2007): *Journal of Environmental Science and Technology* 42, 530-535.
14. Abramowitz, D.A. (1990): *Critical Review in Biotechnology* 10: 241-251.
15. Boyle, A.W., Silvin, C.J., Hasset, J.P., Nakas, J.P. and Tanenbaum, S.W. (1992): *Biodegradation* 3:285-298.
16. Funk, S.B., Roberts, D.J., Crawford, D.L. and Crawford RL. (1993): *Applied Environmental Microbiology* 59:2171-2177.
17. Lamar, R. and Dietrich, D.M. (1990): *Applied Environmental Microbiology* 56:3093-3100.
18. Michel, F.C., Reddy, C.A. and Forney, L.J. (1995): *Applied Environmental Microbiology* 61:2566-2571.
19. Radke, C., Cook, W.S. and Anderson, A. (1994): *Applied Microbiology and Biotechnology* 41:274-280.
20. Quensen, J.F., Boyd, S.A. and Tiedje, J.M. (1990): *Applied Environmental Microbiology* 56:2360-2369.
21. Sondossi, M., Sylvestre, M. and Ahmad, D. (1992): *Applied Environmental Microbiology* 58:485-496.
22. Strom, P.F. (1985): *Applied Environmental Microbiology* 50:899-905.
23. Thomas, D.R., Carswell, K.S. and Georgiou, G. (1992): *Biotechnology Bioengineering* 40:1395-1402.
24. Perfumo, Amedea, Ibrahim, M. Banat, Marchant, R. and Vezzulli, L. (2007): *Chemosphere* 66: 179-184.
25. Rupassara, S.I., Larson, R.A., Sims, G.K. and Marley, K.A. (2002): *Bioremediation Journal* 6 (3): 217-224.
26. Marchiol, L., Fellet, G., Perosa, D. and Zerbi, G. (2007): *Plant Physiology and Biochemistry* 45 (5): 379-87.
27. Wang, J., Zhao, F., Meharg, A.A., Raab, A., Feldmann, J. and McGrath, S.P. (2002): *Plant Physiology* 130 (3): 1552-61.
28. Greger, M. and Landberg, T. (1999): *International Journal of Phytoremediation* 1 (2): 115-123.
29. Meagher, R.B. (2000): *Current Opinion in Plant Biology* 3 (2): 153-162.
30. Mendez, M.O. and Maier, R.M. (2008): *Environ Health Perspect* 116 (3): 278-83.
31. Subramanian, M.O., David, J. and Shanks, J.V. (2006): *Biotechnology Progress* 22 (1): 208-216.
32. Hannink, N., Rosser, S.J., French, C.E., Basran, A., Murray, J.A., Nicklin, S. and Bruce, N.C. (2001). *Nature Biotechnology* 19 (12): 1168-72.
36. Baker, A.J.M. and Brooks, R.R. (1989): *Biorecovery* 1 (2): 81-126.
37. Burken, J., Vroblesky, D. and Balouet, J.C. (2011): *Environmental Science and Technology* 45(15): 6218-6226.
38. Sorek, A., Atzmon, N., Dahan, O., Gerstl, Z., Kushisin, L., Laor, Y., Mingelgrin, U., Nasser, A., Ronen, D., Tsechansky, L., Weisbrod, N. and Graber, E.R. (2008): *Environmental Science and Technology* 42 (2): 536-542.
39. Vroblesky, D., Nietch, C. and Morris, J. (1998): *Environmental Science and Technology* 33 (3): 510-515.
40. Vassil, A.D., Kapulnik, Y., Raskin, I. and Salt, D.E. (1998): *Plant Physiology* 117 (2): 447-53.
41. Salt, D.E., Smith, R.D. and Raskin, I. (1998): *Annual Review of Plant Physiology and Plant Molecular Biology* 49: 643-668.

42. Federal Remediation Technology Roundtable (FRTR). (2006): Remediation Technologies Screening Matrix Reference Guide, Version 4.0.
43. Fragoeiro, Silvia Isabel de Sousa. (2005): Use of Fungi in Bioremediation of Pesticides. *Cranfield University Ph.D. Thesis.*
44. Shanahan Peter. (2004): Bioremediation. *Waste Containment and Remediation Technology, Spring 2004, Massachusetts Institute of Technology, MIT Open Course Ware.*
45. Shannon, M.J. and Unterman, R. (1993): Evaluating Bioremediation: Distinguishing fact from Fiction. *Annual Review of Microbiology* (24):15(24):47.
46. US Microbics. (2003): Annual Report FY-2003. http://www.clu-in.org. Online manual: *Technology Practices Manual of Surfactants and Cosolvents,* CH2MHILL.

Pages: 139-168

WASTE GENERATION AND UTILIZATION

Edited by: **Dr. Priya Bajaj; Dr. B. Tabassum** and **Dr. Pawan Kumar 'Bharti'**

ISBN: 978-93-5056-792-0

Edition: **2016**

Published by: **Discovery Publishing House Pvt. Ltd., New Delhi (India)**

CHAPTER - 8

Impact of Solid Waste on Ecology of Sahastradhara River at Dehradun, India

Jaswant Ray;[1] **Bipin Kumar**[2] and **Pawan Kumar 'Bharti'**[3]

ABSTRACT

Sahastradhara hill-stream is a fast developing tourist spot of north India. Many restaurants, shops, Dhabas and hotels are developed for the needs of tourists. Hotels and restaurants are increasing their number in a tremendous way. Due to the hotels, Dhaba and restaurants, a huge amount of solid waste is generated and dumped openly to a dumping site near crossing bridge (behind Buddha temple).

The preliminary study of solid waste generated at this site was carried out on the basis of percentage composition of materials in solid waste. Besides the solid waste, the amount of sewage is increasing day-by-day due to the increasing number of tourist in Sahastradhara region. The major source of drinking water is the Sahastradhara stream and the sewage ultimately going dumped into the same water body into downstream. Increasing amount of waste may creates many negative impacts to the aquatic ecosystem of river.

1. Research Scholar, Department of Zoology, Mewar University, Chittodgarh, (Rajasthan), India.
2. Department of Zoology, SSN College (University of Delhi), Alipur, Delhi - 110032, India.
3. Society for Environment, Health, Awareness of Nutrition and Toxicology (SEHAT-India), 1775, Sohanganj, Near Clock Tower, Delhi - 110007, India.

The present papers deals with the alteration in water quality and changes in aquatic biodiversity and ecology of river Sahastradhara at Dehradun (Uttarakhand).

Keywords: Sahastradhara river, Solid waste generation, Environmental pollution, Aquatic ecology.

INTRODUCTION

Water is not only essential for life but predominant inorganic constituent of living matter forming in general nearly three quarters of the weight of living cells. It makes some 5 per cent of the body weight of an adult human and can forms as 98 per cent of the mass of certain jellyfish. Organisms that contain relatively small amounts of water are generally in dormant state or show very slow development; seeds and certain invertebrates that live in arid environments are examples (Bharti, 2012). On the other hand high rainfall over a landmass in variably means a large biomass per unit area.

Everything originated in the water and everything is sustained by water all life on earth depends on water. Water is very essential for the survival of all living organism there is a wide variety of beneficial uses of water. Man uses water for many purposes, drinking, irrigation, fisheries, industrial purposes, transportation and waste disposal. The origin of water on the earth is not clear so far. However, the current presumption is that the primordial earth had no oceans and perhaps volatile constituents bound in the earth crust oozing to the surface through volcanoes rock movements and hot springs, condensed to form the ocean and the atmosphere. This way come into being and eventually become an indispensable component of earth's environment.

Modern civilization is dependent on water for irrigation, industry, and domestic needs, shipping and of increasing importance for sanitation and disposal waste. Most of our water bodies such as: ponds, lakes, streams and rivers have become polluted and a consequence of increasing industrialization, urbanization and other development activities. Today many of the rivers of the world revives millions of litter of sewage, domestic wastes and industrial and agriculture effluents containing substances varying form simple nutrients to highly toxic substances *viz;* nitrates, selenium, cadmium, mercury, chlorinated hydrocarbons etc. In U.S.A. every major river has become seriously polluted. The great lakes, which furnish the greatest single sources of water to America and Canada, have already been polluted. Massive pollution turned Rhine into a dead river in the heart of Western Europe.

Himalayas are the cradle of a large number of streams and mighty rivers. Lesser Himalayas consists of a main part of Uttaranchal *i.e.* Kumaon and Garhwal Himalaya. Dehradun, Hardwar and Rishikesh are the main religious and beautiful cities, situated in the foothills of Garhwal Himalaya.

A hill-stream Sahastradhara, a major tributary of river Song flows downward through Dehradun valley. Dehradun valley rests in the arms of the Himalaya in the North and Shiwalik in the South and transversely bordered by Ganga in the South-East. Yamuna in the North-West forms an intermontane valley ecosystem extending from 29° 55′ to 30° 30′ N latitude and 77° 35′ to 78° 20′ E longitude with the area of about 2000 sq km., ranging from 330 meter to 1800 m asl (Valdiya, 1975).

The main sources of water in Himalayas are glaciers. The glaciers are an important resource of fresh water stored in the solid state and regulated by climate. Glacier melts and the water pass through heavy and porous sediment materials in the form of river. Water is the basic requirement of all living organisms. Lotic habitats are those exiting in relatively fast running streams, springs, river and brooks. The lentic habitats represent lakes, marshes, swamps, ponds and wetlands. A hill-stream consists of two major zones, *(i)* Rhithron and *(ii)* Potamon. Aquatic biodiversity is mainly occurring in potamon zone due to the slow velocity of running water.

Water quality characteristic of aquatic environment arise from a multitude of physical, biological and chemical interactions. The water bodies, lakes, rivers, dams and estuaries are continuously subject to a dynamic state of change with respect to the geological age and geochemical characteristics. This is demonstrated by continuous circulation, transformation and accumulation of energy and matter through the medium of living thing and their activities (Adefemi *et al*. 2007).

The dynamic balance in the aquatic ecosystem is upset by human activities, resulting in pollution which meter, is manifested dramatically as fish kill, offensive taste, odour, colour and unchecked aquatic weeds. The over production of higher tropic levels biomass and the subsequent decay of dead plants could lead to oxygen depletion, death of aquatic organisms and development of anaerobic zone where bacteria action produce foul odours and bad tastes (Forstner and Wittman, 1979).

Water quality includes: all physical, chemical and biological factor that influence the beneficial use of water, Lotic habitats are those exiting in relatively fast running streams, springs, river and brooks. The lakes represent lentic habitats; marshes and swamps represent ponds and wetland. The above classification of fresh water environment is based on currents and ratio of the depth of surface area.

The biotic community in the streams and rivers is quite different from that in the ponds, lakes and other stagnant water bodies. The differences in the community are largely due to differences in the physical and chemical conditions of their environments. The physiological changes, adaptations and other characteristics are also entirely different.

A hill-stream consists of two major zones, *(i)* Rithron and *(ii)* Potamon. Aquatic biodiversity is mainly occurring in Potamon zone due to the slow velocity of running water.

In case of industrial units, effluents in most of the cases are discharged into pits, open ground, or open unlined drains near the factories, thus allowing it to move to low-lying depressions resulting in groundwater pollution. The industries, which are burgeoning at a fast rate, produce about 55,000 million m^3 of wastewater per day, out of which 68.5 million m^3 is discharged into river and streams. Thus the magnitude of damage caused to our water resources can be estimated from the fact that about 70 per cent of rivers and streams in India contain polluted water. Therefore, water contaminated by human waste is often discharged directly into watercourses or seeps into the groundwater table from faulty septic tanks or pit latrines. The level of faecal coliform bacteria in most rivers often exceeds the WHO (World Health Organization) standards and is responsible for causing a number of gastrointestinal ailments among the population. All of India's 14 major river systems are heavily polluted, mostly from the 50 million cubic meters of untreated sewage discharged into them each year. The domestic sector is responsible for the majority of the wastewater generation in India. Combined, the 22 largest cities in the country produce over 7267 million litres of domestic wastewater per day, of which slightly over 80 per cent is collected for treatment (Rao and Mamtha, 2004).

Use of fertilizers and pesticides to improve soil fertility and crop protection has created an environmental menace. Both these products find their way into the food chain and have implications on human health. Fertilizers and pesticides have entered the water supply through runoff and leaching to the groundwater table and pose a hazard to human, animal and plant populations. Some of these chemicals such as: hexachlorocyclohexane (HCH), dichlorodiphenyltrichloroethane (DDT), endosulfan, methyl malathion, malathion dimethoate, and ethion are considered as extremely hazardous by the WHO and are banned or are under strict control in developed countries (Rao and Mamtha, 2004). Degradation of water quality creates water scarcity and limits its availability for human use and ecosystem and thereby impacts the optimum management of water resources. Pollution of surface and groundwater resources occurs through point and diffuses sources.

Metals that are naturally introduced into the water body come primarily from such sources as rock weathering, soil erosion, or the dissolution of water-soluble salts. Naturally occurring metals move through aquatic environments independently of human activities, usually without any detrimental effects. Humans consume metallic elements through both water and food. Some metals such as: sodium, potassium, magnesium, calcium, and iron are found in living tissue and are essential to human life biological anomalies arise when they are depleted or removed. Probably less well known is that currently no less than six other heavy metals including molybdenum, manganese, cobalt, copper, and zinc, have been linked to human growth, development, achievement, and reproduction (Vahrenkamp, 1979). Even these metals, however, can become toxic or aesthetically undesirable when their concentrations are too great. Several heavy metals, like: cadmium, lead, and mercury, are highly toxic at relatively low concentrations, can accumulate in body tissues over long periods of time, and are nonessential for human health.

The toxic heavy metals entering the ecosystem may lead to geo-accumulation, bioaccumulation and biomagnifications. Heavy metals like: Fe, Cu, Zn, Ni and other trace elements are important for proper functioning of biological systems and their deficiency or excess could lead to a number of disorders. Food chain contamination by heavy metals has become a burning issue in recent years because of their potential accumulation in biosystems through contaminated water, soil and air. Therefore, a better understanding of heavy metal sources, their accumulation in the soil and the effect of their presence in water and soil on plant systems seem to be particularly important issues of present-day research on risk assessments (Lokeshwari and Chandrappa, 2006).

The water bodies have a complex and fragile ecosystem; however they have self-cleaning ability but excess load always disturb the natural system and therefore readily accumulate pollutants. In some tourist hilly regions, there are not any more industrial pollution, but tourist's anthropogenic activities may alter the water quality of hill-streams and the physico-chemical characteristics of water of some tourist spot may affect the biological diversity of that water body.

Pollutants originating from the anthropogenic activities affect the water chemistry and there by the ability to predict the location and severity of potential impact can be achieved only through knowledge of hydro-chemical processes in pristine waters of similar physico-chemical characteristics. If a sufficiently detailed knowledge has pristine, or baseline, water chemistry is available, the effects of local pollution, stemming from land use and atmospheric deposition of acidic oxides for example can be quantified.

The objectives characterised the water chemistry of these geologically young environments and to determine the nature and degree of anthropogenic impacts on stream ecology and chemistry of a hill-stream. The impact on water chemistry of anthropogenic pollution from industrial, agricultural, sources, quarrying and tourists activity has concerned environmentalists and scientists for the past three decades. In consequences, the chemistry of headwater streams, lakes and lowland rivers has been monitored widely in Europe and North America in an effort to define and quantifying these anthropogenic impacts.

Ecological study of hill-stream describes the distribution and abundance of aquatic living organisms and also their contribution into environment. Biological diversity mainly influenced by the physicochemical characteristics of the aquatic ecosystem through the food chain. The biotic community in the stream exhibited the quantitative and qualitative fluctuations due to varied nutrient dynamics and ultimately changed the different trophic status of species community and limnological status of aquatic ecosystem. Physico-chemical and biological parameters play an important role in population dynamics of phytoplankton, zooplankton, benthos and fishes. Various parameters that affect the population dynamics of phytoplankton may be broadly classified as light intensity, photoperiod, chlorophyll content, nutrient availability, transparency, turbidity, temperature, velocity, water column depth. Light intensity, duration and water column depth are the basic parameters and others are the derived ones.

The present study deals with the impacts of solid waste dumping on heavy metal concentrations in river water, biological diversity, primary productivity and physico-chemical characteristics of stream water, which gives a baseline data about the eco-biological status of river. The purpose of this work is to provide preliminary observations of the ecology of natural water from Sahastradhara river and to make geo-chemical comparison between 'Sahastradhara' water and water from other regions of the country. The present work is aimed towards developing baseline data for river water quality of *'Sahastradhara'* river and to understanding the ecological processes active in Himalayan river water.

Study Area

Sahastradhara is situated 15 km. Far Away from Dehradun in Northeast side. Site is connected by city bus service. This site is main attraction and interesting place for picnic tourist spot. The trickling waters from the nearly caves enhance the scenery; so many people go there to enjoy picnic. Sahastradhara is well known for *sulfur springs* and streams of sulfur water gush out of mountain cavities in a spectacular way, tourist rest house and P.W.D.I/H are available for stay there. Sahastradhara river originated basically from the hills of Mussoorie. Upstream of Sahastradhara is connected with river Badli near village *Karligarh*. River Badli is divided in to two branches *Jhandu Nala* and *Dhadola* at 840-1310 masl.

Geologically, Sahastradhara hills are enriched with limestone. It is also famous for limestone quarrying, which is prohibited by Government after the appeals of M.C. Mehta (1985, *R.L.E case Dehradun vs. state of U.P.*). Geographically, Sahastradhara is situated in the globe on Latitude 29.57° - 31.20° N and Longitude 77.35° - 79.20° E (Bharti, 2004). The water of Sahastradhara is very beneficial for skin disease due to sulfur. Skin disease can be cure after bathing regularly in this water. The downstream of

Sahastradhara meets with Kali Rao, which is mostly dry during study period and quarrying is running regularly in its basin. This stream meets with Song River, which is a tributary of River Ganga.

The famous tourist spot of north India 'Sahastradhara' was selected for the study purpose. The sampling site is situated in Sahastradhara valley, 15 km., far from Dehradun. Five sampling stations were selected along with this stream after significant distances, in which two stations were selected in upstream direction and two in downstream direction.

Sampling Points

The descriptions of selected five sapling locations are given below:

(i) Sampling station S_1 (*Karligarh Village*): This site is situated just 1.5 km., far away (towards upstream) from main tourists spot (Sulfur spring). This is the first upstream sampling site. This site is very close to village Karligarh.

(ii) Sampling station S_2 (*Parking bridge*): This sampling site is just before 700 meter from S_1 site (downward). The velocity of water is more at this site than the other sites. This is the second up stream sampling station. The next sampling point is main tourist spot.

(iii) Sampling station S_3 (*Main tourist spot*): This site is main tourist spot of Sahastradhara due to the sulfur spring. People bath here and dump flower and food materials for fishes such as: bread, rice and supplementary food. This site is just near the 'Drone temple'. Tourists visit here for recreational purpose throughout the year and create anthropogenic activities.

(iv) Sampling S_4 (*Main crossing bridge*): This site is just 500-meter downward form main tourists spot. This is first downstream sampling station near 'God Buddha temple'. People and shopkeepers dump solid waste along with this site. Recently, a solid waste dumping site is developed here due to waste generated by local restaurants, dhabas, shops and hotels.

(v) Sampling station S_5 (*Bus stand*): This is the second downstream and last sampling station just 600-meter downward from crossing bridge or sampling station S_4. After this site, Sahastradhara stream immediately joins Kali Rao River, which is further connected with Song River.

All five stations can be finding in the following maps:

Material and Methods

To assess the water quality of Sahastradhara river, five sampling stations were selected. Water samples were collected in plastic Jericanes and analyzed according to APHA (1995) and Trivedi and Goel (1984) with the help of Atomic absorption spectrophotometer. The details of materials and methods are given below:

Fig. 8.1: **Satellite Imagery of sampling stations at Sahastradhara stream**

Material

Following materials and accessories were used in water sampling:

1. *Sampling bottles*: 300ml capacity BOD bottles were used for collecting the samples. These were washed with chromic acid and then rinse well with tap water followed by rinsing with distilled water. Then these were oven dried at 160° - 180° for 3 hours.

2. *Pipettes*: Pipettes were washed in same manner as in above. All the pipettes used were of Borosil glass certified grade pipettes used were of 1ml capacity (micro pipettes), 5ml capacity and 10ml capacity.
3. *Reagents and Glassware*: Some reagents were taken for on spot analysis and sample preservation. Glassware used in study *viz*; conical flask, beaker, burettes etc., were of Borosil glass certified grade. All the glassware were washed with chromic acid and then rinsed well with tap water and then with distilled water.
4. *Jeri canes*: Jeri cane used for carrying the samples from sampling sites to laboratories. Jeri cane made of plastic and washed well with water and then rinsed well with distilled water.
5. *Chemical bottles*: Some small chemical bottles were used for transporting some necessary chemical urgently required during the sampling for immediately analysis for selected parameters.
6. *Bag*: A bag of large carrying capacity was taken during the sampling for the collection of all water, soil and sediment samples.
7. *Thermometer:* Mercury thermometer was used for on spot measurement of the soil and water samples.
8 *pH meter*: A handy pen pH meter was used for on spot evaluation of the pH of surface water.

Sampling

Grab sampling was generally applied during the sampling. A grab sample is an ordinary sample which is taken from a particular place representing the whole water quality. This type of sample is valid only when it is certain that the water quality is not changing in a short time and effluent discharges, if any, are fairy regular. It is advisable to collect and analyze the grab samples separately at various timings, if the water quality is known to change with time. In such cases the schedule of timings shall be dependent on the frequency of discharge or change in water quality. This approach is used in studies to understand diurnal changes in pH, free CO_2, alkalinity, dissolved oxygen, etc., by collecting a 2 or 3 hour sample round the clock. In any kind of water, at least for dissolved oxygen, several grab samples spread over the whole day or even the night shall be important in limnological study.

The sampling of water from stream banks can be easily carried out using a wide mouthed polythene bottle but a sampler has to be used if the studies are to be undertaken at various strata of water.

Stream water samples were analyzed by standard methods (APHA, 1995; Wetzel, 1975; Trivedi and Goel, 1984 and Santhanam *et al.* 1989). The trace heavy metals were analyzed in the laboratory by Atomic absorption spectrophotometer *AAS 4129 model*.

The samples were taken in BOD bottles and plastic Jeri cane for physical, chemical and heavy metals analysis. Solid waste was evaluated manually and volume density was estimated as per Bharti (2004); and Bharti (2012).

Sample Digestion and Dilution

Samples were collected in Borosil BOD bottles and some Jeri canes for laboratory experiments. Some parameters were determined immediately on sampling sites, for rest parameters and heavy metals; samples were stored in refrigerator at 4°C. Heavy metals may be analyzed in the 6 months period from the preservation date.

Samples were taken in Jeri canes for determination of the parameters like: conductivity, total solids, pH (hydrogen ion concentration), COD, free CO_2, total alkalinity, total hardness Ca/Mg, chlorides, lead, manganese, zinc, calcium and magnesium. Caps of cans were closed tightly after filling up of cane.

For dissolved oxygen/biochemical oxygen demand, samples were collected in sterilized 300 ml capacity BOD bottles. The bottles were filled completely with sample water up to the rim and stopper was placed only avoiding any kind of air bubble inside it. DO was immediately fixed by adding 2 ml each of alkaline potassium iodide and manganese sulphate ($MnSO_4$) at sampling spot. While the sample for BOD was incubated for 5 days in BOD incubator at 20°C.

Collected, preserved, diluted water samples were prepared for the evaluation of metal concentrations with the help of AAS 4129.

Metals enter in the surface water ecosystem through the disposing of waste materials and various. For every metal a standard was required and concentration may be detected by AAS. Diluted and completely digested samples were required for metal detection by AAS 4129. Metal elements were determined with the help of Atomic absorption spectrophotometer (Model AAS 4129). Alan Walsh first developed the technique of atomic absorption spectrophotometry in 1955, and since then it has emerged as a powerful tool in quantitative analysis of more than 70 metals. The major advantages of the method are that it is free from any kind of interferences and very small concentrations are possible to be measured (De, 2002). The AAS is based on the principle that atoms of elements, which normally remain in ground state under flame condition, absorb energy when subjected to radiation of specific wavelength. The absorption of radiation is proportional to the concentration of atoms of the element. The absorption of radiation by the atoms is independent of the wavelength of absorption and temperature of the atoms. These to feature provide AAS a distinct advantage over flame spectroscopy.

Solid Waste near Sahastradhara

Rivers always attract to the people especially nature lovers since the ancient times. People feel harmony, peace and internal satisfaction near the springs, streams or rivers. In the recent time, rivers are the part of tourisms. Many tourist places are established near or very closed to the rivers. Rivers or streams have a very old relation with tourisms not only in India but abroad.

A river basin is made up of a mosaic of contrasting and often competing biophysical, economic and social circumstances, and community interests. Only along limited reaches of a river basin is it possible to identify much commonality of attitude or purpose by the inhabitants. More typically, the segmentation of natural and human components of the basin is reflected in conflicting attitudes towards the single unifying element present – the river system.

Those living upstream tend to value the riverine environment primarily for its aesthetic appeal and perhaps its recreational role, rather than its economic function. Further downstream, the value of water for economic purposes becomes paramount to service agricultural, urban and industrial needs. The emphasis is on maximising the quantity of water available, with some level of biophysical degradation acceptable as a trade-off against economic viability and regional development. In the lower reaches of the basin, the riverine environment is degraded further from contaminated effluent, so that aquatic life, wetlands, estuaries, and the coastal zone, are frequently compromised by eutrophication and sedimentation.

Tourism

Tourism and associated anthropogenic activities may cause effects on water ecosystem and can alter the water quality of that river or stream in many ways. The direct addition or dumping the waste material directly into river water can change many physico-chemical parameters of river water, so that the water quality can degrade drastically after increment in such type of activities and ultimately the entire aquatic ecosystem may disturb. The ecology of river water especially the living organisms of water column may realise the changes in their surrounding environment settings and few of them can show few indication to support or oppose the increasing pollution in the ecosystem. These few species are commonly called as biological indicators of pollution.

During the time of tourist activities especially at hot tourist spots, awareness for environment protection should be increased. Strict rule and regulations should be adopted for all individuals. Anthropogenic activities, which accelerated the rate of pollution or environmental degradation, should be avoided or banned or appropriate alternate should be adopted in those cases. A significant amount of solid waste has been generated along with Sahastradhara river as it is a fast growing tourist place near Dehradun.

Anthropogenic Activities

Water is an important substance required by all living organisms and for all anthropogenic activities. The problem of environmental pollution due to toxic metals has begun to cause concern now in most major metropolitan cities (Bharti, 2007a). Most of our water resources are gradually becoming polluted due to the addition of foreign materials from the surroundings. These include organic matter origin from plant and animal, land surface washing, Industrial and sewage effluents.

In some tourist hilly regions, there are not any more industrial pollution, but tourist's anthropogenic activities may alter the water quality and the water quality of lakes of some tourist spot may affect the water quality of that water body.

These are the major human activities which were observed during the study period in Sahastradhara region:

- Dispersion of Polythene wrappers.
- Generation of feacal material.
- Clothes washing.
- Mass bathing.
- Addition of food materials directly into stream water.
- Development of a solid waste dumping site near fourth site.
- Vehicle movement.
- Interference with vegetation composition.

Solid waste Generation

Sahastradhara hill-stream is a fast developing tourist spot of north India. Many restaurants, shops, Dhabas and hotels are developed for the needs of tourists. Hotels and restaurants are increasing their number in a tremendous way. Due to the hotels, Dhaba and restaurants, a huge amount of solid waste is generated and dumped near fourth sampling site (very closed to Buddha temple).

The manual study of solid waste generated at this site was carried out on the basis of percentage composition of materials in solid waste.

Table 8.1: Per cent composition of solid waste for various category waste materials

S.No.	Material	% Composition
1.	Wood products and woody toys	20
2.	Plastic and polythene	22
3.	Cartoons and papers	28
4.	Leaves and straw	8
5.	Waste Food materials	10
6.	Hairs and bones	5
7.	Glass and metals	3
8.	Ash	2
9.	Others	2

So, the major degradable material was wood products, papers, leaves, waste food and ash and the contribution of degradable materials into total solid waste is 68 per cent. The degradable material will never create a problem in near future, but rest 32 per cent of non-degradable solid waste will certainly harmful for the health of Sahastradhara river and its water quality also.

Table 8.2: Per cent composition of solid waste

S.No.	Material	% Composition
1.	Degradable	68
2.	Non-degradable	32

Besides the solid waste, the amount of sewage is increasing day-by-day due to the increasing number of tourist in Sahastradhara region. The major source of drinking water is the Sahastradhara stream and the sewage ultimately going dumped into the same water body into downstream. Increasing amount of waste may creates many negative impacts to the aquatic ecosystem of river.

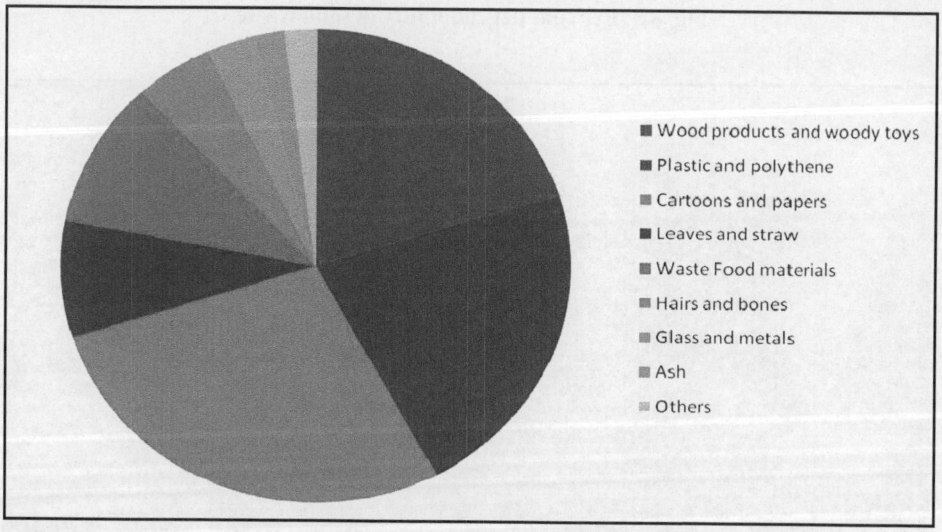

Fig. 8.2: **Per cent composition of solid waste**

Traffic Density

The study area is a fast developing tourist place near Dehradun. A large number of tourists are visited here throughout the year, and this number is going increase every year. Tourists, generally used the bus service, but sometimes, they prefer their vehicle for their comfortableness. So, the numbers of vehicle are also increasing day-by-day. Vehicle plays an important role in this fast going era, so that every person uses the vehicle and contributes to traffic volume density. Expensive and luxury vehicles are the mark of prestigious in the fashionable time. So, few persons are using vehicle only for the purpose.

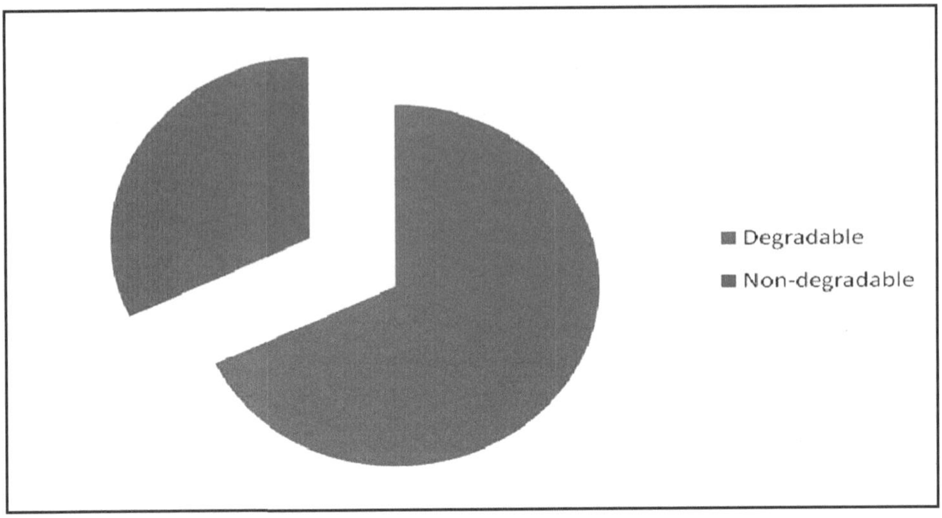

Fig. 8.3: **Per cent degradability of solid waste**

Fig. 8.4: **A scene of mass bathing in Sahastradhara river**

A B

C D

Fig. 8.5 (A-D): **Few anthropogenic activities near Sahastradhara river**

Vehicle volume is season dependable. A study was conducted for the evaluation of traffic load in Dun valley during the day times and nighttime in winter, summer and rainy seasons. A two days based survey was carried out for the assessment of traffic volume density in Sahastradhara Valley. Season-wise data is given for all type of vehicles (Bharti, 2012).

Table 8.3: Traffic Volume density in daytime (6.00 AM to 6.00 PM)

S.No.	Vehicle Type	Winter	Summer	Rainy
1.	Trucks and tankers	10	15	8
2.	Buses	10	12	9
3.	Tractors and trailers	8	11	6
4.	JCBs and Earth Moving	5	6	2
5.	Jeeps and Sumo type	10	17	4
6.	Three wheeler	6	11	3
7.	Bikes and scooter	15	23	5
8.	Bicycle	4	7	2

Table 8.4: Traffic Volume density in nighttime (6.00 PM to 6.00 AM)

S.No.	Vehicle Type	Winter	Summer	Rainy
1.	Trucks and tankers	1	3	0
2.	Buses	0	1	0
3.	Tractors and trailers	0	2	0
4.	JCBs and Earth Moving	0	1	2
5.	Jeeps and Sumo type	1	2	0
6.	Three wheeler	0	1	0
7.	Bikes and scooter	1	6	0
8.	Bicycle	0	1	0

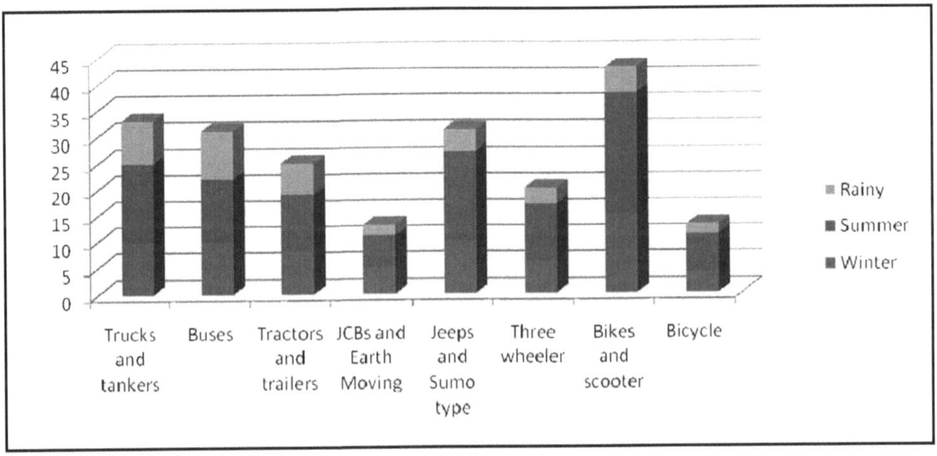

Fig. 8.6: **Traffic density in day hours**

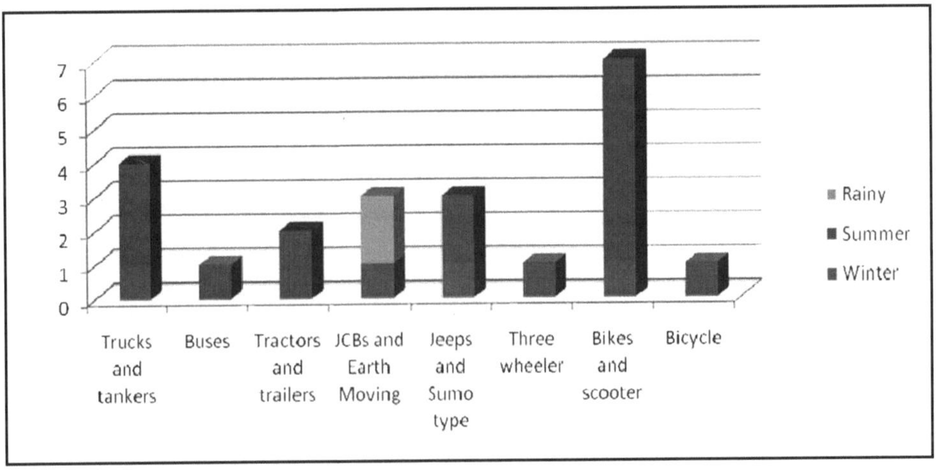

Fig. 8.7: **Traffic density in night hours**

Impact on River Ecology

The impact on water quality of anthropogenic pollution from industrial, agricultural, sources, quarrying and tourists activity has concerned environmentalists and scientists for the past two decades. Plankton is the primary producer of any aquatic ecosystem, which can be as an indicator of water quality. Dissolved oxygen is decreases or increases in an aquatic ecosystem due to the plankton. Plankton takes sunlight directly and makes food for the total ecosystem through the photosynthesis process. Plankton may vary at place-to-place and season-to-season.

Temperature plays a vital role in all physico-biochemical reactions and self-purification power of aquatic system. Organic matter, which is oxidized, is highly influenced by the temperature. Temperature fluctuation measurement is useful to determine the trends of bio-chemical and biological activities. The Sahastradhara stream has a difference in the fluctuation of water temperature was recorded maximum (17.7°C ± 0.4) in the month of May and minimum (13.1°C ± 0.66) in January. The temperature of water decreases form September and increases from January onward. Badola and Singh (1981) observed similar trend in the river Alaknanda in the Garhwal region. The maximum value of velocity of Sahastradhara stream was recorded in the month of May (0.64m/s ± 0.257) and minimum (0.58m/s ± 0.1315) in December. During the study period it has been observed that form January onward the velocity starts increasing up to April. Similar observation has been recorded by Joshi *et al.* (1995) in western Ganga canal at Hardwar.

The seasonal fluctuation of pH depends chiefly on amount of free carbon-dioxide, which is ultimately related to the rate of photosynthesis and also the decomposition of organic matter. The pH of natural water was controlled in a greater extent by the interaction of hydroxyl ions, resulting form the dissociation of carbonic acid and form hydroxyl ion arising from the hydrolysis of bicarbonate. In this study, it was recorded that the pH was always slightly alkaline. The pH of stream water was recorded highest (8.02 ± 0.1166) in December and lowest (7.4 ± 0.1414) in the month of April. Various workers in their studies have shown similar results in other rivers of Garhwal region. Sharma (1986) has also indicated the same trend of pH values on seasonal basis in the Bhagirathi River, Garhwal Himalayas.

The dissolved oxygen showed an inverse relationship with temperature as reposted by Das and Srivastava (1956) and Dobriyal (1985). The dissolved oxygen in water is often attributed to the fact that the oxygen is dissolved more during the period of active photosynthesis. Hutchinson (1957) reported that when the water has low temperature has greater capacity for holding dissolved gases. The highest value of dissolved oxygen was recorded (9.85 mg/l ± 0.776) in the month of January and the lowest value of dissolved oxygen was observed (6.68 mg/l ± 0.387) in the month of May.

Table 8.5: Physical parameters of Sahastradhara stream

Parameters	Site - I	Site - II	Site - III	Site - IV	Site - V
Temperature (°C)	15.75±1.14	15.37±1.63	15.0±1.41	15.75±1.6	15.75±2.277
(Range)	(14 - 18)	(13 - 17.5)	(13 - 17)	(13.5 - 18)	(12 - 18)
Velocity (m/s)	0.3±0.14	0.9±0.1	0.35±0.05	0.8±0.02	0.65±0.05
(Range)	(0.3 - 0.4)	(0.28 - 0.32)	(0.8 - 1.0)	(0.78 - 0.82)	(0.6 - 0.7)
Turbidity (JTU)	2.75±1.47	3.25±1.30	4.5±1.15	3.75±1.48	4.75±1.48
(Range)	(1.0 -5.0)	(2.0 - 5.0)	(3.0 - 6.0)	(2.0 - 6.0)	(3.0 - 7.0)
Total solids (mg/l)	1218±183.2	1234.2±89.8	1277.25±122.6	1305.7±166.1	1290.75±146.1
(Range)	(955 - 1427)	(1090 - 1332)	(1115 - 1443)	(1135 - 1520)	(1148 - 1535)
TDS (mg/l)	1093.25±175	1094.25±120.5	1140.5±134.6	1189±158.01	1134.25±176.1
(Range)	(840 - 1278)	(895 - 1217)	(1010 - 1322)	(1039 - 1380)	(965 - 1420)
TSS (mg/l)	124.75±14.39	140.0±28.16	136.75±40.95	116.75±13.8	156.5±41.69
(Range)	(113 - 149)	(119 - 195)	(105 - 207)	(105 - 140)	(115 - 211)

This trend was also stated by Khanna *et al.* (1992) in Ganga river at Hardwar. The higher value of dissolved oxygen during winter months can be attributed to increased solubility of oxygen at lower water temperature and high photosynthetic rate.

Free carbon dioxide released during the decomposition of certain substances and respiration of living organism since higher temperature accelerate the decomposition of organic substances as well as the respiratory activity of the biota and shown direct relationship between the water temperature and free carbon dioxide (Hynes, 1970). The maximum value of free carbon dioxide was observed (2.2 mg/l ± 0.155) in May and minimum value in January (1.70 mg/l ± .066). Free carbon dioxide and dissolved oxygen showed a negative relationship to each other. The similar observations have also been reported by Quadri and Shah (1989) in some fresh water ecosystem. The highest rate of photosynthesis decreases free carbon-dioxide content and higher rate of decomposition increases free carbon dioxide. An inverse relationship between dissolved oxygen and free carbon-dioxide has been reported by Khan and Siddiqui (1971).

Chloride was found in form of chloride ion, and one of the major inorganic anions present in natural water. The maximum chloride concentration was recorded (17.14mg/l ± 1.33) in the month of May and minimum in the month of January (11.36 mg/l ± 2.008), chloride and hardness showed a positive relationship to one another. Chopra and Patrick (1994) also stated similar trend in aquatic ecosystem in the river Ganga at Rishikesh. The maximum calcium concentration was observed (15.99mg/l ± 5.53) in the month of May while the minimum value of calcium was observed (80.336mg/

l ± 2.64) in the month of January. Similar type of relationship of calcium was observed by Ahemad and Hasnain (2001) in fresh water bodies. Khanna and Singh (2000) also reported similar trend of calcium distribution in river Suswa, Raiwala, Dehradun. Sahastradhara stream may be regarded as rich in calcium and other geochemical nutrients. Calcium is one of the essential nutrients, which plays an important role in biological system. In fact, Calcium content in water is responsible for bone growth of children.

Magnesium is also an essential and beneficial element, but it is toxic at higher concentration. The recommended acceptable limit of magnesium for domestic purpose is 30mg/l in the river. The amount of magnesium in the river Sahastradhara was found maximum (57.2mg/l ± 7.24) in the month of May while the minimum value of magnesium was recorded (52.2mg/l ± 6.55) in the month of January. Castante *et al.* (1985) in river Parana and Meybeck (1984) in river Zaire also reported similar trend of magnesium availability in natural water.

Table 8.6: Chemical parameters of Sahastradhara stream

Parameters	Site - I	Site - II	Site - III	Site - IV	Site - V
pH	7.625±0.43	7.6±0.28	7.75±0.15	7.75±1.66	7.6±0.339
(Range)	(7.2 - 8.1)	(7.3 - 8.1)	(7.5 - 7.9)	(7.6 - 8.0)	(7.2 - 8.1)
Free CO2 (mg/l)	1.6525±0.39	1.75±0.017	1.825±0.25	1.74±0.09	1.87±0.21
(Range)	(1.40 - 1.69)	(1.62 - 1.92)	(1.62 - 2.20)	(1.65 - 1.85)	(1.62 - 2.20)
D O (mg/l)	8.41±1.62	8.46±1.18	8.65±0.95	7.55±0.87	7.49±1.36
(Range)	(7.04 - 11.08)	(6.84 - 10.07)	(7.04 - 9.47)	(6.04 - 9.06)	(6.04 - 9.47)
BOD (mg/l)	1.875±0.162	1.98±0.23	2.25±0.18	2.0±0.14	2.05±0.15
(Range)	(1.60 - 2.0)	(1.7 - 2.2)	(2.0 - 2.5)	(1.8 - 2.2)	(1.9 - 2.3)
COD (mg/l)	2.55±0.32	2.6±0.25	2.9±0.22	2.68±0.22	2.7±0.18
(Range)	(2.1 - 3.0)	(2.2 - 2.9)	(2.6 - 3.2)	(2.4 - 3.0)	(2.4 - 2.9)
Hardness (mg/l)	196.25±8.2	200.0±15.41	222.5±19.2	200.0±18.71	198.75±21.02
(Range)	(190 - 210)	(185 - 220)	(200 - 250)	(180 - 230)	(185 - 235)
Alkalinity (mg/l)	250.0±134.7	262.5±140.8	305±172.1	292.5±168.8	317.5±175.2
(Range)	(150 - 480)	(140 - 500)	(170 - 600)	(130 - 570)	(120 - 540)

Sodium at lower concentration has no adverse effect on human health. The maximum sodium concentration was recorded (9.44 mg/l ± 1.016) in the month of May and minimum value of sodium was observed (7.1mg/l ± 0.663) in the month of January. Pande and Mishra (2000) observed similar results on Sahastradhara stream. Sodium is one of the most common cation present in the water bodies. Potassium is naturally occurring elements, like: the sodium, however its concentration remains lower than sodium. The potassium is released by the clay mineral, weathering and leaching form the growing vegetation and decomposition of organic matter. Potassium concentration was observed highest in the month of May (17.2 mg/l ± 0.67) and lowest in the month of January (15.2 mg/l ± 0.812). Similar results were obtained by Sarin *et al.* (1989) and Subramanian (1989) observed the similar trend on the river Brahmaputra.

The quantitative fluctuation of the planktonic diversity has shown a significant effect on the ecology of river. All natural water contains a variety of plankton as the natural flora and fauna. The phytoplankton community is a heterogeneous group of tiny plants adapted to suspension in the fresh water. The present study showed that the maximum number of total plankton were recorded (1523.6 ± 26.56) in the month of January and minimum (718.6 ± 19.33) in the month of May.

Phytoplankton was recorded maximum (1371 ± 25.77) in the month of January and minimum (633 ± 9.32) in the month of May. Eddy (1993) pointed out that plankton production is mainly influenced by temperature. Badola and Singh (1981) reported high values of plankton during January to March in freshwater of Kumaon Lake. According to Das and Pathani (1978) increment in turbidity will reduces the plankton production in a water body due to low light penetration and low rate of photosynthesis. According to Khanna (1993) the plankton were maximum in the month of winter probably due to low temperature, high content of dissolved oxygen low velocity and transparency of water and other suitable conditions. Allen (1920) stated that water currant is the chief factor influencing the plankton of stream San Joaquin River and its tributaries near Stockton in California.

Zooplankton were recorded maximum (152.6 ± 13.00) in the month of December and minimum (82 ± 13.02) in the month of May. Total diatoms were recorded maximum (1048.8 ± 34.02) in the month of January and minimum (495 ± 9.25) in the month of April. Green algae were recorded maximum (241.2 ± 29.77) in the month of January and minimum (106.4 ± 6.28) in the month of May. Blue Green algae was recorded maximum (81 ± 4.05) in the month of January and minimum (27.6 ± 3.98) in the month of May. Juttner *et al.* (1995) also reported the similar trend of diatom communities in Himalayan Hill Streams. Similar observations have been reported by Khanna *et al.* (1998) in relation to phytoplanktonic communities of Ganga canal at Haridwar. Khanna and Singh (2000) also reported the similar trend of planktonic diversity in Suswa River, Raiwala, Dehradun. Similar observations were also reported by Nautiyal (1982) in Alaknanda River and Khanna (1993) in river Ganga at Hardwar.

Table 8.7: Major elements of Sahastradhara stream

Parameters	Site - I	Site - II	Site - III	Site - IV	Site - V
Chloride *(mg/l)* (Range)	12.78±1.73 (11.36 - 15.62)	13.73±1.93 (11.36 - 16.58)	15.26±2.1 (12.78 - 18.46)	13.49±3.25 (9.94 - 18.46)	11.6±3.06 (8.52 - 16.58)
Calcium *(mg/l)* (Range)	84.67±3.58 (80.16 - 88.17)	85.67±4.28 (80.160 - 92.184)	91.68±10.13 (77.154 - 104.21)	89.18±8.26 (79.158-99.19)	88.43±6.19 (80.16 - 96.19)
Magnesium *(mg/l)* (Range)	48.66±3.09 (45 - 53)	57.33±3.29 (55 - 62)	64.66±2.36 (63.0 - 68.0)	55.33±2.49 (52.0 - 28.0)	51.0±5.29 (45.0 - 55.0)
Sodium *(mg/l)* (Range)	7.375±0.96 (6 - 8.5)	7.725±0.506 (7.0 - 8.2)	8.75±0.75 (8.0 - 9.5)	8.87±1.14 (7.0 - 10.0)	9.25±1.35 (7.5 - 11.0)
Potassium *(mg/l)* (Range)	15.13±0.74 (14 - 16)	15.75±0.901 (14.5 - 17.0)	16.62±0.65 (16.0 - 17.5)	16.5±0.79 (15.5 - 17.5)	17.0±1.35 (16.0 - 18.0)

It is well established that the primary productivity is controlled by several physico-chemical and biotic interactions. The rate of production of organic mater per unit time is termed as productivity. There are two levels of production, primary and secondary. The amount of new organic matter resulting from photosynthesis is termed as primary productivity. The animal and plant communities inhabiting water bodies are considered as the direct manifestation of the productivity. The maximum net primary productivity was observed (0.335 ± .093) in the month of December and minimum (0.170 ± .04) in the month of May. The maximum gross primary productivity was observed (.796 ± .123) in the month of January and minimum (.569 ± .0379) in the month of May. The maximum net community respiration was observed (.479 ± .0575) in the month of January and minimum (.399 ± .0102) in the month of April. The higher productivity in the present studied was concomitant with temperature range from 14°C to 18°C. Singh and Swaroop (1980) observed positive correlation with productivity and water temperature. A positive correlation existed between gross primary productively and calcium in Cavery (Lakshminarayan, 2001). Vashney *et al.* (1983) present study a positive correlation was recorded between gross primary productivity and dissolved oxygen while the negative correlation between gross primary productivity and temperature and free carbon dioxide.

Net production efficiency shows the positive correlation with dissolved oxygen, while the negative correlation between net production efficiency and carbon dioxide. The maximum mean value of net production efficiency was observed (43.79%) in the month of January and minimum (29.88%) in the month of April. Similar trend was observed by Yeragi and Shaikh (2003) on the primary productivity of Tansa River. Singh *et al.* (1980) and Kar *et al.* (1978) however, recorded low and high productivity in summer and winter respectively.

Table 8.8: Planktonic diversity of Sahastradhara stream

Parameters	Site - I	Site - II	Site - III	Site - IV	Site - V
Total plankton (n/l) (Range)	1130.25±316.8 (700 -1540)	1133±316 (725 - 1525)	1101.5±323.9 (693 - 1480)	1063.75±346.9 (700 - 1490)	1163.25±339.4 (730 - 1583)
Phytoplankton (n/l) (Range)	1018.25±286.1 (625 - 1380)	1023.75±291.5 (635 - 1380)	992.5±296.3 (615 - 1345)	951.25±318.2 (635 - 1340)	1037.5±259.5 (640 - 1410)
Zooplankton (n/l) (Range)	112±31.61 (75 - 160)	109.25±27.09 (77 - 145)	109±28.6 (78 - 140)	112.5±31.72 (65 - 150)	125.75±36.66 (90 - 173)
Total diatoms (n/l) (Range)	764.75±206.6 (492 - 1022)	784.5±218.5 (645 - 1015)	772.25±247.3 (480 - 1064)	732.5±236.5 (495 - 1035)	807±250.5 (495 - 1108)
Green algae (n/l) (Range)	190.5±59.86 (105 - 275)	179.5±64.96 (98 - 278)	161±40.72 (102 - 205)	164.5±57.21 (105 - 228)	157.5±50.13 (102 - 220)
Blue green algae (n/l)(Range)	63±24.53 (21 - 83)	57.25±21.57 (27 - 87)	59.25±17.72 (33 - 76)	54.25±25.86 (27 - 83)	58±32.04 (23 - 97)

Table 8.9: Primary productivity of Sahastradhara stream

Parameters	Site - I	Site - II	Site - III	Site - IV	Site - V
Net primary productivity (mg/l) (Range)	0.271±.069 (0.200 - 0.355)	0.220±.0215 (0.200 - 0.255)	0.336±.108 (0.140 - 0.500)	0.231±.086 (0.105 - 0.320)	0.265±.0522 (0.200 - 0.330)
Gross primary productivity (mg/l)(Range)	0.6925±.074 (0.605 - 0.805)	0.640±.0776 (0.600 - 0.705)	0.716±.1344 (0.550 - 1.01)	0.729±.0975 (0.505 - 0.900)	0.676±.0826 (0.580 - 0.810)
Community respiration (mg/l)(Range)	0.420±.0184 (0.405 - 0.450)	0.420±.0635 (0.400 - 0.450)	0.421±.0394 (0.390 - 0.480)	0.498±.156 (0.400 - 0.580)	0.411±.0375 (0.380 - 0.480)
Net production efficiency (%) (Range)	38.77±4.7 (33.05 - 44.09)	34.29±1.101 (33.33 - 36.17)	44.15±15.56 (25.45 - 66.66)	30.485±6.445 (20.79 - 37.03)	38.87±3.069 (34.48 - 42.55)

Sahastradhara stream has a wide biodiversity of small invertebrates, including some benthos, nekton, phytoplankton, zooplankton, which maintain the water quality of aquatic ecosystem. Planktonic genus and other fauna available in the water of Sahastradhara hill stream at Dehradun depicted in Table 8.10.

The endemic fish species about 18 in number occurs in the natural aquatic system of Sahastradhara (Table 8.11). Among these, four to six species may be undertake as sport fishery to enhance or attract the fish anglers on the tourist sites. The limnological and biological status of Sahastradhara stream have shown optimum suitable environment to accelerate the growth and population of endemic fish diversity. There has taken place to increasing use of aquatic resources to cater the needs of tourism. As the present conditions are in sites development of these water bodies has to be taken up for the protection of natural habitats and rehabilitate as fish sanctuaries. The transplantation of healthy stocks of desirable sport fishes have to be done on scientific lines on the basis of optimum biological productivity of the stream. The conservation and management of aquatic ecosystem of hill streams should involve the management of aquatic life including fishes and multiplicity of uses of a whole ecosystem as amenity, ecotourism etc.

Table 8.10 Preliminary study of biotic communities in Sahastradhara stream

Family/Phylum	Genus/Species
Flora: A) Chorophyceae B) Bacillariophyceae C) Rhodophyceae D) Cyanophyceae-	*Ulothrix, Volvox, Cladophora, Chlorella, Vaucheria, Zygnema, Pediasterum Diatoms Batrachospermun Rivularia, Nostoc*
Fauna: A) Protozoans- B) Coelentrata- C) Annelida- D) Arthropods- E) Macroinvertibrate-	*Vorticalla, Amoeba, Paramoecium, Chrysamocha, Volvox Hydra, Ceratella Pheretima Mayfly nymph Snails, Leeches, Flatworms, Beetles*

Table 8.11: Fish diversity in Sahastradhara hill-stream at Dehradun

Scientific Name (Genus/Species)	Local Name
Schizothorax richardsonii (Gray)	Asella
Schizothorax plagiostomus	Dhibrua
Schizothorax sinatus	Maseen
Puntius chola (Ham.)	–
Puntius hexasticus	Khront
Barilius barila (Ham.)	
Barilius bendelisis (Ham.)	Chal
Barilius vagra (Ham.)	Chal
Noemacheilus savona (Ham.)	–
Glyptothorax pectinopterus (McClell.)	–
Mastacembelus armatus (Lac.)	–
Garra lamta (Ham.)	–
Garra gotyla gotyla (gray)	Gunthala
Danio devario (Ham.)	Patukari
Chagunia chagunio (Ham.)	Gelhari
Botia durlo (Ham.)	Baghaua
Chipisoma garua (Ham.)	Raikari
Colisa fasciatus (Block and Schn.)	Khosti

Heavy metals in the water of Sahastradhara hill-stream were detected in very low concentration while upper sites has water free with some metallic contents due to the absence of anthropological activities. However, the area is free from industrial pollution, but due to the increasing tourist activities the water quality is going deteriorate since last few years in a tremendous way. Heavy Metals concentrations are given in Table 8.12 and the increasing trend of Heavy Metals concentrations is indicated by the Fig. 8.8.

Table 8.12: Heavy Metals at all five locations at Sahastradhara stream (ppm)

S.No.	Parameter	Site - I	Site - II	Site - III	Site - IV	Site - V
1.	Cadmium	0.00	0.00	0.00	0.00	0.01
2.	Copper	0.00	0.00	0.00	0.01	0.01
3.	Iron	0.65	0.69	0.72	0.85	1.00
4.	Lead	0.00	0.00	0.01	0.02	0.03
5.	Manganese	0.04	0.06	0.08	0.16	0.21
6.	Zinc	0.01	0.01	0.02	0.03	0.05

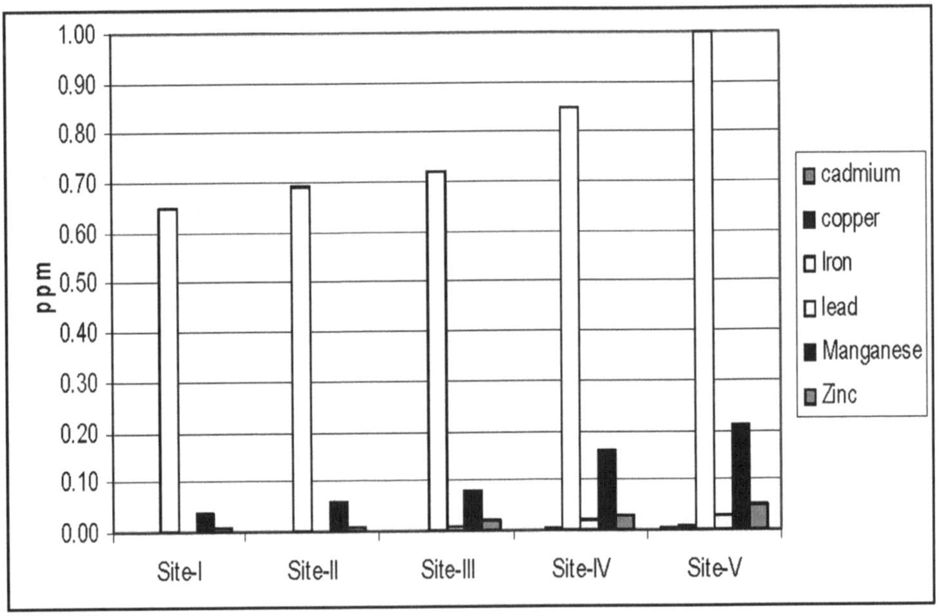

Fig. 8.8: **Showing the Heavy Metals concentrations at various sampling stations**

Heavy Metals were found almost nil or in very low concentrations at all selected site. Heavy Metals like: Cadmium, copper, lead were not found in high concentration at all sites during the study period. Cadmium, copper and lead were absolutely absent in upstreams, while Manganese, Zinc and Iron concentrations were found within the limit in upstream samples. The concentration of iron was maximum observed 1.0 mg/l at fifth station. Lead was found maximum 0.03 mg/l at last downstream site and Zinc concentration was 0.05 mg/l. Malik *et al.* (2009) described the role of Heavy Metals in the surface water of north India. The results of Bharti *et al.* (2010) were also indicated the relation of Heavy Metals with some biological agents in a north Indian water body.

Pollutant sources especially non-point sources of lotic systems are hard to control because they derive, often in small amounts, over a very wide area and enter the system at many locations along its length. Agricultural fields often deliver large quantities of sediments, nutrients, and chemicals like various pesticides to nearby streams and rivers. Urban and residential areas can also add to this pollution when contaminants are accumulated on impervious surfaces such as: roads and parking lots that then drain into the system. Elevated nutrient concentrations, especially nitrogen and phosphorus which are key components of fertilizers, can increase periphyton growth, which can be particularly dangerous in slow moving streams. Another pollutant, acid rain, forms from sulfur dioxide and nitrous oxide emitted from factories and power stations. These substances readily dissolve in atmospheric moisture and enter lotic systems through precipitation. This can lower the pH of these sites, affecting all trophic levels from algae to vertebrates. Mean species richness and total species numbers within a system decrease with decreasing pH. While direct pollution of lotic systems has been greatly reduced in the United States under the government's Clean Water Act, contaminants from diffuse, non-point sources, remain a large problem.

Beside these, few other anthropogenic activities like: dams construction alter the flow, temperature, and sediment regime of lotic systems. Additionally, many rivers are dammed at multiple locations, amplifying the impact. Dams can cause enhanced clarity and reduced variability in stream flow, which in turn cause an increase in periphyton abundance. Invertebrates immediately below a dam can show reductions in species richness due to an overall reduction in habitat heterogeneity. Also, thermal changes can affect insect development, with abnormally warm winter temperatures obscuring cues to break egg diapause and overly cool summer temperatures leaving too few acceptable days to complete growth. Finally, dams fragment river systems, isolating previously continuous populations, and preventing the migrations of anadromous and catadromous species.

Conclusion

Sahastradhara hill-stream ecosystem has suitable conditions for the habitation and survival of different biotic communities including plankton, nekton and benthos. In the Sahastradhara hill-stream Calcium and Magnesium level is high especially in the summer season. All the parameters studied had minor differences at different sites during the observation. Water quality of

Sahastradhara stream has widely affected by tourists activities hence industrial pollution is no more here. Primary productivity is high in winter season whereas production efficiency was influenced by various physico-chemical parameters at different sampling sites.

The sampling site is situated in Sahastradhara valley, 15 km., far from Dehradoon, selected five sampling station along with stream for limnological study. The water samples were collected monthly from different sampling site s_1, s_2, s_3, s_4 and s_5 during 2003 to 2004 in morning period (from 9.00 am to 11.00 pm). First upstream S_1 (Karligarh village), second upstream S_2 (Parking bridge), main tourist spot S_3 (Sulphur Spring), first down steam S_4 (Crossing bridge) and second downstream S_5 (Bus stand) were the sampling stations with a distance of about 1 km for each. The samples were taken in BOD bottles and plastic Jeri cane for physical, chemical and biological parameters. The samples for different parameter were analyzed with the help of the procedure described by Mark (1977), APHA (1995), Mathur (1982), Trivadi and Goel (1984), Santhanam *et al.* (1989), and Bharti (2012a).

The water quality is quite rich in natural nutrients which play an important implication for use the drinking purpose after making sure the bacterial and other hygienic condition after clean technology. The conservation measures must be directed towards understanding of the intricate relationship between all biotic organisms either plants or animals along with surrounding environment.

A huge quantity of solid waste is generated at any tourist place and the study area is not an exceptional case. It has been noticed and examined that the entire quantity of solid waste generated at Sahastradhara is being dumped near the stream in a very rough manner. This dumped solid waste can cause various environment health hazards. So, the disposal practises for the solid waste should be proper and managed. Even the solid waste should be dumped anywhere very far from the stream basin. It should be keep in the mind that the leaching of pollutants from solid waste dumping site can also impacts on stream environment. Analytical results of the river water samples indicating that solid waste site is significantly contributing to increased the heavy metals concentration in aquatic ecosystem. Increasing tourist activities can impart to deteriorate the aquatic environment (Bharti, 2008).

Awareness for environment protection should be increased during the time of tourist activities especially at hot tourist spots. Strict rule and regulations should be adopted for all individuals. Anthropogenic activities, which accelerated the rate of pollution or environmental degradation, should be avoided or banned or appropriate alternate should be adopted in those cases. The present chapter described the various pollution sources especially due to the tourist activities and other anthropogenic activities and their effects on the environment in a tourist place.

Quantity of solid waste generated at tourist places, traffic density in different seasons, the degradation of organic matter and many other things can contribute to environment pollution significantly. Water quality alterations at various stations especially heavy metals of Sahastradhara stream have already been discussed in previous section. These activities can alter the physico-chemical parameters, planktonic and benthic diversity, heavy metal concentration and many other basic characteristics of a natural hill-stream. The diversity of river water may also change their population size, distribution, density and behaviour.

The rate of pollution due to the tourist's activities or other anthropogenic activities should be minimized in an integrated and sustainable manner. Currently, Tourism is one of the hottest industries in India also. On the other hand, environment is also important. So, the pollution abatement should be on top preferences and all the steps should be of eco-friendly manners. Tourisms should be promoted in all regions, but environment conservation is the first priority and above the all aspects.

Both the things can be managed easily with the help of strict regulations and appropriate management practices in the tourisms industry and that is the only way for sustainable development and the protection of aquatic environment.

REFERENCES

Adefemi, O.S.; Asaolu, S.S. and Olaofe, O. (2007): Assessment of the Physico-chemical Status of Water Samples from Major Dams in Ekiti State, Nigeria, *Pakistan Journal of Nutrition*, 6 (6): 657-659.

Ahamed, S. and Hasnain, S.I. (2001): Snow and Stream Water Chemistry of the Ganga Headwater Basin, Garhwal Himalaya, India, *Hydrological Sciences Journal* 46(1): 103-111.

Allen, W.E. (1920): A Quantitative and Statistical Study of the Plankton of the San Joaquin River and its Tributaries in a Near Stockton California in 1913. *Univ. Calif. Publ. Zool.* 22(1): 1-24.

APHA (1995): Ecological Methods for the Examination of Water. *American Public Health Association*, 1015 fifteen street NW, Washington, 19: 1-1134.

Badola, S.P. and Singh, H.R. (1981): Hydrobiology of the River Alaknanda of Garhwal Himalaya *Indian J. Ecol.*, 8(2): 269-276.

Bharti, P.K. (2004): Limnological Study of Sahastradhara Hill-Stream, Dehradun, *M.Sc. Thesis, Gurukula Kangri University, Hardwar, India,* pp. 102.

Bharti, P.K. (2007a): Effect of Textile Industrial Effluents on Ground Water and Soil Quality at Panipat (Haryana). *Ph.D. Thesis submitted to Gurukula Kangri University, Haridwar,* pp. 191.

Bharti, P.K. (2007c): Any Means to Save Lalita River?, *Down To Earth*, 15(17): 3.

Bharti, P.K. (2008): Status of Water Quality and Ecotourism Enhancement in Sahastradhara Stream at Dehradun. In: Third Uttarakhand State Science Congress organised by UCOST, Dehradun held on 10-11 November, 2008 at IIT, Roorkee.

Bharti, P.K. (2010): Sandushan - (Eutrophication), *Vigyan Pragati,* January 2010, pp. 29-31.

Bharti, P.K. (2012a): Hill-stream Ecology, *Biotech Books*, pp. 246.

Bharti, P.K. and Malik, D.S. (2005a): Significance of Rivers in Vedic literature, *Gurukula Shodha Bharti*, Vol. 4, pp. 217-221.

Bharti, P.K. and Malik, D.S. (2005b): Sahastradhara Nadi ke Vibhinna Sthhano par Machhliyon ke Anukool vaas Sthhano ke liye Upyukt Dashaayen, in Proceedings of (in Hindi) National Symposium: Uttaranchal me Maatyasyki ki Bhaavi Sambhaavnaye' organized by department of zoology, H.N.B. Garhwal University, Srinagar on 28-29 October 2005, pp. 84-87.

Bharti, P.K.; Malik, D. S. and Yadav, R. (2008): Influence of Heavy Metals on Abundance of Cyanophyceae Members in Three Spring-fed Lake in Kempty, Dehradun, *Journal of Ecology and Fisheries*, 1(1): 35-38.

Bharti, P.K.; Malik, D.S. and Yadav, R. (2010): Influence of Heavy Metals on Abundance of Cyanophyceae Members in Three Spring-fed Lake in Kempty, Dehradun, In: 'Advances in Aquatic Ecology, Vol. III' ed. by V.B. Sakhare, *Daya Publishing House, New Delhi*, pp. 107-111.

Bharti, Pawan K. (2007a): 'Where is Environmental Science going in India?' *Current Science*, 92 (4): 414.

Bharti, Pawan Kr. (2007b): 'Why are Indian Standards not so Strict?', *Current Science*, 93(9): 1202.

Chopra, A.K., Patrick, Nirmal, J. (1994): Effect of Domestic Sewage on Self-purification of Ganga Water at Rishikesh. *A. Bio.science*, 13(11): 75-82.

Das, S.M. and Pathani, S.S. (1978): A Study on the Effect of lake Ecology on Production of Mahaseer (*Tor tor and T. putitora*) in Kumaon lake. *Indian Matsya*. 4: 25-31.

Das, S.M. and Srivastava, V.K. (1956): Studies of Fresh water Plankton II Correlation between Plankton and Hydro-biological Factors *Proc. Nat. Acad. Sci. India*, (13) 26: 243-253.

Dobriyal, A.K. (1985): Ecology of Limnofauna in the Small Streams and their Importance to the Village Life in Garhwal Himalya. *Uttar Pradesh J. Zool*. 5 (2): 139-144.

Eddy, S. (1934): A Study of Freshwater Plankton Communities. *Illinois Biol. Monogr*. 12 (4): 1-93.

Forstner, U. and G.T.W. Wittman, (1979): Metal Pollution in the Aquatic Environment. Berlin, Spring-Verlag, pp. 486.

Hutchinson, G.C. (1957): A Treatise on Limnology, Geography, Physical and Chemical, Vol. I, New York: *John Wiley and Sons, Inc.*, pp. 1-1015.

Hynes, H.B.N. (1970): The Ecology of Running Waters. *Liverpool University Press, Liverpool, 4th Impression*: 1-555.

IUPAC (1994): Atomic Weights of the Elements, 1993, International Union of Pure and Applied Chemistry, *Pure Appl. Chem.*, 66: 2423.

Jain, C.K. (1992): Effect of Waste Disposals on Quality of Water of River Kali (Uttar Pradesh). Tech, Report No. TR-148, *National Institutute of Hydrology*, Roorkee, India.

Jain, C.K. (1996): Application of Chemical Mass Balance Approach to Upstream/downstream River monitoring data. *J. Hydrol* 182: 105-115.

Joshi, B.D., Bisht, R.C.S. and Semval, V.P. (1995): Primary Productivity in Western Ganga Canal at Hardwar. *Indian J.Ecol*. 22(2): 123-126.

Juttner I., Heike Rothfritz and Steve J. Ormerod (1995): *University of Wales, Cardiff, CFI 3TL UK* - 'Diatom Communities in Himalayan Hill Streams, pp. 589-597.

Kar, O.K., P.C. Mishra, M.C. Das and R.C. Das (1978): Pollution Studies in River Ib. III Plankton, Pollution and Primary Productivity, 175.

Khan, A.A. and Siddiqui, A. (1971): *Hydrobiologia*, 37:447.

Khanna, D.R and Singh. R.K. (2000): Seasonal Fluctuations in the Plankton of Suswa River at Raiwala Dehradun. *Env. Conservations J.* 1(2 and 3): 89-92.

Khanna, D.R. (1993): Ecology and Pollution of Ganga River, *Ashish Publishing House*, New Delhi. pp. 1-241.

Khanna, D.R., Badola, S.P., Sing, H.R. and Dobriyal, K., Anoop (1992): Observations on Seasonal Trends in Diatomic Diversity in the River Ganga at Sapt-sarover, Hardwar. In: Recent Research in Cold Water: Fisheries, Ed. by K.L. Sehgal, *Today and Tomarrow printers and publishers*, New Delhi: 99-107.

Khanna, D.R., Bhutiani, R. and Chandra, K. S. (2005): Modeling to Assess Effect of Light on Phytoplanktonic Growth Dynamics: A Review, *Env. Conservations J.*, 6(3): 103-107.

Khanna, D.R., Malik, D.S. and Rana, D.S. (1998): Phytoplanktonic Communities in Relation to Certain Physico-chemical Parameters of Ganga canal at Hardwar. *Him. J. Env. Zool.*, Vol. 12: 193-197.

Lakshminarayana and R.K. Someshekar. (2001): Ecology of Polluted Water by Arvind Kumar Vol. 1, Chapter II, pp. 51-60, *APH Pub. Corp.* New Delhi - 110 002.

Lokeshwari, H., and Chandrappa, G.T. (2006): Imapct of Heavy Metal Contamination of Bellandur Lake on Soil and Cultivated Vegetation. Current Science, 91(5), pp. 622-27.

Malik, D.S. and Bharti, P.K. (2005a): Nutrient Dynamics in Rhithron zone of Shivalik Himalayan Stream Sahastradhara, Dehradun (Uttaranchal), *Env. Cons. J.* 6 (2): 63-68.

Malik, D.S. and Bharti, P.K. (2005b): Fluctuation in Planktonic Population of Sahastradhara Hill-Stream at Dehradun (Uttaranchal), *Aquacult.* 6 (2): 191-198.

Malik, D.S. and Bharti, P.K. (2005c): Primary Production Efficiency of Sahstradhara Hill-Stream, Dehradun, *Env. Cons. J.* 6 (3): 117-121.

Malik, D.S. and Bharti, P.K. (2007a): Water Resources Conservation in Vedas, *Gurukula Shodha Bharati*, Vol. 7, pp. 231-235.

Malik, D.S. and Bharti, P.K. (2007b): Macro-zoobanthos as Pollution Indicator in River Saung at Dehradun (Uttaranchal), *J. Exp. Zool. India*, 10 (1): 221-222.

Malik, D.S. and Bharti, P.K. (2007d): Ecology of Sahastradhara Hill-stream at Dehradun (Uttaranchal), In: 'Advances in Aquatic Ecology, Vol. I' ed. by V.B. Sakhare, *Daya Publishing House, New Delhi*, (ISBN 81-7035-483-8) pp. 1-11.

Malik, D.S.; Bharti, P.K. and Yadav, R.; Kumar, P. and Chauhan, P. (2008): Dispersion of Heavy Metals in Textile Effluent and Pond Environment in Panipat Industrial Area, *Env. Cons. J.* 9 (3): 77-81.

Malik, D.S., Bharti, P.K.; Yadav, R. and Deepmala (2008): Distribution of Heavy Metals in Pond Sediment in Textile Industrial Area at Panipat (Haryana), *Journal of Ecology and Fisheries*, 1(1): 39-44.

Malik, D. S., Yadav, R. and Bharti, P.K. (2009): Role of Aquatic Macrophytes in the Remediation of Metal Pollutants, In: 'Aquatic Ecology II', *Narendra Publishing House*, New Delhi, pp. 145-158.

Malik, D.S., Bharti, P. K.; Negi, K.S. and Yadav, R. (2009): Distribution of Metals in Water of an Artificial Lake at Mussoorie, Uttarakhand, In: 'Aquatic Biology and Aquaculture' edited by V.B. Sakhare, Ambajoagi, MS, *Manglam Publication*, New Delhi, pp. 77-95.

Malik, D.S., and Bharti, P.K. (2006): Sahastradhara me Matasya vinod evam paryatan, in Proceeding of National Seminar on 'Meethajal Matsyiki' organized by Rashtriya matsya anuvanshik sansadhan bureau, Lucknow.

Malik, D.S., Bharti, P. K.; Negi, K.S. and Yadav, R. (2009): Distribution of Metals in Water of an Artificial Lake at Mussoorie, Uttarakhand, In: 'Aquatic biology and aquaculture' edited by V.B. Sakhare, Ambajoagi, MS, *Manglam Publication,* New Delhi, pp. 77-95.

Mani, V.; Kaur, H. and Mohini, M. (2005): Toxic Metals and Environmental Pollution, *J. Ind. Poll. Cont.,* 21(1): 101-107.

Nautiyal, P. (1982): Some Aspects of Bio ecology of Tarputitora in Relation to Hydrobiology of some Garhwal Hill-Stream. *D.Phill. Thesis;* Garhwal University.

Pande, R.K. and Asha Mishra (2000): Water Quality Study of Freshwaters of Dehradun (Sahastradhara stream and Mussoorie lake). *Aquacult.* Vol. 1: 57-62.

Quadri, M.Y. and Shah, G.M. (1984): Hydro-Biological Feature of Hoassar. A Typical Wetland of Kashmir-I, Biotope. *Indian J. Ecol.,* 2(2): 203-206.

Rao, S.M. and Mamtha, P. (2004): Water Quality in Sustainable Water Management, Current Science, 87(7):942-947.

Santhanam, R.; Velayntham, P. and Jegatheesan, G. (1989): A Manual of Freshwater Ecology. *Daya Publishing House* Delhi - 1100 06: 3-17, 53-92.

Sarin, M.M., Krishnaswamy, S.K., Trivedi, J.R. and Sharma, K.K. (1992): Major ion Chemistry of the Ganga Source Waters: Weathering in High Altitude Himalaya. In: *Proc, Indian acad. Sci. (Earth Planet Sci.)* 1, 89-98.

Schwoerbel, J. (1991): Handbook of Limnology, *Ellis Horwood Limited, Chichester, England:* pp. 95-114.

Shrama, R.C. (1986): Effect of Physico-chemical Factors on benthic fauna of Bhargirathi River Garhwal Himalaya. *Indian. J. Ecol.* 13(1): 133-137.

Singh, S.N.; Gupta, M.L.; and Prakash, P. (1980): Hydro-biological Studies of some eutrophic ponds of Rohtash, Bihar. *Environment and Ecology.* 16 (2): 457-462.

Subramanian, V. (1989): Chemical and Suspended Sediment Characteristics of River of India. *J. Hydrol,* 44: 37-55.

Trivedi, R.K. and Goel, P.K. (1984): Chemical and Biological Methods for Water Pollution Studies. *Enviro Media Publication, Karad.* pp. 1-251.

Vahrenkamp, H., (1979): Metalle in Lebensprozessen: Chemie in Unserer Zeit, 7: 97-105.

Valdiya, K.S. (1975): Emergence of the Himalayas, Science Today, 9: 14-18.

Vashney, P.K.; R. Vijayalakshmi, Nair and S.H.H. Abidi (1983): Primary Productivity in near shore Water of Thai Maharashtra Coast, India. *J.Mar. Sci.* 12:27-30.

Wetzel, R.G. (1975): Limnology, *W.B. Saunders Co. Philadelphia,* pp. 743.

Yeragi, S.G. and Nisar Shaikh (2003): Studies on Primary Productivity of Tansa River. *J. Natcon* 15 (1): 125-130.

Pages: 169-190

WASTE GENERATION AND UTILIZATION

Edited by: **Dr. Priya Bajaj; Dr. B. Tabassum** and **Dr. Pawan Kumar 'Bharti'**

ISBN: 978-93-5056-792-0

Edition: **2016**

Published by: **Discovery Publishing House Pvt. Ltd., New Delhi (India)**

CHAPTER - 9

Are We Experiencing an E-waste Tsunami? E-waste Management in Mysore, India

Nichola A. Ramchurjee[1-2] and C.E. Ramchurjee[1]

ABSTRACT

Electronic waste (E-waste) or waste electrical and electronic equipment (WEEE) is drawing rapid attention across the globe as the quantity being generated is rapidly rising. This paper increases the awareness of the rapid growth of e-waste and its effect on communities in Mysore, Karnataka and the socio-economic factors and consumer choices contributing to this phenomenon. The paper highlights the various issues of e-waste management, such as: the impact of e-waste, status of e-waste in Mysore and the management strategies used in the reduction of e-waste. It also focus on the informal recycling effect on the state and the health effects on the people. There are suggestions to the manufacturing companies on how to tackle the e-waste disposal and recycling techniques. Urgent needs arise to document the issues related to e-waste generation and management in order to deal with this important and toxic waste stream.

Keywords: E-waste, issues of E-waste management, Status of e-waste, recycling techniques, Health hazards.

1. Department in Environmental Science, University of Mysore, Mysore (Karnataka), India.
2. 667 East 232nd Street, Apt #3A, Bronx, N.Y. 10466, New York, USA.

INTRODUCTION

When electronic devices reach the end of their useful life; they become waste (e-waste) or waste electrical and electronics equipment (WEEE) (Onwughara *et. al.* 2010). The electronic industry is the world's largest and fastest growing manufacturing industry. During the last decade, it has assumed the role of providing a forceful leverage of the socio-economic and technological growth in a developing society. The consequence of its consumer oriented growth combined with rapid product obsolescence and technological advances are a new environmental challenge - the growing menace of 'Electronic Waste' or 'E-waste' that consists of obsolete electronic devices. The composition of this waste stream, that is, its constituents including toxics and its resource potential, varies significantly by products. This makes e-waste very difficult to manage. Rapid product innovation, miniaturization and replacement, especially for information and communication technology (ICT) products and consumer equipment are fueling the increase of e-waste (Balde *et. al.* 2015).

It is an emerging problem as well as a business opportunity of increasing significance, given the volumes of e-waste being generated and its content of both toxic and valuable materials. The fraction including iron, copper, aluminum, gold and other metals in e-waste is over 60 per cent, while plastic accounts for about 30 per cent and the hazardous pollutants comprise 2.7 per cent (Agarwal, 1998). Solid waste management is already a mammoth task in Mysore, Karnataka, India and e-waste is finding an easy way into developing countries in the name of free trade which is further complicating the problems associated with waste management.

Global Scenario

The growing amount of e-waste has posed a significant challenge to waste management in both developed and developing countries. Rapid technology innovation and ever-shortening product lifespans are among the factors contributing to the growing amount of e-waste (Baldé *et. al.* 2015). Every year 20 to 50 million tonnes of e-waste are generated worldwide (Schwarzer *et. al.* 2005). Electronic waste (e-waste) now makes up five per cent of all municipal solid waste worldwide (Greenpeace International, 2015).

Figure 9.1 shows e-waste generation by the top eight countries taking European countries as a whole. The global quantity of e-waste generation in 2014 was around 41.8 million tonnes, that's an average of about 43 lbs (20 kgs.), or the weight of eight bricks, for each of the billion people on Earth (Lewis, 2013). This figure is expected to grow to 49.8 million tonnes in 2018, with an annual growth rate of 4-5 per cent (Table 9.1). About 6.5 Mt of e-waste was reported as formally treated by national take-back systems. Not all e-waste laws have the same scope as the comprehensive scope in this report. In total, 0.7 Mt of e-waste is thrown into the waste bin in the 28 EU Member States. The amount of e-waste that is disposed of in waste bins is unknown for other regions. The quantities of the collection outside formal take-back systems are not documented systematically (Baldé *et. al.* 2015).

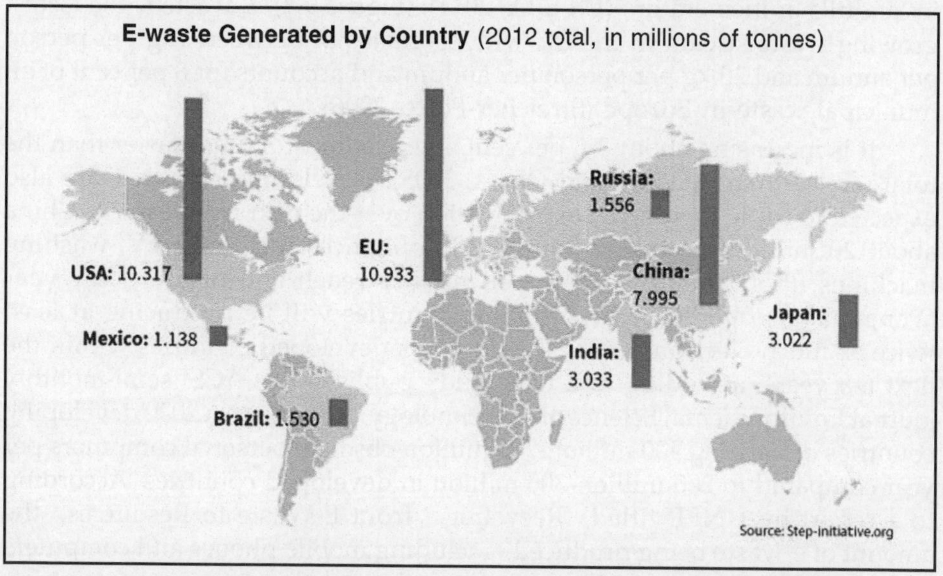

Fig. 9.1: **E-waste generation by country (2012 total, in millions of tonnes)**

Table 9.1: Shows the growth and forecast of the generation of e-waste from 2010-18

Global Quantity of E-waste Generated			
Year	E-waste Generated (Mt)	Population (billion)	E-waste Generated (kg/inh.)
2010	33.8	6.8	5.0
2011	35.8	6.8	5.2
2012	37.8	6.9	5.4
2013	39.8	7.0	5.7
2014	41.8	7.1	5.9
2015	43.8	7.2	6.1
2016	45.8	7.3	6.3
2017	47.8	7.4	6.5
2018	49.8	7.4	6.7

Forecasted data from 2015-18.

In developed countries, e-waste constitution is 5 per cent of the total municipal solid waste (MSW) generation and in the United States is 2-5 per cent of the US municipal solid waste stream and is growing rapidly (Kang and Schoenung, 2005). In 2012, the United States generated 3.412 million tons of e-waste. Of this amount, only 1 million tonnes or 29.2 per cent was recycled, according to the EPA (up from 25% in 2011). The rest was trashed in landfills or incinerators (US EPA, 2014), (Figure 9.2). E-waste is the fastest growing waste stream in the EU with estimates of between 1kg per person per annum and 20 kg per person per annum and accounts for 8 per cent of all municipal waste in Europe (Streicher-Porte, 2006).

It is increasing about 3-5 per cent a year, almost 3 times faster than the total waste stream (Darby and Obara, 2005). Developing countries are also expected to triple their e-waste production over the next five years. In China about 20 million electronic household appliances including TV, washing machines, PCs) and 70 million cell phones reach end-of-life every year (Yongguang, *et al.* 2006). Developing countries will be producing at least twice as much electronic waste (e-waste) as developed countries within the next 6-8 years, according to a new study published in ACS' semi-monthly journal Environmental Science and Technology. It foresees in 2030 developing countries discarding 400 million-700 million obsolete personal computers per year compared to 200 million-300 million in developed countries. According to a report by UNEP titled, 'Recycling - from E-Waste to Resources,' the amount of e-waste being produced - including mobile phones and computers - could rise by as much as 500 per cent over the next decade in some countries, such as: India (UNEP, 2012).

Developing countries will be producing at least twice as much electronic waste (e-waste) as developed countries within the next 6-8 years, according to a new study published in ACS' semi-monthly journal Environmental Science and Technology. It foresees in 2030 developing countries discarding 400 million-700 million obsolete personal computers per year compared to 200 million-300 million in developed countries (Science Daily, 2010).

On March 25, 2009, the House Science and Technology Committee approved funding for research on reducing electronic waste and mitigating environmental impact, regarded as the first federal bill to address electronic waste directly (CQ Politics, 2009). A fee similar to the one in California was added to the cost of purchasing new televisions, computers, and computer components in Alberta, the first of its kind in Canada, in February 2004. Saskatchewan also implemented an electronics recycling fee in February 2007, followed by British Columbia in August 2007. Nova Scotia in February 2008, and Ontario in April 2009. In 2007, Manitoba issued the Proposed Electrical and Electronic Equipment Stewardship Regulation by which the sale of regulated products is forbidden unless covered by the stewardship programme. "Products covered under this legislation include TVs, computers, laptops, and scanners." (Feszty and Calder, 2007). Hong Kong's Waste Disposal Ordinance bans the import of batteries and cathode rays. There is no current legislation in place to bar the entrance of other electronics into the ports of Hong Kong. South Korea, Japan and Taiwan ensure manufacturer responsibility by demanding that they recycle 75 per cent of their annual production.

In China, rapid economic growth, coupled with urbanization and growing demand for consumer goods, has increased the consumption of EEE in large quantity, thus made the WEEE manifold rapidly, posing a severe threat to the environment and the sustainable economic growth as well. Waste Electronic and Electrical Equipment treatment, the recovery technologies, and the current status of WEEE and corresponding responses adopted are important to the industrial sectors in China's economy. Serious adverse impacts on the environment and human healthfrom e-waste recycling have occurred in the past and continue to occur in China today, due to a lack ofnational management strategies. China has madegreat efforts to face the challenges of the approaching peak increase in the domestic generation of e-waste and the illegal shipment of e-waste from other countries. It was found that the material and the financial flows of e-waste in China had their own specific characteristics. Nearly 60 per cent of the generated e-wastes were sold to private individual collectors and passed into informal recycling processes. More than 90 per cent of Chinese citizens are reluctant to pay for the recycling of their e-waste. This is due to their traditional understanding that there remained value in these end-of-life products. Regulations concerninge-waste in China have been drafted but their deficiencies are obvious. The extended producer responsibilities (EPR) have been introduced but are not well-defined (Liu, 2006). Guiyu, China is infamous for its involvement in primitive e-waste processing and recycling activities. Freshwater samples were collected in and outside of Guiyu for dissolved metal analysis. It was found that dissolved metal concentrations were higher in Lianjiang and Nanyang River within Guiyu than the reservoir outside of Guiyu (Wong *et al*. 2007).

Chinese laws are primarily concerned with eliminating the import of e-waste. China has ratified the Basel Convention as well as the Basel Ban Amendment, officially banning the import of e-waste. In October 2008, the Chinese State Council has approved a "draft regulation on the management of electronic waste." This regulation is intended to promote the continued use of resources through recycling and to monitor the end-of-life treatment of electronics. Under this new regulations, recycling of electronics by the consumer is mandated. It also requires the recycling of unnecessary materials discarded in the manufacturing process. However, to stem the negative effects of this activity, China has banned the import of e-waste in 2000. Nevertheless, the labor-intensive nature of electronics recycling has perpetuated a black market in the trade, taking advantage of China's abundant, cheap, and skilled labor force.

National Scenario - Status of E-Waste in India

Over the last few decades, India has become a major destination for e-waste exports from the developed nations. Due to the rapid developmental activities, India, faces a fast increasing load of WEEE originating from both inland and through illegal imports (Streicher-Porte *et al.* 2005). Moreover, Indians have been generating rapidly increasing amounts of E-waste domestically (Skinner, 2010). Studies so far reveal that the total e-waste generation in India is approximately 146,000 tonnes (Consumer Voice, 2007; SIMs Recycling Solutions, 2008; Beary, 2008) to 3.3 lakh tonnes a year and is expected to touch 4.7 lakh tonnes by 2011 (MAIT). 'The projected growth for e-waste generation for India is about 34 per cent year on year' says Sinha (Associate Director of Toxics Link) (Kukday, 2007). Of the total e-waste generated in the country, western India accounts for the largest population at 35 per cent, while the southern, northern and eastern regions account for 30, 21 and 14 per cent, respectively.

As stated by Agarwal *et al.* (2005), the report by Toxics Link, a New Delhi based NGO, estimated that in India businesses and individual households make approximately 1.38 million personal computers obsolete every year. Schluep *et al.* (2009) stated that the amount of EEE (computers, printers, washing machines, mobile phones and TVs) put on the market in 2007 was estimated to be 823.6 K tonnes. In the same year of 2007, the estimated domestic WEEE arising for computers, printers, washing machines, mobile phones, and TVs was 439 K tonnes. Figure 9.2 shows the growth of some EEEs in India during the last six years. Consumer electronics, industrial electronics, communication and broadcast equipment show considerable growth during the last six years from 2005-06 to 2010-11.

E-waste Generation and Recycling 2000-12

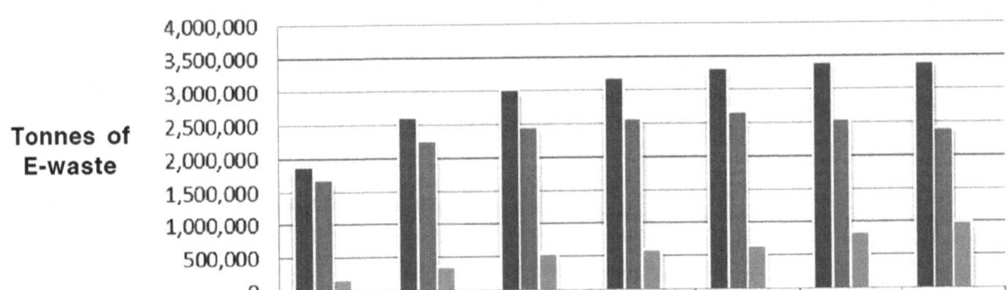

	2000	2005	2007	2009	2010	2011	2012
■ Total e-waste generated	1,900,000	2,630,000	3,010,000	3,190,000	3,320,000	3,410,000	3,420,000
■ E-waste trashed	1,710,000	2,270,000	2,460,000	2,590,000	2,670,000	2,560,000	2,420,000
■ E-waste recycled	190,000	360,000	550,000	600,000	650,000	850,000	1,000,000
■ Percent Recycled	10.0%	13.7%	18.3%	18.8%	19.6%	24.9%	29.20%

Fig. 9.2: **EPA data from "Municipal Solid Waste Generation, Recycling and Disposal in the United States, 2012," Feb 2014. These EPA numbers are for 'selected consumer electronics' which include products such as: TVs, VCRs, DVD players, video cameras, stereo systems, telephones, and computer equipment**

A Central Pollution Control Board (CPCB) report said 65 cities in India generate morethan 60-70 per cent of the total e-waste, which comes from 10 states namely: Maharashtra, Tamil Nadu, Andhra Pradesh, Uttar Pradesh, West Bengal, Delhi, Karnataka, Gujarat, Madhya Pradesh and Punjab, Table 9.2 (NIIR Project Consultancy Service (npcs), 2012; Raghupathy, *et.al.* 2012). From Table 9.2, it is noted that Karnataka is in the 7th position among the e-waste generators. As regards to the cities, Bangalore is 2nd and Hyderabad is 5th in generation of e-waste. A study released by the Electronics Industry Association of India (ELCINA) at the electronics industry expo – 'Componex Nepcon 2009' had estimated the total e-waste generation in India at a whopping 4.34 lakh tonnes by end 2009 (CBS News.com, 2009). The CPCB has estimated that it will exceed the 8 lakh tonnes or 0.8 Mt mark by 2012 (CPCB, Ministry of Environment and Forests, Government of India, 2008). The estimated total number of Personal Computers (PCs) emanating each year from businesses and individual households in India will be around 1.38 million.

The dumping of e-waste, particularly computer waste into India from developed countries has further aggravated the problem associated with waste management and hence computer waste management is a major focus of this study. Environmental and occupational hazards associated with e-waste processing and the prevailing stream of waste management systems is analyzed to develop an appropriate strategy for betterment (Mundada *et al.* 2004).

Table 9.2: Shows E-waste/WEEE generation in top ten states

S. No.	States	WEEE (tonnes)	Percentage (%)
1.	Maharashtra	20270.59	18.49
2.	Tamil Nadu	13486.24	12.30
3.	Andhra Pradesh	12780.33	11.66
4.	Uttar Pradesh	10381.11	9.47
5.	West Bengal	10059.36	9.18
6.	Delhi	9729.15	8.87
7.	Karnataka	9118.74	8.32
8.	Gujarat	8994.33	8.20
9.	Madhya Pradesh	7800.62	7.11
10.	Punjab	6958.46	6.35
	Total	**109578.93**	**100**

Issues of E-Waste Management in India

Pollutants in E-Waste

Electronic wastes can cause widespread environmental damage due to the use of toxic materials in the manufacture of electronic goods. Hazardous materials such as: lead, mercury, cadmium and hexavalent chromium in one form or another are present in such wastes primarily consisting of cathode ray tubes (CRTs), printed board assemblies, capacitors, mercury switches and relays, batteries, liquid crystal displays (LCDs), cartridges from photocopying machines, selenium drums (photocopier), electrolytes, plastic casing, cables and polyvinyl chloride (PVC) cable insulation that release highly toxic dioxins and furans when burned. All electronic equipment contain printed circuit board which are hazardous because of their content of lead (in solder), brominated flame retardants (typically 5-10% by weight) and antimony oxide, which is also present as a flame retardant (typically 1-2% by weight). **Table 9.3**, shows the major pollutants occurring in waste electrical and electronic equipment (Janzand Bilitewski, 2008).

Table 9.3: Shows the major pollutants and their occurrence in waste electrical and electronic equipment

Pollutant	Occurrence
Arsenic	Semiconductors, diodes, microwaves, LEDs (Light-emitting diodes), solar cells.
Barium	Electron tubes, filler for plastic and rubber, lubricant additives.
Brominated flame-proofing agent	Casing, circuit boards (plastic), cables and PVC cables.
Cadmium	Batteries, pigments, solder, alloys, circuit boards, computer batteries, monitor cathode ray tubes (CRTs).
Chrome	Dyes/pigments, switches, solar.
Cobalt	Insulators.
Copper	Conducted in cables, copper ribbons, coils, circuitry, pigments.
Lead	Lead rechargeable batteries, solar, transistors, lithium batteries, PVC (polyvinyl chloride) stabilizers, lasers, LEDs, thermoelectric elements, circuit boards.
Liquid crystal	Displays.
Lithium	Mobile telephones, photographic equipment, video equipment (batteries).
Mercury	Components in copper machines and steam irons; batteries in clocks and pocket calculators, switches, LCDs.
Nickel	Alloys, batteries, relays, semiconductors, pigments.
PCBs (polychlorinated-biphenyls)	Transformers, capacitors, softening agents for paint, glue, plastic.
Selenium	Photoelectric cells, pigments, photocopiers, fax machines.
Silver	Capacitors, switches (contacts), batteries, resistors.
Zinc	Steel, brass, alloys, disposable and rechargeable batteries, luminous substances.

Impacts of E-wastes on Human Health and the Environment

The problems associated with electronic waste are now being recognized. E-waste is highly complex to handle due to its composition. It is made up of multiple components some of which contain toxic substances that have an adverse impact on human health and environment if not handled properly. Often, these problems arise out of improper recycling and disposal methods (Joshi, 2009). This underlines the need for appropriate technology for handling and disposal of these chemicals. If improperly managed, such substances may pose significant human and environmental health risks. Toxic substances can be found within the following types of emissions or outputs:

1. Leachates from dumping activities.
2. Particulate matter (coarse and fine particles) from dismantling activities.
3. Fly and bottom ashes from burning activities.
4. Fumes from mercury amalgamate 'cooking', desoldering and other burning activities.
5. Wastewater from dismantling and shredding facilities.
6. Effluents from cyanide leaching and other leaching.
7. Activities (Sepúlveda *et al*. 2010).

The degree of health risks and hazards posed to workers and the environment varies greatly depending on the individuals involved and the nature of operations. According to Liu *et al*. 2009, the pollution generated by e-waste processing brings about toxic or genotoxic effects on the human body, threatening the health not only of workers but also of residents and future generations living in the local environment. Studies done on China have shown that the rudimentary recycling techniques coupled with the amounts of e-waste processed have already resulted in adverse environmental and human health impacts, including contaminated soil and surface water (Frazzoli *et al*. 2010; Wang *et al*. 2011; Zhao *et al*. 2010; Tsydenova and Bengtsson, 2011). Health problems have been reported in the last few years, including diseases and problems related to the skin, stomach, respiratory tract and other organs (Nordbrand, 2009). According to Prakash and Manhart, 2010, workers suffer high incidences of birth defects, infant mortality, tuberculosis, blood diseases, anomalies in the immune system, malfunctioning of the kidneys and respiratory system, lung cancer, underdevelopment of the brain in children and damage to the nervous and blood systems. Table 9.4, shows the hazardous substances, their occurrences and impact on environment and human health.

Table 9.4: Hazardous substances, their occurrences and impact on environment and human health

Substance	Occurrence in E-waste	Environmental and Health Relevance
Arsenic	Small quantities in the form of gallium arsenide within light emitting diodes	Acutely poisonous and on a long-term perspective injurious to health
Barium	Getters in CRT	May develop explosive gases (hydrogen) if wetted
Beryllium	Power supply boxes which contain silicon controlled rectifiers, beamline components	Harmful if inhaled
Cadmium	Rechargeable NiCd-batteries, fluorescent layer (CRT screens), printer inks and toners	Acutely poisonous and injurious to health on a long-term perspective
Chlorofluorocarbon (CFC)	Cooling unit, insulation foam	Combustion of halogenated substances may cause toxic emissions
Chromium VI	Data tapes, floppy-disks	Acutely poisonous and injurious to health on a long-term perspective causes allergic reactions
Gallium arsenide	Light-emitting diode (LED)	Injurious to health
Lead	CRT screens, batteries, printed wiring boards	Causes damage to the nervous system, circulatory system, kidneys kidneys causes learning disabilities in children
Lithium	Li-batteries	May develop explosive gases (hydrogen) if wetted
Mercury	Found in the fluorescent lamps that provide backlighting in LCDs, in some alkaline batteries and mercury wetted switches	Acutely poisonous and injurious to health on a long-term perspective
Nickel	Rechargeable NiCd-batteries or NiMH batteries, electron gun in CRT	May cause allergic reactions
PCB (polychlorinated biphenyls)	Condensers, transformers	Cause cancer, effects on the immune system, reproductive system, nervous system, endocrine system and other health effects. Persistent and bioaccumulation
PVC (polyvinyl chloride)	Cable insulation	High temperature processing of cables may release chlorine, which is converted to dioxins and furans
Rare Earth Elements (Yttrium, Europium)	Fluorescent layer (CRT-screen)	Irritates skin and eyes
Zinc sulphide		Toxic when inhaled
TBBA (tetrabromo-bisphenol-A) • PBB (polybrominated biphenyls) • PBDE (polybrominateddiphenyl ethers)	Fire retardants for plastics (thermoplastic components, cable insulation) TBBA is presently the most widely used flame retardant in printed wiring boards and covers for components	Can cause long-term period injuries to health acutely poisonous when burned
Toxic organic Substances	Condensers, liquid crystal display	
Toner Dust	Toner cartridges for laser printers/copiers	Health risk when dust is inhaled risk of explosion

(*Source:* Report on Assessment of Electronic Wastes in Mumbai-Pune Area - MPCB, March 2007).

Management of E-waste: Existing Legislations and Policy related to E-waste

Despite a wide range of environment legislation in India there are no specific laws or guidelines for electronic waste or computers waste. As per the Hazardous Waste Rules (1989), e-waste is not treated as hazardous unless proved to have higher concentration of certain substances. Though PCBs and CRTs would always exceed these parameters, there are several grey areas that need to be addressed. The import of this waste therefore requires specific permission of the Ministry of Environment and Forests. However, India is a signatory to the Basal Convention. (Basel Convention is the United Nations Environment Programme) on the control of Transboundary Movement of Hazardous wastes and their disposal and has created the Draft Hazardous Materials (Management, Handling and Transboundary movement) Rules, 2007 (dated: September 28, 2007), which has become a part of the Environment Protection Act, 1986 (Draft Hazardous Materials (Management, Handling and Transboundary Movement, Rules, 2007).

As the collection and re-cycling of electronic wastes is being done by the informal sector in the country at present, the Government has taken the following action/steps to enhance awareness about environmentally sound management of electronic waste (CII, 2006). Several Workshops of Electronic Waste Management was organized by the Central Pollution Control Board (CPCB) in collaboration with Toxics Link, CII etc. Action has been initiated by CPCB for rapid assessment of the E-waste generated in major cities of the country (Raghupathy, *et.al*. 2012). A National Working Group has been constituted for formulating a strategy for E-Waste Management. A comprehensive technical guide on "Environmental Management for Information Technology Industry in India" has been published and circulated widely by the Department of Information Technology (DIT), Ministry of Communication and Information Technology. Demonstration projects have also been set up by the DIT at the Indian Telephone Industries for recovery of copper from Printed Circuit Boards.

Although awareness and readiness for implementing improvements is increasing rapidly, the major obstacles to manage the e-waste safely and effectively remain. These include:

1. The lack of reliable data that poses a challenge to policy-makers to design an e-waste management strategy and to an industry wishing to make rational investment decisions.
2. Only a fraction of the e-waste (estimated 10%) finds its way to recyclers due to absence of an efficient take back scheme for consumers.
3. The lack of a safe e-waste recycling infrastructure in the formal sector and thus reliance on the capacities of the informal sector pose severe risks to the environmental and human health.

4. The existing e-waste recycling systems are purely business-driven that have come about without any government intervention. Any development in these e-waste sectors will have to be built on the existing set-up as the waste collection and pre-processing can be handled efficiently by the informal sector, at the same time creating numerous job opportunities.

Management Strategies

Experience shows that simply prohibiting or competing with informal recyclers is not an effective solution. The future of e-waste management depends not only on the effectiveness of stakeholders including: industry players, local and national governments, customs authorities, regulatory agencies, intergovernmental organizations, non-governmental organizations, operators of recycling services and also community participation (Lundgren, 2012).

There are numerous options for dealing with e-waste. One of the option for dealing with e-waste is to reduce the volume. Designers should ensure that the product is built for re-use, repair and/or up-gradeability. Stress should be laid on the use of less toxic, easily recoverable and recyclable materials which can be taken back for refurbishment, remanufacturing, disassembly and reuse. Recycling and reuse of material are the next level of potential options to reduce e-waste. Recovery of metals, plastic, glass and other materials reduces the magnitude of e-waste.

Take back Policies Programmes

Implementation of take back policies programmes. Producers must be responsible for the entire lifecycle of their products. In developed countries, several efforts have been made on this front. Several dozen cities in the states of California and Massachusettes, including San Francisco, also have passed resolutions supporting 'producer take back' rules. Wipro Infotech has launched an e-waste disposal service for end customers. Others offering recycling options include Dell (dell.com), HP (hp.com) and Apple (apple.com) (Raymond, 2007).

Extended Producer Responsibility

A sustainable electronics life-cycle system should take into account environmental justice, the precautionary principle, and EPR. Most waste-related policies in recent years have been based on the EPR principle which requires electronics producers to take financial responsibility for the disposal of their products. In an effective EPR scheme, the true cost of waste management is internalized within the retail price by the producer. The aim is to provide an incentive to produce less toxic equipment that is cheap and easy to recycle. Companies are further pressured to address the life cycle issues of products, especially end-of-life issues. This, in turn, drives innovation, such as: in business models, take-back logistics and design changes, to reduce the environmental impact of products (Nimpuno and Scruggs, 2011).

E-waste Recycling: Impacts of Informal Recycling

The accrued electronic and electric waste in India is dismantled and sorted manually to fractions such as: printed wiring boards, cathode ray tubes (CRTs), cables, plastics, metals, condensers and other, and now-a-days invaluable materials like batteries. It is a livelihood for unorganized recyclers and due to lack of awareness, they are risking their health and the environments as well. The valuable fractions are processed to directly reusable components and to secondary raw materials in a variety of refining and conditioning processes. No sophisticated machinery or personal protective equipment is used for the extraction of different materials. All the work is done by bare hands and only with the help of hammers and screwdrivers. Children and women are routinely involved in this operations. Waste components which does not have any resale or reuse value are openly burnt or disposed of in open dumps. Pollution problems associated with such backyard smelting using crude processes are resulting in fugitive emissions and slag containing heavy metals of health concern. CRT breaking operations result in injuries from cuts and acids used for removal of heavy metals and respiratory problems due to shredding, burning and the use of strong acids to retrieve precious metals such as: gold. Working in poorly ventilated enclosed areas without masks and technical expertise results in exposure to dangerous and slow poisoning chemicals. Polychlorinated biphenyls (PCBs) in older capacitors and transformers, and brominated flame retardants on printed circuits boards, plastic casings, cables and polyvinyl chloride (PVC) cable insulation can release highly toxic dioxins and furans when burned to retrieve copper from the wires. On a broader scale, analyzing the environmental and societal impacts of e-waste reveals a mosaic of benefits and costs. Proponents of e-waste recycling claim that greater employment, new access to raw materials and electronics, and improved infrastructure will result.

Informal recycling enables the hazardous employment for thousands of people in poverty. Actions should be taken to mitigate existing problems at the local level (Williams, *et al.* 2008). In addition, workers need to be informed of the effects of e-waste processing on environmental and human health (Wang *et al.* 2011). Awareness raising programmes and activities are also needed on issues related to ESM and OSH, and on how to form cooperatives and integrate into the formal sector. It has to be noted, however, that a common feature of the informal waste sector is that it consists of poor people with little or no formal education; many are illiterate. This should be kept in mind when considering the role of information and education (Nimpuno and Scruggs, 2011). The economic stimulus driving the growth of the informal industry represents a key challenge. While there is a need to enforce appropriate legislation which specifically targets e-waste, enforcement is a challenge in areas of the world with limited resources for governance

(Hicks, Dietmar and Eugsterb, 2005). Cheap, safe and simple processing methods appropriate for introduction into the informal sector are lacking, and researchers are only just beginning to look into this (Sepúlveda *et al.* 2010). As a consequence, regulation has to be combined with incentives for informal recyclers not to engage in destructive processes, such as: a financial incentive to deliver parts to central collection sites rather than processing them themselves (Williams *et al.* 2008). Integrating the informal sector into the formal, together with the creation of cooperatives, could result in reduced pollution and better resource management.

Green Design

Most companies today design their products for planned or perceived obsolescence. This is reinforced through marketing and retailing practices, and affordability and convenience have taken over from product durability as primary drivers (Clapp, 2005). The ETBC provides a list of criteria for full assessment to minimize potential environmental, human health and social impacts, including to:

1. Be carbon neutral.
2. Maximize design for reparability, reuse and durable use.
3. Plan for recyclability and ease of disassembly.
4. Minimize toxicity.
5. Minimize use of raw virgin materials.
6. Invest in solutions that go beyond our current dominant technologies.
7. Actively engage communities and stakeholders.
8. Reuse and apply zero waste policies (ETBC, 2011).

Land Filling

Land filling of e-wastes can lead to the leaching of lead into the groundwater. If the CRT is crushed and burned, it emits toxic fumes into the air. These products contain several rechargeable battery types, all of which contain toxic substances that can contaminate the environment when burned in incinerators or disposed of in landfills. The cadmium from one mobile phone battery is enough to pollute $600m^3$ of water. The quantity of cadmium in landfill sites is significant, and considerable toxic contamination is caused by the inevitable medium and long-term effects of cadmium leaking into the surrounding soil. Because plastics are highly flammable, the printed wiring board and housings of electronic products contain brominated flame retardant, which are clearly damaging to human health and the environment (Alastair, 2004).

E-waste Scenario in Karnataka

The State of Karnataka has enacted legislation that governs management and disposal of Waste Electrical and Electronic Equipment (WEEE).

Government of India's Environment (Protection) Act, 1986 and the Karnataka E-waste (Management and Handling) Act was passed in 2001. The two main objectives of the act is to establish a proper system for the collection and recycling of discarded electronic devices and to limit the amount of toxic substances. This legislation is enforced by the Karnataka State Pollution Control Board (KSPCB). Based on Restrictions on Hazardous Substances (RoHS), KSPCB has designated e-wastes as universal wastes. This is due to the fact that, when processed with precaution, these wastes do not pose any danger to the environment or the people. Compared to hazardous wastes, the universal wastes are regulated by less stringent rules for handling and transportation.

E-waste Recycling firm Started Formally first in Karnataka

Parthasarathy's ISO 14001 model, developed with help from Germany's GTZ and Switzerland's EMPA uses a simple, indigenous method that manually dismantles goods like: computers, printers, cartridges and other peripherals, segregates and pulverizes, all in an environmentally benign manner. 'Less than five per cent of waste generated reaches the organized recycling sector', says P. Parthasarathy director of India's first e-recycling firm, the Bangalore-based E-Parisara. E-Parisara's 50-odd customers are all major corporate, including: IBM, Lucent-Alcatel, Hewlett Packard, Intel, Infosys and Motorola (Begum, 2013).

An Electronic Waste Recycling Fee is therefore collected from consumers who buy covered electronic devices. This fee is collected by the retailers and is then transferred to the Board. The Karnataka State Integrated Waste Management Board manages the payment system and performs an annual evaluation of the fee.

An estimated 30,000 computers become obsolete every year from the IT industry in Bangalore alone (SIMs Recycling Solutions, 2008). Home to more than 1200 foreign and domestic technology firms, Bangalore figures prominently in the danger list of cities faced with e-waste hazard. As many as 1000 tonnes of plastics, 300 tonnes of lead, 0.23 tonnes of mercury, 43 tonnes of nickel and 350 tonnes of copper are annually generated in Bangalore (Beary, 2008). There are only two formal recyclers in the south of India (at Chennai and Bangalore) and one in western India. Currently, there are no formal recyclers operating in the north or the east (MAIT, E-waste, Indian perspective). Over 1 million poor people in India are involved in the manual recycling operations (Toxicslink, 2003).

Research Methodology and Study Area

The present study was conducted in the Mysore city area from January to June 2014. For this research, both primary and secondary data were utilized. The primary data was collected from key personnel and the secondary data was collected from Pollution Control Board (PCB), NGOs, processing units and formal units. This study used a survey questionnaires to investigate and collect information from the primary sources. A pilot study was conducted in core areas where e-waste processing was done, KSSIDC Industrial Estate, Hebbal, Nanjangud, V.V. Mohalla, Saraswathipuram, and K.T Street. From the results of the pilot survey, questions were designed keeping in view the specialization in processing like: segregation, collection and extraction of specific components like: plastic, CRT tubes, and precious metals. However, personnel involved in the informal handing of e-waste were reluctant to provide information due to the ban imposed on informal e-waste recycling by the PCB. Another problem encountered was that the respondents were unable to answer the questions because they had not kept any records of the quantity of e-waste processed, frequency of health problems experienced etc.

Mysore also known as Mysuru, is the third largest city in the state of Karnataka, India. It is situated at the base of the Chamundi Hills and spreads across an area of 128.42 km^2 (50 sq mi) (Figure 9.3). It is located about 146 km (91 mi) southwest of the state capital Bangalore, the top IT destination in India.

Fig. 9.3: **Shows the location of Mysore in relation to Bangalore, the top IT destination in India**

A Situation Analysis of the Mounting E-waste Challenge in Mysore

E-waste is increasing and is seen as a threat to the deteriorating environment in Mysore. According to Beary 2005, Bangalore figures prominently in the danger list of cities faced with e-waste hazard and this has spilled over to its closest neighbor Mysore, where it can be seen more and more IT firms are opening their door in this once peaceful and green city. Because of it close vicinity and its pollution problems, many people including natives and foreigners are shifting their home base and businesses to Mysore. With little awareness among the majority about the magnitude of the problem, e-waste has been accumulating almost unrestricted and is becoming one of the most serious management challenges. Many experts have cautioned against the potentially harmful impacts of e-waste and hence the need for its safe disposal. E-waste is no longer a subject for academic discussions at environmental forums. Instead, there is a growing realization that the issue may assume dangerous proportions over the next few years if left unaddressed. However, efforts are being made to involve the IT companies to take more responsibilities for the management of e-waste. But, the limitation of having almost no available data on the number of unregistered companies, tracking them remains a problem. The PCB is taking steps to ensure safe disposal, with the adaptation of the Hazardous Waste (Management and Handling) Rule 2003 with major amendments covers various aspects in detail. However, implementation has not been very effective.

Formal Disposal Site - Treatment Storage and Disposal Facility (TSDF)

There is no formal e-waste disposal site in Mysore. The Pollution Control Board, in association with GTZ, a German Engineering Firm, has set up an e-waste disposal landfill site, with an investment of 55 crores, at Dobbaspet about 50 kms from Bangalore near Tumkur Road. The landfill has been operating since February 2009, despite encountering opposition from activists, local residents and politicians fearing a hazardous impact on health and environment. The landfill is spread over 93 acres with a potential storage capacity of 40,000 tonnes of industrial and biomedical waste every year and actual storage capacity of 800,000 tonnes - enough to last for two decades. Industries registered in Karnataka have to pay between Rs. 1,500 and Rs. 2, 500 for each tonnes of waste they supply to the TSDF.

Informal E-waste recycling in Mysore

Informal e-waste recycling is carried out in certain parts of Mysore that are highly congested, densely populated by minority communities with low-income. These recyclers are engaged in various forms of partnerships in the e-waste business. It could be a single individual or partnerships at various levels based on the financial investments. The informal recycling process has several levels of management. The physical flow of e-waste begins with agents, waste dealers and even ordinary kabadiwalas who acquire any type of e-waste such as: computers, mobile phones, televisions, kitchen appliances etc. from the public and private sectors. After segregation, both agents and small waste dealers sell the waste to the mediating waste dealers. Small waste dealers sell some of the waste to the public as second hand goods while the remaining is diverted to the open market. From the mediating waste dealers, the scrap flows to the service industry as parts for repair and maintenance of old computers. Again, some residuals in the service industry get back into the open market while the rest is sold to large waste dealers. From the large waste dealers it is channeled in three ways: *(i)* recycling of certain parts; *(ii)* selected waste sold to specific individuals and *(iii)* certain parts come back to the open market. At the other end of this chain, there is a network of dealers operating from large cities like: Mumbai and Delhi through agents, intermediaries and company agents. All of them approach large dealers in Bangalore and Mysore to acquire scrap directly or through the open market (Manasi, 2013).

Institutions' Role in E-waste Management

The present legislation does not seem to be effective in addressing the rising e-waste problems adequately. The stakeholders have started taking notice of the growing hazards of e-waste disposal in conjunction with a growing agreement that recycling and resource recovery used to be environmental-friendly. This has led to several organization staking up various initiatives in e-waste management. Such partnerships as the Indo-German-Swiss e-waste initiative involving several partners - Ministry for Environment and Forests, Central Pollution Control Board, BMZ, German Technical Cooperation, SECO and EMPA - is an example to the coordinated efforts and management of e-waste. The Indo - German-Swiss e-waste initiative is a joint project involving India, Switzerland and Germany. The vision of this initiative is to establish a clean e-waste channel aimed at establishing.

(a) Convenient collection and disposal system for large and small consumers to transfer all e-waste safely.

(b) Voluntary system for producers concerned over the care of their products post their useful life.

(c) Financially secure system that makes environmentally and socially responsible e-waste recycling viable.

The initiative also aims to *(a)* reduce risks to the population and the environment from unsafe handling of e-waste; *(b)* focus on knowledge transfer and skills up-gradation of all the stakeholders through trainings and seminars and *(c)* target the informal recyclers to ensure safe participation in future E-waste management and facilitate their growth and integration within the formal structure.

In Karnataka state, the role of the (Karnataka State Pollution Control Board) KSPCB, is to enforce laws, which governs emerging issue such as:

e-waste. The KSPCB received its first application in 2005 for re-cycling e-waste in Karnataka and was the first to give such authorization to E-Parisara followed by other formal recyclers.

Conclusion

E-waste management in Mysore is largely unorganized and in the initial stages of working towards proper management. However, this is difficult as there are no accurate estimates available on the quantity of e-waste generated and recycled, given the magnitude of the problem and poor accountability. The primary and secondary data, interviews with various categories of people and estimation of e-waste suggests that the generation of e-waste in Mysoreis increasing due to high obsolescence rates, lack of policy for disposal forproducers, consumers and manufacturers and lack of awareness. The manufacturers need to undertake green initiatives like take-back programmes and extended producer responsibility (EPR) for taking responsibility for environment friendly disposal of their end of life products as they are the largest contributor of e-wastes. The government and regulatory agencies have a major role to play by formulating guidelines, benchmarks, creation of awareness and monitoring the implementation of standards. The consumers should adhere to the standards and policies of the government for disposal of their end of life products. The NGOs and civil society action groups should create awareness for the producers and consumers on the hazards associated with improper disposal, extending the useful life of products and reuse. There is an urgent need for all stakeholders to engage in dialogue to find sustainable solutions on the issue of e-waste. One of the foremost requirements is to have sustainable legislation on electronic and electrical waste.

REFERENCES

Agarwal, R. (1998): India: The World's Final Dumpyard! January, *Basel Action News*, 1, www.ban.org

Agarwal, Singhmar A. Kulshrestha, M. and Mittal, A. K. (2005): Municipal Solid Waste Recycling and Associated Markets in Delhi, India. *Resources Conservation and Recycling*, 44(1): 73-90.

Alastair, I. (2004): Mapping Environmental Justice in Technology Flows: Computers Waste Impacts in Asia Global Environmental Politics, Massachusetts Institute of Technology, 4:4.

Baldé, C.P. Wang, F. Kuehr, R. and Huisman, J. (2015): The Global E-waste Monitor – 2014, United Nations University, IAS – SCYCLE, Bonn, Germany.

http://i.unu.edu/media/unu.edu/news/52624/UNU-1stGlobal-E-Waste-Monitor-2014-small.pdf

Beary, H. (2005): Bangalore Faces E-waste Hazards, http://news.bbc.co.uk/2/hi/south_asia/4222521.stm

Beary, H. (2008): Bangalore faces e-waste hazards, http://www.news.bbc.co.uk/1/hi/world/south_asia/4222521.stm.

Begum, Kousar Jahan Ara. (2013): Electronic Waste (E-Waste) Management in India: A Review, http://iosrjournals.org/iosr-jhss/papers/Vol10-issue4/H01044657.pdf

CBS News.com (2009): "Following the Trail of Toxic E-waste", 60 Minutes, http://www.cbsnews.com/stories/2008/11/06/60minutes/main4579229.shtml

CII. (2006): E-Waste Management, Green Business Opportunities, Confederation of Indian Industry, Delhi, 12(1).

Clapp, J. (2005): Distancing of waste: Overconsumption in a Global Economy, TIPEC Working Paper 01.10 (Trent International Political Economy Center).

http://www-rohan.sdsu.edu/faculty/dunnweb/rprnts.2005.10.10Clapp.pdf.

Congressional Quarterly (CQ) Politics. (2009): "House Panel Approves Bill to Aid Disposal of Unwanted Electronics.".

Chatterjee, S. and Kumar, K. (2009): Effective Electronic Waste Management and Recycling Process Involving Formal and Non-formal Sectors, *International Journal of Physical Sciences*, 4(13): 893-905.

Consumer Voice. (2007): E-Waste: *The next hazard wave*. 3: 6.

CPCB, Ministry of Environment and Forests, Government of India. (2008): 'Guidelines for Environmentally Sound Management of E-waste,' http://www.cpcb.nic.in/latest/27.06.08%20guidelines%20for%20E-Waste.pdf

Darby, L. and Obara, L. (2005): "Household Recycling Behaviour and Attitudes towards the Disposal of Small Electrical and Electronic Equipment." *Resources Conservation and Recycling*, 44(1): 17-35.

Draft Hazardous Materials (Management, Handling and Transboundary Movement, Rules, 2007), http://www.govtindustry-environment.com/Draft%20Rules,%2007%20-%20K.P.Nyati.pdf.

E-waste, Indian perspective. http://www.nswai.com/images/newsletters/nov2007.pdf.

Electronics Take Back Coalition (ETBC). 2011. State legislation. Available: http://www.electronicstakeback.com/promote-good-laws/state-legislation/ [8 Dec. 2011].

Feszty, K. and Calder, J. (2007): E-waste Legislation Grows in Canada, Green Supply Line.

Frazzoli, C. Orisakwe, O. E. Dragone, R. and Mantovani, A. (2010): Diagnostic Health Risk Assessment of Electronic Waste on the General Population in Developing Countries' Scenarios. *Environmental Impact Assessment Review*, 30: 388-399.

Greenpeace International. (2015): The E-waste Problem,

http://www.greenpeace.org/international/en/campaigns/detox/electronics/the-e-waste-problem/#a0

Hicks, C. Dietmara, R. and Eugsterb, M. (2005): The Recycling and Disposal of Electrical and Electronic Waste in China – Legislative and Market Responses. *Environmental Impact Assessment Review*, 25: 459-471.

Janz, Alexander and Bilitewski, Bernd. (2008): 'Hazardous Substances in Waste Electrical and Electronic Equipment' in Rakesh Johri, E-waste: Implications, Regulations and Management in India and Current Global Best Practices, TERI, New Delhi, pp. 93.

Kukday, K. (2007): Making Profit from Mining of E-waste, http://timesofindia.indiatimes.com/business/india-business/Making-profit-from-mining-of-e-waste/articleshow/2107581.cms

Joshi, Sandeep. (2009): 'Growing E-waste Causing Concern', *The Hindu*, 28 February, 2009.

Kang, H.Y. and Schoenung, J.M. (2005): "Electronic Waste Recycling: A Review of US Infrastructure and Technology Options." *Resources Conservation and Recycling* 45(4): 368-400.

Lewis, T. (2013): World's E-Waste to Grow 33% by 2017, Says Global Report, http://www.livescience.com/41967-world-e-waste-to-grow-33-percent-2017.html

Liu, Q. Cao, L. Li, K. Q. Miao, X. H. Li, G. Fan, F. and Zhao, Y. C. (2009): "Chromosomal Aberrations and DNA Damage in Human Populations Exposed to the Processing of Electronics Waste," *Environmental Science and Pollution Research*, 16(3): 329-338.

Lundgren, Karin. (2012): The Global Impact of E-waste: Addressing the Challenge; International Labour Office, Programme on Safety and Health at Work and the Environment (Safe Work), Sectoral Activities Department (SECTOR), Geneva.

MAIT. "E-waste growth in India" http://www.mait.com/pressupdate.1jsp?id=77

Manasi, S. (2013): Emerging Trends in E-waste Management: Status and Issues: A Case Study of Bangalore City, *Working paper (Institute for Social and Economic Change)*, 297,

http://www.isec.ac.in/WP%20297%20-%20S%20Manasi.pdf

Mundada, M. N. Kumar, S. and Shekdar, A.V. (2004): E-waste: A New Challenge for Waste Management in India. *Int. J. Environ. Studies,* 61(3): 265-279.

NIIR Project Consultancy Service (npcs). (2012): E-waste in India: A growing Industry, http://www.niir.org/information/content.phtml?content=144

Nimpuno, M. and Scruggs, C. (2011): Information on Chemicals in Electronic Products: A Study in Needs, Gaps, Obstacles and Solutions to Provide and Access Information on Chemicals in Electronic Products (TemaNord). http://www.chemsec.org/get-informed/globalinitiatives/unep-cip-study-on-electronics

Nordbrand, S. (2009): Out of Control: E-waste Trade Flows from the EU to Developing Countries.

(SwedWatch). http://www.swedwatch.org/en/reports/e-waste-export-outcontrol

Onwughara, N.I. Nnorom, I.C. Kanno, O.C. and Chukwuma, R.C. (2010): Disposal Methods and Heavy Metals Released from Certain Electrical and Electronic Equipment Wastes in Nigeria: Adoption of Environmental Sound Recycling System, *International Journal of Environmental Science and Development*, 1(4): 290-296, http://dx.doi.org/10.7763/IJESD.2010.V1.57.

Prakash, S. and Manhart, A. (2010): Socio-economic Assessment and Feasibility Study on Sustainable E-waste Management in Ghana (Freiburg, Öko-Institut).

Raghupathy, L. Krüger, C. Chaturvedi, A. Arora, R. Henzler, Mikael P. (2012): E-waste Recycling in India – Bridging the gap between the informal and formal sector, https://www.google.com/url?sa=t&rct=j&q=&esrc=s&source= web&cd= 1&cad=rja &uact=8&ved=0CB4QFjAA&url=http%3A%2F%2 Fweeerecycle. in%2 Fpublications %2 Fresearch_papers%2FE_Waste_India_ISWA_ Conference. doc&ei=Sw9nVa69K4 iuyQSyqoPYAw&usg=AFQjCNG4lK9SDpNjTIC-BTUyEUiEEJjz2Q&sig2=BH69jqCm_iLMNYvBoNkxFw&bvm=bv.93990622,d.aWw

Raymond, J. (2007): Environment: Easy to be Green. Newsweek. 2007, http://www.newsweek.com/id/56722.

Schluep M. Hagelueken, C. Kuehr, R. Magalini, F. Maurer, C. Meskers, C. Mueller, E. and Wang, F. (2009): Recycling - from E-waste to Resources. United Nations Environment Programme and United Nations University, Germany, http://isp.unu.edu/news/2010/files/UNEP_eW2R_publication.pdf

Schwarzer, S. De Bono, A. Giuliani, G. Kluser, S. and Peduzzi, P. (2005): "E-waste, the Hidden Side of IT Equipment's Manufacturing and use," *UNEP DEWA/GRID-Europe Environment Alert Bulletin*, 5, http://www.grid.unep.ch/product/publication/download/ew_ewaste.en.pdf.

Science Daily. (2010): Is there a Difference in E-waste Production between Developing and Developed Countries? https://www.causesinternational.com/ewaste/e-waste-facts

Sepúlveda, A. Schluep, M. Renaud, F.G. Streicher, M. Kuehr, R. Hagelüken, C. Gerecke, A.C. (2010): "A Review of the Environmental Fate and Effects of Hazardous Substances Released from Electrical and Electronic Equipment during Recycling: Examples from China and India," *Environmental Impact Assessment Review*, 30: 28-41.

SIMs Recycling Solutions. (2008): E-waste Guide, http://www.ewaste.in.

Sinha, D. (2004): The Management of Electronic Waste: A Comparative Study on India and Switzerland. (Master's Thesis, University of St. Gallen, 2004).

Skinner, A. Dinter, Y. Lloyd, A. and Strothmann, P. (2010): The Challenges of E-waste Management in India: Can India Draw Lessons from the EU and the USA? *ASIEN*. 117: 7-26.

Streicher-Porte, M. Widmer, R. Jain, A. Bader, H. P. Scheidegger, R. and Kytzia, S. (2005): Key Drivers of the E-waste Recycling System: Assessing and Modelling E-waste Processing in the Informal Sector in Delhi. *Environ. Impact Assess. Rev*. 25: 472-491.

Streicher-Porte, M. (2006): SWICO/S.EN.S, the Swiss WEEE Recycling Systems, and Best Practices from other European Systems. *Proceedings of the 2006 IEEE International Symposium on Electronics and the Environment, IEEE*.

Toxicslink. (2003): Scrapping the hi-tech Myth: Computer Waste in India. Published in Toxics, http://www.toxicslink.org/pub-view.php?pubnum=37.

Tsydenova O. and Bengtsson, M. (2011): Chemical Hazards Associated with Treatment of Waste Electrical and Electronic Equipment. *Waste Management*, 31: 45-58.

UNEP (2012): "Recycling - from E-Waste to Resources," "As E-waste Mountains soar, UN urges Smart Technologies to Protect Health." United Nations-DPI/NMD - UN News Service Section.

US EPA. (2014): "Municipal Solid Waste Generation, Recycling and Disposal in the United States; Tables and figures for 2012," http://www.epa.gov/epawaste/nonhaz/municipal/pubs/2012_msw_dat_tbls.pd

Wang, H. Han, M. Yang, S. Chen, Y. Liu, Q. and Ke, S. (2011): "Urinary Heavy Metal Levels and Relevant Factors among People Exposed to E-waste Dismantling", in *Environment International*, 37(1): 80-85.

Williams, E. Kahhat, R. Allenby, B. Kavazanjian, E. Kim, J. and Xu, M. (2008): Environmental, Social and Economic Implications of Global Reuse and Recycling of Personal Computers. *Environmental Science and Technology*, 42(17): 6446-54.

Wong, C.S.C. Wu, S. C. Duzgoren-Aydin, N. S. Aydin, A. and Wong, M. H. (2007): Trace Metal Contamination of Sediments in an E-waste Processing Village in China. *Environmental Pollution*, 145: 434-442.

Yongguang, Z. Qingdong, Y. *et al*. (2006): "A Research into the Recycling System of Waste Electrical and Electronic Equipment in China." *2006 IEEE International Conference on Service Operations and Logistics, and Informatics* (IEEE Cat. No. 06EX1352C): pp. 6.

Zhao, X.R. Qin, Z.F. Yang, Z.Z. Zhao, Q. Zhao, Y.X. Qin, X.F. hang, Y.C. Ruan, X.L. Zhang, Y, F. Xu, X. B. (2010): Dual Body Burdens of polychlorinated biphenyls and polybrominateddiphenyl ethers among Local Residents in An E-waste Recycling Region in Southeast China. *Chemosphere* 78(6): 659-666.

Index

❑❑❑❑